Disciplinary Dialogues on Social Change

Disciplinary Dialogues on Social Change

Gender, Early Childhood and Theatre

Editor

Nitya Rao

ACADEMIC FOUNDATION
NEW DELHI

www.academicfoundation.org

First published in 2016
by

ACADEMIC FOUNDATION
4772-73 / 23 Bharat Ram Road, (23 Ansari Road),
Darya Ganj, New Delhi - 110 002 (India).
Phones : 23245001 / 02 / 03 / 04.
Fax : +91-11-23245005.
E-mail : books@academicfoundation.com
www.academicfoundation.com

Cataloging in Publication Data--DK
Courtesy: D.K. Agencies (P) Ltd. <docinfo@dkagencies.com>

"Education for Social Change: Multidisciplinary Perspectives" (Workshop) (2013 : New Delhi, India)
Disciplinary dialogues on social change : gender, early childhood and theatre / editor, Nitya Rao.
pages cm
Papers presented in a workshop, "Education for Social Change: Multidisciplinary Perspectives", held on 30 and 31 August 2013 in New Delhi, India.
ISBN 9789332703483

1. Early childhood education--India--Congresses. 2. Child care--India--Congresses. 3. Well-being--India--Congresses. 4. Sex discrimination against women--India--Congresses. 5. Theater and society--India--Congresses. I. Rao, Nitya, editor. II. Title.

LB1139.3.I4D57 2013 DDC 372.210954 23

Typeset, printed and bound by The Book Mint, New Delhi.
www.thebookmint.in

CONTENTS

Section II
Gender, Socialisation and Theatre

About the Editor/Contributors

Editor:

Nitya Rao is Professor of Gender and Development at the University of East Anglia, Norwich, United Kingdom. She has worked extensively in the field of women's rights, employment and education for close to three decades. Located mainly in South Asia, her research interests include exploring the gendered changes in land and agrarian relations, migration and livelihoods, education, intra-household relations and identities. She has published extensively on these themes. Her book on the theme of land as a resource in the struggle over gendered identities entitled: *Good Women Do Not Inherit Land: Politics of Land and Gender in India* was published in 2008, with a second paperback edition in 2012.

Contributors

Indu Agnihotri is presently Director, Centre for Women's Development Studies (CWDS), New Delhi. Prior to this, she was Associate Professor, Department of History, Vivekananda College, University of Delhi. She has been involved with the women's movement and with women's studies in India for nearly four decades now. Her academic interests lie in women's studies, history, labour and gender issues.

Hanne M. de Bruin holds a PhD in Indology from Leiden University, The Netherlands. She has published extensively on the Kattaikkuttu theatre in particular and popular theatre in India in general, women performers, stigma, and Tamil culture. Hanne was one of the co-founder of the Kattaikkuttu Sangam and Kattaikkuttu Gurukulam of which she is at present the Executive Director. Together with her husband P. Rajagopal, she is involved in creating new productions and equipping a new generation of young graduates of the Kattaikkuttu Gurukulam with adequate skills and knowledge to face the competitive world of the professional arts.

A. Mangai is the pseudonym of Dr V. Padma. She teaches English in Stella Maris College, Chennai. She has been actively engaged in Tamil theatre as an actor, director and playwright for almost three decades. She has been one of the founder members of Chennai Kalai Kuzhu, Shakthi, Palkalai Arangam, Voicing Silence and Marappachi. She hopes that her academic, activist and artistic selves can find a vibrant intersection. Her fields of interest are: theatre, gender and translation studies. She writes in both Tamil and English.

Archana Mehendale is an independent researcher working in the areas of child rights, right to education, child labour, and early childhood rights since two decades. She is particularly interested in studying the role of law and policy in affecting social change. She has written three articles for the report on *Status of Young Child in Karnataka,* which was brought out by Sutradhar and FORCES in 2003-04. Her policy papers titled "Early Childhood Education and International Law" and "Early Childhood Education in India: Law and Policy", were published by ICICI Centre for Elementary Education in 2010-11. She recently collaborated with the Centre for Early Childhood Education and Development, Ambedkar University, Delhi, to research on Right to Early Childhood Development.

Amit Mitra is a New Delhi based independent researcher. He has a wide experience of working with marginalised agrarian communities, gender and education. Informal sector labour markets, water, farming, forests and other natural resources and also governance are key focal areas as are adaptation to climate change and disaster risk reduction. His skills range from designing large-scale socio-economic surveys and data management systems and policy research to grass-roots-level activities with a strong gender and child rights perspective. With a good understanding of social development and proficiency in a wide range of social research methodologies and techniques, including participatory research, he has been able to improvise the same to ensure process ownership by the participants.

Jolly Rohatagi is an artist and teacher, who has worked for the last three decades in the fields of development through art with children, women and persons with disability, education in the formal and non-formal sector, design and product development, an integrated approach to education through multimedia interpersonal art, use of art for therapy and recreation, marketing of handicrafts, local and international, and preparing educational kits and training materials for the urban and rural poor, and tribals, with special emphasis on women and children. She has been involved with documentation and action research to support the marketing of a range of handicraft products produced by the poor.

Adarsh Sharma is presently a freelance consultant in the field of Early Childhood Education (ECE) and human development. She is the Country Coordinator of Asia Pacific Regional Network for Early Childhood (ARNEC) and has also been its steering committee member from 2006 to 2011. Her professional career spans over a period of four decades in the field of child development. She has worked at the University of Delhi and G.B. Pant University of Agriculture and Technology as Professor. She was associated recently in setting up of the Center of Early Childhood Education and Development (CECED) of Ambedkar University, Delhi as a Visiting Professor (2009-2012). After working for over two decades at the National Institute of Public Cooperation and

Child Development (NIPCCD), a premier organisation of child development, she retired as its Executive Director in 2005.

Rekha Sharma Sen is Associate Professor of child development in the School of Continuing Education at Indira Gandhi National Open University, New Delhi, engaged in developing open and distance learning programmes in the sector of Early Childhood Care and Education (ECCE) and disability. She served as Chair Professor at the Centre for Early Childhood Development and Research (CECDR), Jamia Millia Islamia, New Delhi from 2011 until 2014. Her areas of publication include, ECCE, early literacy, creativity, disability, and gender in open and distance learning. She has authored chapters in innovative textbooks for classes I to V of the Primary Education Programme (Prashika) of Eklavya, Bhopal, as well as in the NCERT and CBSE textbooks for senior secondary classes. She has been member of several government committees including the Working Group for Development of the National Policy on ECCE and National Curricular Framework for ECCE (2010). She is an active member of the Alliance for Right to Early Childhood Development, a voluntary body of activists working to secure the rights of the young child.

Rajalakshmi Sriram is Professor and Chair of the Department of Human Development and Family Studies, at the Maharaja Sayajirao University of Baroda, Gujarat. She has been committed to engaging in basic and applied research as well as in ensuring that the benefits of research and technical know-how of higher education enrich the lives of people. She has published numerous journal articles and chapters in books, and has also prepared communication materials on effective parenting, fathering and domestic violence. During the last decade, her research and applications have focused on understanding fathering and promoting involved fathering, through awareness and advocacy.

Mina Swaminathan has had a long and varied career embracing three disciplines. A leading practitioner, teacher-educator and writer on ECCE, Chair of the 1972 Committee leading to Integrated Child Development Services (ICDS), trainer of generations of teachers and trainers, and editor of an ECE journal, she has written three widely popular teachers' manuals. An activist deeply involved in gender studies, her interests range from maternity entitlements and day care, to a feminist interrogation of science. The third strand, drama and theatre, she has used as tools both for self-expression, and to explore issues. She is also a prolific writer.

Foreword

"Age cannot wither her, nor custom stale her infinite variety" (Shakespeare's *Antony and Cleopatra*) came to my mind as I sat through a workshop, "Education for Social Change: Multidisciplinary Perspectives", held on 30 and 31 August 2013 in New Delhi, to celebrate the 80th birthday of Mina Swaminathan. This book is based on the papers presented at the workshop, and covers some of the areas to which she has devoted large parts of her life, with passion and conviction added to skills; not only for improvement of the spread and quality of child education, but even more, for the rights and needs, often unrecognised, of both children and women, such as day care for labouring women. She has played a substantial role in getting professional, political and national attention focused on issues relating to gender equity, and ECCE (early childhood care and education). In all her work, communication, especially the innovative use of drama and theatre, has been critical.

The importance of ECCE for all-round development of the young child is obvious from the fact that India still has the largest number of underweight and malnourished children in the world, as well as children with low birth weight, with the consequent adverse impact on their cognitive abilities in later life. Mina has been a pioneer here in drawing attention to these and other facts. She has used pedagogic methodologies like drama and folk theatre with great impact. Her life-long experience in many of these fields was brought together in the project Action for Child Care and Education Strategies and Services (ACCESS), a programme for networking of stakeholders to support training, research and advocacy on ECCE at MS Swaminathan Research Foundation (MSSRF). The results of this unique project have been summarised in a fascinating book titled *As the Salt in the Seas*, compiled by Mina and L.S. Saraswathi.

Mina has an admirable ability to reinvent herself and start afresh. Moving base to Chennai when nearly 60, she demonstrated her resilience by taking up new challenges, including a change of working language from Hindi to Tamil, working closely with Integrated Child Development Services (ICDS) in training of both Anganwadi Workers (AWWs) and supervisors, and into new projects at MSSRF, entering energetically and enthusiastically into untried fields.

Her high levels of innovation, the ability to think creatively and pragamatically, usher in new ideas and projects, and learn from mistakes, has been inspirational. MSSRF has derived immense advantage from her leadership in its programmes and priorities. Project ACCESS demonstrated clearly the value of working closely with mass media, leading to the setting up of *The Hindu* Media Resource Centre at MSSRF to foster meaningful linkages between science and society, with media serving as the bridge; while a programme titled *Every Child a Scientist* was started at Wayanad in Kerala and in Chennai, to kindle the spirit of innovation and enquiry in the minds of children. Also, a Touch and Smell Garden, together with a computer-aided Braille programme on plant sciences, were set up for visually impaired children in Chennai, to give all children the joy of experiencing the gifts of nature.

Mina's versatility is reflected in her ability to bridge different disciplines, and all with some depth of understanding, rather than superficially. This was demonstrated in the drafting of the Women Farmer's Entitlement Bill, 2011, introduced by me as a Private Member's bill in the Rajya Sabha. Extensive consultations were organised with a range of stakeholders—academics, lawyers and activists—by Mina in the process of drafting this Bill. While it was unfortunately not taken up for discussion during my tenure in the Rajya Sabha, and thereafter lapsed, Mina has continued to advocate for the principles enshrined in this draft legislation, and is currently working with a women farmers' network to draft such a legislation.

Her political commitment and conviction, acting fearlessly and speaking out when necessary on behalf of the marginalised, makes her stand out as an activist. Although holding a Tripos in Economics from Cambridge, she has never cared for personal power or positions. This was a characteristic even from her younger days when she stepped down from the Committee on Status of Women (before Vina Mazumdar took over as Chair), because it was inactive and elitist in orientation, and she colourfully called it a "Ladies' Tea Party".

Mina's five-decade long involvement in the fields of education, childcare, creative and educational drama, and gender equality and justice, helped her recognise what was needed and how to achieve it. In 1972, she was the principal author of the ICDS programme in her capacity as Chairperson of a Committee set up by the Central Advisory Board of Education. Her wide experience and her total commitment to a holistic approach in dealing with social issues are principally responsible for providing a methodology for operationalising the pro-woman mandate of MSSRF. I hope that the Uttara Devi Centre for Gender and Development which she established will carry forward the unfinished task of taking her goals to their logical end. It is our duty to ensure that the many buds she has helped to create do not end up as 'blossoms in the dust', but are enabled to flower and bear fruit.

I am glad that the papers in this fascinating book capture not only Mina's unique qualities and unparalleled contributions, but even more, express their tribute in the form of excellent papers from each contributor in their respective domains. I am grateful to the authors for their papers which are both scholarly and sensitive. We are all deeply indebted to Nitya Rao for conceiving such a seminar and editing this book. I would also like to thank Indu Agnihotri and the Centre for Women's Development Studies, of which Mina was a founder member, for hosting the seminar and facilitating this publication; as well as to Smt Anuradha Desai of the Venkateswara Group for making it financially possible. Finally, our thanks goes to the Academic Foundation and to Shri Sanu Kapila for ensuring the reader friendliness of this publication.

—M.S. Swaminathan
Emeritus Chairman and Chief Mentor
MS Swaminathan Research Foundation, Chennai

NITYA RAO

Introduction

Disciplinary Dialogues on Social Change

Introduction

This book has grown from a two-day multi-disciplinary workshop held in New Delhi on 30-31 August 2013, to celebrate the long, varied and distinguished career of Mina Swaminathan, a leading practitioner, trainer and writer in the field of education, focusing specifically on ECE (early childhood education), gender and communication. Her concern with innovative educational strategies for children, adults and teachers led her to use drama and theatre extensively, as tools to explore a variety of wider social issues, from oppressive social relationships to alternate sexualities. This not only prepared the ground for interrogating assumptions about gender roles, relations and processes of socialisation, but has also contributed to setting in motion a process of social change and women's empowerment, with emphasis on issues ranging from maternity entitlements and the right to development of children below six, to a curriculum for gender studies, and using theatre and creative communication strategies for advocacy.

Rather than viewing these fields and disciplines as independent silos, this book seeks to bring together different perspectives and social concerns in relation to education, viewed as a broad field of learning, questioning and deepening understandings. It highlights the important role of not just analysis and interpretation of evidence, but equally effective communication. It is innovative in examining the links between theory, research and practice, including advocacy for policy change, in the realms of early childhood education and gender studies, focusing on the use of theatre as a political tool for mobilisation and change. As the papers demonstrate, while the themes appear distinct, there are strong conceptual and practical connections in terms of the relationships between children, teachers and parents, and gendered constructions of meaning across all domains of life.

A key link in fact is the shift in discourse from ECE in the 1960s to ECCE (early childhood care and education) in the 1980s. With the recognition that children needed not just education, but also care, in a world where women, though primarily responsible for caregiving, have multiple roles and responsibilities, established firmly the link with gender studies. In fact, Mina Swaminathan's book *Who Cares?* was presented at the Third World Conference on Women, Nairobi, 1985, where childcare was recognised as an issue for serious consideration by the women's movement. Theatre becomes a partner in the project of mobilisation and empowerment, especially in contexts where people are non-literate and live in oral cultures.

The book is organised in two main sections: the first on early childhood care and education, and the second on gendered socialisation and transformations, through theatre and alternate communication pathways. What is clear is the overlap between these themes, with issues of gender (and fatherhood) impacting on early childhood, as well as being implicated in different forms of theatre and strategic communication. This chapter therefore tries to draw out some of the key interlinkages between these fields of study in policy and practice.

Rights of the Child and Women's Work

Feminist researchers have for the past four decades emphasised the invisibility of women's work, locating women's subordination in the realm of their almost sole responsibility for domestic labour and care work (Edholm *et al.*, 1978: 123).[1] Not only are the everyday, reproductive tasks allocated to women less recognised than the more visible, productive tasks allocated to men, but activities performed in the public realm get socially recognised and valued,

1. See, for instance, Molyneux (1979); and Beneria (1982).

while work within the home is both invisible and limits opportunities for social mobility. This understanding has led to efforts to value women's unpaid work, especially care work, while at the same time supporting the expansion of paid work.[2] An underlying assumption is that contributions to visible and recognised work shape relative bargaining power and agency within a household.

While childcare and socialisation starts at home, with the mother primarily responsible for these tasks, the women's movement, however, seeing this mother-child conflation as one of the major reasons for women's subordination, focused on establishing women's rights as 'persons'. This involved claiming equal rights in the public sphere—be it in resource control, employment or education. While these have all been legitimate areas for advocacy, in the process, the issue of childcare has lost priority. It has more recently been put on the agenda by the child rights movements to protect the rights of the child. The link between women empowerment and improved child well-being—a central element of social reproduction—has however been overlooked.

While not entering the debate of why this might be the case, suffice to say that this tension reflects a larger tension between women's rights as human rights and women's rights as instruments for attaining development goals such as child well-being. Framing of the link between the mother and child in instrumental terms in international discourse takes away the transformative edge from feminist agendas and claims. Perhaps as a reaction, while clearly vital for a majority of Indian women, the women's movement itself has struggled to find a way to take forward the childcare agenda without diluting that of women's rights.

To a large extent, this tension still remains. While a few feminist organisations may be sensitive to women's childcare needs and provide facilities during meetings and workshops, this is not the usual norm. Neither the public nor the private sector ensure high quality childcare that could potentially support women's work and

2. Engagement in the production of goods and services for consumption in the household is now included in the definitions of work adopted by the System of National Accounts in 1993 as a result of a decade of feminist advocacy (Hirway, 2009).

household well-being more generally (see Mehendale, this volume). Recent research in Tamil Nadu, which has seen a fertility transition, reveals that reproductive success, which includes both bearing a child and raising it successfully, is central to women's agency (Rao, 2014). While mediated by factors like age and stage in the life cycle, and social location—especially of caste and class—this shift seems to also be a response to the poor quality and arduous nature of work available to women, the still steep gender wage gaps, and the social welfare programmes of the state government, in particular, the provision of free rice.

Unless good quality and reliable childcare is assured, women, especially poor women, will never be able to engage with better quality work, that brings them sufficient returns for their labour. The assumption that visible, paid work, irrespective of its quality and/or status enhances women's power and agency, is challenged by several papers in this volume (de Bruin, Mitra and Rao), demonstrating that despite working and earning, certain professions are either seen to be inappropriate to the status of a 'respectable' woman (e.g., performance), or patriarchal ideologies and their practice, both materially and symbolically, restrain women's agency.

Women's time is at a premium. According to the Government of India's (GoI's) Time Use Survey 1998 (2000), 53 per cent of the total work done, is performed by women. This includes both productive and reproductive work. A figure like this however challenges the dominant patriarchal notion of the man as the head of household, the main breadwinner and provider. Hence, not surprisingly, a similar Time Use survey has not been repeated in the last 15 years.

While performing the bulk of the work, women remain excluded from the realm of politics and decision-making. Their illiteracy is often blamed for this, conflated somehow with the lack of knowledge or the inability to understand issues and make decisions. While this is not necessarily the case, as literacy cannot really be equated to knowledge or understanding, it is true that the styles and forms of communication, the language used, may be different. Educational programmes are always planned and executed from the standpoint of the middle classes—alternate knowledges and ways of both thinking and communication are often ignored.

Recent debates about quality education have turned the spotlight on the processes and experiences of learning, the value systems embedded within curricula, classroom practices, and how all these are gendered. So it is not just poverty or culture that keeps girls out of school, but equally the school environment and culture, the lack of adequate support for learning to girls, including their need to take care of their young siblings, when their mothers go to work. Childcare then is essential not just to facilitate women's work, but equally to ensure that older girls don't drop out of school in order to take care of their young siblings.

While attention to childcare can then help facilitate both women's empowerment and gender equitable education, it is surprising that it is still lagging behind on the policy agenda in India. In fact, in South East Asia, one finds early childhood care and education as the central issue of discussion, advocacy and policy attention, within the education sector, especially in the Philippines, Singapore and Malaysia, all countries where women's participation in the workforce is high (UNICEF and UNESCO, 2012). In South Asia, Bangladesh Rural Advancement Committee (BRAC), a large NGO (non-governmental organisation) in Bangladesh, realised the central role of childcare, and over the past decade has focused its education programme on this sector, rather than primary education.

Where does theatre and communication fit in this discussion? It is well acknowledged that learning needs to be joyful, to develop creative capacities and analytical skills, rather than rote memorisation. For adults, it is important for learning to be linked to their real-life experiences, to generate 'critical consciousness' in the terms of the Brazilian adult educator, Paolo Freire (1970). Yet, drama, sport or other creative activities are hardly encouraged as a part of the learning process; if at all, they are seen as extracurricular.

There is a gender dimension to this too. Gendered socialisation is about regulating behaviour, not just skills. This includes regulation and control over the body—dress, physical movement, eye contact, etc. Girls are trained to be quiet, passive, and dress to cover their bodies. I remember working with the literacy campaign—*arivoli iyakkam*—in Pudukkottai district of Tamil Nadu in the early 1990s. Learning to cycle was included as part of the campaign—the idea was to help girls and women overcome their fear of learning in general, but also become more confident of their bodies and physical movement (Rao, 2002). Performing in public still remains taboo for a lot of girls and women (de Bruin's paper in this volume), even though theatre is one medium which they relate to easily, understand well, and can engage with in a meaningful way.

While traditional modes of communication including story-telling and theatre are now used by international and local agencies to convey 'development messages' to women, this is not a medium that has been explored for two-way communication. For women too used to express their feelings and emotions around what is just a priority, and what is not. Interestingly enough, during the same period in Pudukkottai, in workshops with women quarry workers, role-plays proved to be an excellent tool to get an insight into their everyday social and gender relations, *vis-à-vis* the quarry contractor, their men, upper caste groups and so on. The unequal power relations that women were unable to articulate in words, they could express very candidly through role play (Rao, 2001).

The transformatory potential of alternate ways of learning and communication is tremendous. Apart from challenging gendered bodily movements and expression, it allows suppressed thoughts and emotions to be expressed in a somewhat fictionalised form, it opens up alternatives which seem real and within reach, it gives the confidence and support of the collective to their ideas, and facilitates negotiation for greater equity in everyday lives. This ultimately is the process of social change. It is multidimensional, and not straightforward, yet entry points can be both practical and strategic, providing opportunities for creative communication and action.

Many of these ideas have been tried and tested by Mina Swaminathan over a career spanning six decades. She recounts some of these experiences in chapter 1, an abbreviated oral history of her life. Education, gender, theatre—these would be considered very different disciplines in the academe today—yet they came together in her work, each receiving attention in almost equal measure—given the interlinkages she found between them. For her, they are not different disciplines, but rather parts of a whole, each contributing to the larger cause of social justice and change.

And these were not all. There is a further dimension to her work that is not covered by the papers in this book. Women's empowerment is driven also by access to a range of resources, including, but not just, childcare. While she has always advocated for equal wages and labour rights, in recent years, she has advocated strongly for land rights for women, land being a key resource in rural India. She is an example of lifelong learning, willing to be challenged by peers and younger colleagues, as she acknowledges in chapter 1. Yet at the same time, she has remained a supportive and nurturing teacher, though in her own way, using a pedagogy that is critical and questioning.

Content of the Book

The contributors to this book include well-established academics and activists, deeply involved in these fields, both conceptually and in practice. Each of them has had a special relationship with Mina Swaminathan, at different stages of her life and career. While most of the papers are academic/research articles, we also include one graphic story (by Jolly Rohatagi and Mina Swaminathan), to illustrate the use of other forms of communication as equally valid for generating debate around new themes and concepts. In this case, the woman's right to choose, and here, to choose a family based on warm human relationships rather than on conventional marital choices, is illustrated; not only that, but in a rural setting, usually held to be more conservative and traditional.

The book is organised in two sections, the first on early childhood care and development and the second on gender and theatre. Given the interlinkages, this division is an artificial one, created more for organisational ease.

The papers in the first part cover a range of themes from scientific aspects of brain development to processes of learning and socialisation, as well as rights. Adarsh Sharma in her paper on brain development research provides an overview of the scientific knowledge about the biology of early brain development, and the mechanisms underlying learning capacity, behaviour regulation, and physical and mental development across the life span. The plasticity of the brain, its ability to change and adapt, the influential role of early relationships, and epigenetics, are delineated. This understanding about early brain development, including structure and functional aspects, leads to a framework for effective interventions and practices. The purpose is to illustrate how practices can be underpinned by an understanding of neuroscience to promote child development during the foundational years. But interestingly enough, what emerges as crucial is the positive support of adults through instructional and parenting practices; childhood outcomes are complex and cannot have biomedical/biological explanations alone.

Rekha Sharma Sen, in her paper "Acquiring Literacy in Pre-primary and Class 1: Meaning-making in a Trilingual Environment", demonstrates how young children learning English, Hindi, and Urdu simultaneously make sense of reading and writing. Based on observation of 32 teaching events, involving eight teachers, in one section each of pre-primary and Class 1 in a school, her research found that reading and writing activities were carried out in a strikingly similar manner across the two classes as well as across the three languages. Reading was essentially conceptualised by the teachers as an incremental process of learning to decode and was being taught mechanically through three sequential stages—letter recognition and naming, reading words (in isolation of the text) through a spelling based approach emphasising drilling and memorisation, followed by reading sentences/text in the same way. The teaching process did not account for variation in children's prior learning due to varying exposure to the languages in their socio-cultural milieu. Meaning-making while learning to read was completely relegated to the background. A combination of whole word approach, phonics and organic reading, premised on children's active agency, may enhance children's motivation to read and positively influence their ability to read and write meaningfully.

Archana Mehendale in her review of the "Right to Childcare in India" notes that childcare is presently seen as a need of mothers and their young children falling within the private domain of the family, and at times provided for externally by the private sector. Childcare as a 'right' finds only weak references in law and policies, thereby indicating the reluctance of the state to articulate its commitment. This paper critically examines the notion of right to childcare in India, analyses its contents by identifying who is entitled to this right and upon whom the obligation is placed. The review is contextualised within historical factors that shaped it as part of 'labour welfare'; and contemporary factors like privatisation and reduction in government's welfare functions, which have had implications on the way right to childcare has been enunciated.

While not explicitly engaging with a gender analysis, these papers point to the importance of socio-cultural contexts and norms, parenting practices and differences in the experiences of children as significant elements in shaping both child learning and general well-being. Rajalakshmi Sriram in her paper "Harnessing Fathering Potentials to Ensure Child Well Being" engages directly with a key gender problem, namely, fathers' involvement in child well-being. Moving from viewing fathers from a role-deficit perspective, which compares fathers and mothers on a similar template, the paper recognises father's needs, potentials and contributions across varied contexts and circumstances. Fathering, she demonstrates, not only contributes to children's well-being, but benefits women, even reduces violence, and contributes positively to a man's adult development. This is a well-recognised concept within the Indian notion of *Grihastha*. This paper highlights the ways in which fathers can be and are involved in young children's lives based on Indian evidence. It also focuses on the available opportunities to promote fathers' engagement with children. Drawing from the author's practical involvement in awareness and advocacy, the paper puts forth several strategies that can be used by practitioners to enhance father's involvement with young children.

The second section is explicitly written from a feminist perspective. Starting with a paper by Hanne M. de Bruin entitled

"Gender at Crossroads", which reflects, from a mixed academic and practical-emotional perspective, on the entry of girls and young women into Kattaikkuttu, a popular form of Tamil theatre. How has their entry changed performances and how have these performances been received by rural audiences? How empowering can theatre be for rural young women, in view of the fact that they continue to suffer from the double stigma of being an exponent of a low-status theatre as well as a woman performer?

Kattaikkuttu actor, director, teacher and playwright, P. Rajagopal is a strong advocate of opening up Kattaikkuttu training and onstage performances to girls and women. The transmission of his artistic knowledge and skills to women has broken the myth that they cannot or should not perform in this physically demanding ritual theatre which, traditionally, was men's prerogative. The Kattaikkuttu Young Professional Company is the first-ever mixed gender Kattaikkuttu theatre company and has shown actresses in leading male and female roles in both all-night, traditional and shorter, innovative performances. In fact, these professional young women artists contribute to the company's regional popularity.

In spite of this groundbreaking work, there is still no wholehearted acceptance of rural women as professional performers in society. Nor does society appears yet to have accepted even the genre in which they have been trained, Kattaikkuttu, as a legitimate and worthy form of theatre. How can rural women be enabled for freedom of choice, and to opt for a career in the performing arts? How can such a choice ensure them financial security and social dignity? And what are the challenges which the artistic métier poses to today's young women performers? These are some of the questions the paper seeks to address.

Mangai, in "Voicing Silence: Staging Feminist Consciousness", seeks to document the work of Voicing Silence over a decade (1993-2013) in building up a discourse of feminist theatre, mobilising the perspectives of women in the field of theatre—artists, directors and social groups using theatre as a tool for communication, celebrating the many voices of women through *Kulavai* (a woman's chant) festivals, and addressing specific needs of communities like

Dalit women, transgender persons, etc. Through its multi-fronted activities including production of plays, conducting workshops and organising meets at different levels, Voicing Silence hoped to gather the synergy of feminist consciousness. The 1990s saw the momentum of women's theatre/feminist theatre at the national and regional levels and Voicing Silence certainly played a crucial role in that process.

In "Lok Doot (the People's Messenger): Theatre for Communication", Jolly Rohatagi and Mina Swaminathan, through a graphic narration, demonstrate an element of the work they jointly did between 1975 and 1983. Lok Doot, the theatre group at Mobile Creches, consisting of a few talented staff members, grew out of the literacy programme on the construction sites, from a felt need for greater communication with the construction labour for whom it was intended. Starting as a series of humorous sketches to motivate people to join the literacy classes, the repertoire was gradually transformed by the two leaders, a drama teacher and an artist respectively, into an ongoing dialogue between the actors and the audience, using a variety of forms and techniques. Gender issues were introduced at two levels: a) by mirroring the life and difficulties of a woman construction worker; and b) through a new literacy primer which, by introducing the sign for the 'eee' sound in Hindi as early as the second lesson, which gave women both voice and role. Issues affecting the life of the people were dealt with, on the one hand, through traditional stories, tales, and myths as content, and on the other, using the people's own idiom—its sayings, language, songs, dances and folk art to tell the tale. Form and content both were drawn from the people, to make this a medium for two-way communication.

The last two papers deal with processes of gendered socialisation in tribal communities in India, and the implications for strengthening the voice and agency of girls and women. Amit Mitra examines the deep-rooted, underlying patriarchal gender ideologies that end up disadvantaging girls (and women) even in supposedly non-discriminatory institutions such as the school, using qualitative insights and observation from Dungarpur in Rajasthan. While challenging the myth of gender equality amongst tribal communities such as the Bhils (even though marginally better than caste groups), the paper examines both the home and the school as social institutions. The everyday activities and 'performances' therein, engrain particular gendered modes of behaviour in children. This paper points to the links across institutions in shaping gender relations, often intensifying and reproducing gender inequalities rather than challenging them.

In the final paper of this volume, Nitya Rao examines the trade-offs in the choices of women and girls, between maintaining their own identity as persons and keeping up wider social relationships, including with their children and parents. While Santal society does not disapprove of female agency and voice, nevertheless normative values around motherhood and expectations from women in terms of the well-being of their children, can constrain this. In particular, the ambiguous position of the girl child poses a dilemma for the mother. While sons will be absorbed and taken care of by the paternal family as legitimate heirs, there is no such obligation towards daughters, except an emotional one. Even if they are looked after, they could be discriminated against, made to perform household chores, and married early. The paper attempts to identify the covariates of social relationships and decisions—the emotive, relational and material—especially between mothers and daughters, in a particular locale, seen as relatively equitable, for well-being. While driven by both the economic situation and social standing of the women concerned, the paper points also to the dynamism of these relationships over time.

Clearly there have been gains for girls and women; many stories of assertion and resistance are visible, as presented also in this volume. Yet progressive, gender-equitable, social change is a slow process, perhaps far too slow. Material constraints and social norms work together to deprioritise both women's practical needs and strategic interests. Interestingly, and encouragingly, there is change on the ground. Men are better prepared and willing to play more responsible fathering roles, to allow greater freedoms to their daughters, although this does not apply to domestic work, seen as 'dirty', or to the realm of marriage. It is institutions of the state and community, deeply patriarchal and male-biased, which now serve to maintain the status quo, of male dominance and female subordination (Elson, 1995). Having built the foundations for equality and social change, feminist mobilisation and advocacy on a larger scale, is perhaps the next step.

References

Beneria, Lourdes (1982). "Accounting for Women's Work", in L. Beneria (ed.), *Women and Development: The Sexual Division of Labor in Rural Societies*. A study prepared for the International Labour Office within the framework of the World Employment Programme. New York: Praeger. pp.119-47.

Edholm, Felicity, Olivia Harris, and Kate Young (1978). "Conceptualising Women", *Critique of Anthropology* 3(9-10): 101-30. *http://coa.sagepub.com/content/3/9-10/101.full.pdf*.

Elson, Diane (1995). *Male Bias in the Development Process*. Manchester: Manchester University Press.

Freire, P. (1970). *Pedagogy of the Oppressed*. New York: Continuum Publishing Company.

Government of India (2000). *Report of the Time Use Survey: 1998-99*. New Delhi: Central Statistical Organisation, Ministry of Statistics and Programme Implementation.

Hirway, I. (2009). "Understanding Poverty: Insights Emerging from the Time Use of the Poor", in R. Antonopoulos and I. Hirway (eds.), *Unpaid Work and the Economy: Gender, Time Use and Poverty in the Global South*. UK: Palgrave Publishers.

Molyneux, Maxine (1979). "Beyond the Domestic Labour Debate", *New Left Review* 1(116): 3-27.

Rao, Nitya (2001). "Transformative Training: An Experiment in Pudukkottai", in R.K. Murthy (ed.), *Building Women's Capacities: Interventions in Gender Transformation*. New Delhi: Sage.

———. (2002). "Cycling into the Future: The Pudukkottai Experience", in P. Fernando and G. Porter (eds.), *Balancing the Load: Women, Gender and Transport*. London: Zed. pp.151-68.

———. (2014). "Caste, Kinship and Life-course: Rethinking Women's Work and Agency in Rural South India", *Feminist Economics* 20(3): 78-102.

Swaminathan, Mina (1985). *Who Cares?: A Study of Childcare Facilities for Low Income Working Women in India*. New Delhi, Indraprastha Press.

UNICEF and UNESCO (2012). *Asia-Pacific End of Decade Notes on Education for All: EFA Goal 1—Early Childhood Care and Education*. Bangkok.

1

MINA SWAMINATHAN and INDU AGNIHOTRI[1]

Gender, Childhood and Creative Communication

An Oral History

I

Early Years

Q. Lets start with your childhood. What are your memories of life in the early years?

My childhood was spent in a protected atmosphere, out of touch with the everyday realities of India in pre-Independence times. My father, a member of the elite Indian Civil Service (ICS), was at the topmost social level, since the ICS were practically the "rulers of the country." Until I was seven, my father served in different districts in Andhra Pradesh, my mother staying with him, so I was brought up mostly by my maternal grandparents, in Bombay. My grandfather was a successful auditor, in one of the earliest Indian audit and accountancy companies, set up by his father. So they must have been fairly wealthy, but the prevailing values of that era were of austere and simple living, spending no more than what was needed. Everybody lived a simple life, reinforced by what they heard from Gandhiji, during the freedom struggle.

My grandparents' two youngest children, my aunts, were only two and five years older than me. We three spent our childhood together, like sisters. I looked on my grandmother, with whom I remained deeply attached to, as my mother, and my mother as a sort of older sister who occasionally came to visit. Life in my grandparents' home was quite different from life with my parents.

---

1. Mina Swaminathan interviewed by Indu Agnihotri.

There was an abundance of good food, and lots of freedom. We used to wander around in buses, going where we wanted because the bus services were so good, and Bombay so safe, that no one worried about us. We joined the Municipal Swimming Pool, learnt to take care of ourselves and our own things, practised yoga, went to the library to borrow books. The big joy of our lives was the Popular Book Store, which had lots of children's books in English. My grandfather had an arrangement with the management that when we girls came, we could take whatever we wanted and he would pay the bill later! So the reading habit was formed early. My grandparents used to take us to the movies from the age of 3, and I have seen many famous Indian movies, like *Achut Kanya* featuring Ashok Kumar. Later, we used to see English movies. So I became a movie buff early in life with the encouragement of elders, quite unusual for girls in those days. My grandfather did not discriminate between sons and daughters, and girls had the same opportunities as boys, also unusual for that time.

Q. So where did you receive formal education?

In 1940, my father moved to Delhi, and at the age of seven I started school there; but as soon as the summer holidays would start each year, I would board the train the very same day and dash off to Bombay. Delhi and Bombay constituted my universe: I was never exposed to rural life. When my father was posted in various districts, I remember visiting him and staying in huge houses on the banks of vast rivers. But those are vague memories, like dreams—my entire childhood was urban. I went to a convent school, but when we came home, we spent the rest of the day playing in the garden or the wild jungle behind the house, or learning and practising cycling. There was no homework; the only extra burden, being music and Sanskrit lessons twice a week. Although we heard about the freedom struggle and were deeply influenced by it, we were not allowed to go to meetings or events, and my first experience of that was at Gandhiji's funeral.

Q. Can you tell me about some significant influences on your life?

There are two unforgettable incidents which shaped my outlook and these happened rapidly one after another. On 14 August 1947, we all sat up at night to hear Jawaharlal Nehru's famous "Tryst with Destiny" speech on the radio at midnight, and the fireworks and celebrations that followed in January 1948. My parents had taken me one evening to the house of a colleague, where the kids were playing badminton in the garden. Suddenly, at about 5'o clock, the adults came out of the house, and shouted, "Stop playing children, Gandhiji has been killed." We came running to sit in front of the radio, to hear the news, and later Nehru's speech: "The Light has Gone Out of Our Lives...." Two days later, we all went for the funeral. There were huge crowds of people, most of whom had walked from the surrounding villages; since there was no public transport at that time, they must have walked day and night. The streets were packed, even the great avenues of New Delhi, with people standing on walls and houses, climbing on trees. And one of my greatest regrets is that even though I was living in Delhi at that time, I never saw Gandhiji alive. These two incidents made a deep impression on me, and were probably the basis of the determination of me and my generation to "serve the country"—that patriotism has remained a constant.

I joined college, much underage in 1948, and passed out at the age of 18 (in the year strict age regulation was imposed!) and went to Cambridge, where I was the same age as any other 18-year-old undergraduate, although I already had a BA degree from India.

Q. Would you agree that it was learning from reading, but no exposure to reality?

Yes, I floated through school, always coming out top of the class, without actually doing any work. So I never developed good work habits, though I continued to read avidly. Our three main debating issues were politics, religion and sex. The adults appreciated the first two, but the third we had to do secretly! There was no television, and on radio, we were only allowed to listen to AIR. Vividh Bharati had just started and we would listen to that and to US Armed Forces Radio secretly, at night.

So when I came to college, I was familiar with Marx, Sidney and Beatrice Webb, Aldous Huxley, Shaw, Freud, Jung, Eddington and Eisenberg, and many more thinkers, but I knew nothing about poverty, class, caste, and other burning Indian issues. I was a confirmed Socialist by the time I went to college, and was excited by the Avadi declaration of India as a Socialist country! For long, my dream was to go to Soviet countries to study their achievements in child education, and children's programmes, and was careful not to blot my passport with an American visa, lest it prevent me from entering Union of Soviet Socialist Republic (USSR) one day!

I found the teaching at Miranda House, the best women's college at the time, boring and dull; it never inspired us to think or read, nor did it draw on our own reading. The questions asked required only routine information. So, I got involved with debating, drama and music. I was an average student, irritating my teachers with too many questions.

In my first year at college, I enrolled in Physics and Mathematics, out of a passion for science born from reading. But as I had studied no science at all in school (though I had read astronomy and other great scientists in popular books), I made no headway. In the second year, I switched to Economics.

Q. But then how did you land up in Cambridge?

Because my father decided to send me there, and I found it refreshingly different from college life in India, I spent vacations travelling in Europe, polished up my French, and made many friends, Indian, British and European, some lifelong. But looking back, I can see that I did not make the best use of it. I did not work hard, not even recognising the honour of having E.J. Hobsbawm, already an icon, as my alternate Tutor! I realise now that coming from elite homes, we knew deep down that whatever kind of degree we got would be enough for us, so we lazed around focusing on enjoying ourselves—through travel and culture. So, Cambridge did not substantially alter my thinking. I also never developed the Oxford-Cambridge pride that most Indian alumni have, never joined the Oxford-Cambridge Society. This was a rejection, I now see as deliberate. My later life was so different that I never joined that charmed circle.

When I came home from Cambridge at the age of 20, I was convinced, like those with whom I studied science at Delhi University for a year, that in some way or the other we had to "serve the country". None of us knew how we would serve, and in fact, each of us did it in different ways, many by joining the Indian Administrative Services (IAS). But that was the overriding thought in our minds—such was the impact of the freedom struggle and the non-violent achievement of Independence. But my circle of friends at Miranda House, who belonged to the elite, were more concerned with personal goals. In later life, I drifted away from most of them, perhaps because they were not interested in things I was passionate about—only two remained close, and one is no more.

Q. What and how did you learn about the freedom struggle?

I learnt about it indirectly, through my mother, and friends. My mother, brought up in Bombay, had been exposed to the nationalist movement on the streets as a schoolgirl, before her marriage, and was deeply influenced by Gandhian ideals and thinking, and often spoke about it. After her marriage, she became a charming hostess with many accomplishments like swimming, driving, and playing tennis, which she also taught me. But she was no mere housewife. Widely read, she taught herself Sanskrit and Tamil, becoming an accomplished and well-known bilingual writer, writing fiction, drama and essays in Tamil, and later, Indian mythology and legends for children in English, some of which are still in print.

She taught me to read and write Tamil, subscribed to Tamil magazines, through which I was introduced, as a teenager, not only to the serialised classics of nationalist Tamil writers, but also, through her constant singing of his poetry, to the nationalist poet Subramania Bharati.

As my father was still a servant of the British Government, we could not participate in activities like prayer meetings, picketing of shops and burning of foreign cloth, as she had done. But some of my schoolmates did so and I learnt about it from them too, and later from college friends. These were latent but powerful influences.

My father's role was to guide our intellectual development. He encouraged reading, talked about books and ideas and, when he could, read Shakespeare aloud to us. My father was not merely an outstanding bureaucrat, but a scholar, one of the best economists of his generation, a prolific writer in economic journals, knowing several Indian and foreign languages, self-taught.

Q. What were the questions in your mind when you were young and went seeking answers?

After returning from Cambridge, I spent a year travelling to decide what I wanted to do. To my father's great disappointment, I had decided that I wanted to be a school teacher. His friend, Dr VKRV Rao, at that time Head of the Delhi School of Economics (DSE) invited me to do a PhD with him, since a degree from Cambridge counted as an MA in India, and was quite annoyed when I said I didn't want to do a PhD, but wished to "teach children".

So I continued with my *yatra*, travelling around the country looking for work. I went to Kalakshetra where I could have easily got a job, but I was nauseated by the cult atmosphere around Rukmani Devi. I went to Rishi Valley, then under the supervision of one of the great educators of that time, F.G. Pearce. He offered me a job, but I felt that it was not the place for me. When some of the Rishi Valley parents asked me why, I said, "Those children already have everything, they don't need me. I want to work with children who don't have so much, so that I can give them something they need." And that's how I decided to get into the teaching profession and work with poor children. Now, I happily say that I have a PhD from the School of Life!

Meanwhile, I took up a job in the Planning Commission, under the Research Programmes Committee—intended to scrutinise and guide research programmes. I found it boring, although I got to travel—the best thing about that job was that I met some fine people, some of whom became lifelong friends. That was also where I had my first direct experience of sexual harassment at the hands of my boss, an eminent elderly economist!

Around that time, I met Ayesha Jacob, the head of St. Thomas School, one of the persons who influenced me greatly in my teaching career. At that time an 'aided school', a category where the bulk of the expenses were borne by the government, even though it was a private, missionary institution. The fees were very low, attracting children from the surrounding community. The clientele included two distinct groups; clerical employees of the government, who lived in that area, and petty tradesmen from the nearby Paharganj market. The first group set big value on education, because that's how they had got their jobs. Many were Tamil-speaking people, among them, the first generation of educated Tamil migrants, who flocked to seek their fortunes in Delhi, Bombay and Calcutta. But in the trading families, girls had never been sent to school before; these were first generation learners. When I saw this place, I decided that these were the children for whom I could do something useful.

I asked Ms Jacob for a job. She interviewed me and obviously liked me, but said firmly, "We don't take untrained teachers—you may be from Cambridge or anywhere else, but go and get your teacher training first and then I shall employ you".

So in April 1955, I did three things—gave up my job in the Planning Commission, sought admission to the B.Ed course, and got married.

II

The IARI Years[2]

I call these years (1955-1970) by that name because we lived on campus. Although I had a stimulating teaching job at St. Thomas School, the period also marked the early years of our marriage, when I gave a lot of time and energy to being a partner, not merely at home, but also offering social support at work. Every day we went to the lab in the evening, mingled with the students, who were often at our house. We became known as a "partying" group, because every time any of the students crossed one of the milestones, like completing a

2. Indian Agricultural Research Institute.

chapter, it would be celebrated with a party. We became a close-knit group.

This "social lubrication" also extended to conferences and meetings with scientists coming from all over the country. We would often host a tea party for them in our house and make them, sworn enemies who had been glowering at each other all day in meetings holding opposite points of view, play games and laugh uproariously. We also entertained the foreign students, mostly African, who, then as now, were completely ignored by the Indian families on the campus. We invited them over for Christmas dinner, with carol singing, and many would comment: "I've been here two years, but this is the first time I've entered an Indian home." Such is our racism!

Our daily evening walk always ended up at the Botany Department where I would be asked to inspect the ladies' toilets to see if they were in good condition and check what was needed! So because of me, sanitary bins were introduced in the ladies' toilets, a great relief to women scientists and staff.

There was a close integration between my work and family life, which by the late 1960s, culminated in the setting up of the Nehru Experimental Centre, which began catering to the community as a whole.

All this time I was teaching English at St. Thomas, first to higher secondary classes, then lower down, class by class, and by the end of my time there, at the primary and then nursery school level. I must perhaps be the only person who started with the highest class and ended up at the bottom, out of choice! Increasingly I had found that the weaknesses I saw in the classroom had roots in earlier years. So I went on exploring downwards, and have spent most of my life since then working in ECE (early childhood education), with children below six.

I soon became deeply involved in the use of drama as a tool for education, not only to help students understand literature, but to improvise, imagine, create and express, to go beyond the cognitive element so dominating in Indian schools, merely learning by heart, endlessly telling and repeating. Drama was a way of bringing in the social and emotional domains, so that students became aware of the lived reality of a historical period, a story, an argument. This became a lifelong interest, and I am deeply indebted to Ayesha Jacob, for the opportunity. Much of the material I developed was later published, to help other teachers do similar things. My first book on drama in schools was published by National Council of Educational Research and Training (NCERT), and several others followed.

Towards the end of my time there, in 1969, the birth centenary year of Mahatma Gandhi, we produced a big pageant, a dramatic presentation on the life of Gandhiji, starting from his early days in South Africa right up to his death, with the involvement of 1,000 students from classes 6 to 11. Each class was given a segment of the story to dramatise, using the methods of creative drama, to better understand its spirit and feeling. Later, a conventional text was used for presentation. The two-hour pageant was deeply moving and memorable. Shortly after this, I left the school, as the time had come.

Q. *Can you tell us more about the Nehru Experimental Centre?*

The Kothari Commission's vision of locality-based common schools for all children had opened my eyes to the inequities of the existing system. Through the Nehru Experimental Centre, I had started working with the community at IARI. Although its many activities included debates/discussions with postgraduate students, drama, sports for children, I would focus on only two—both concerned with ECE.

In 1960, I came in touch with Rajalakshmi Muralidharan, then at NCERT, who had introduced me to preschool education. I attended several conferences, meetings and workshops, met many others in the same field, and joined the Indian Association for Preschool Education (IAPE), which later became a major vehicle for change in the classroom. Realising that I had to put my learnings into practice, I decided to start a nursery school on campus, to serve the lower levels of staff. I recruited a small band of enthusiastic women, with some having prior training, from the same community as teachers. Although space was provided free by the Institute, there were no grants, and families could not afford much, so fees had to be minimal, as well as the salaries. With application of what I had studied and some ingenuity, we could develop a happy, busy classroom full of learning, at a little cost. Later, I continued my work with still poorer groups, at Mobile Crèches, in Vietnam, and Cambodia. In time, this experience earned me the title of the "prophet of low-cost".

The only thing I regretted was not to start crèches for the children of women agricultural labour working on the huge farm at IARI. But this proposal didn't meet with support from the administration, as the laws on crèches did not (and still do not) extend to agriculture. But this started me thinking about the wider issues of day care.

The second major activity was the attempt to run a Balwadi in a rural area, in one of the villages which the IARI scientists visited. A group of us, both men and women looked around and talked to the women about whether they had a *Balwadi*. The existing one functioned erratically. The *Balwadis* started by Durgabai Deshmukh in the 1950s were intended to extend to the whole country and provide services to all rural women, but often they did not do so, as the design developed by upper-class urban women was unsuited to the needs and issues of rural women, their work burden, timings and caste equations.

We undertook a survey in the month of February and found that between February and May, all the women in the village, a Jat one, left for the field at 6 am for harvesting, and came back around 11 am with big bundles of hay on their heads. The *Balwadi* teacher, who came from far away by bus, rarely reached before 10 am. So they challenged us, "Give us a Balwadi which will take care of our children from 6 am till 11 am, that's all we need. After that, we will take care of our own children." Clearly, they needed a day care arrangement. There was no way to find a trained *Balwadi* teacher who would be there by 6 am in the morning since they all came from far away. Finally one of my colleagues suggested that we contact the 'key' person to do this job—the daughter-in-law of the village Pradhan. This bright young woman, with high school education, was interested and agreed. With her protected position as the daughter-in-law of the village, she wouldn't be criticised by others, if she did not fulfil their expectations. Very practical, but I did not realise at the time that I had fallen into both the caste trap and the family-nepotism trap!

So we started off, with a lot of activities and games, going there every alternate day to work with her, with 30-40 children to care for, and she managed it pretty well. We could not provide food for lack of funds, but the mothers provided some *roti*, and we carried biscuits and sweets for the morning break. That was important in psychological terms, generating goodwill for the project. The village people collected something for a small honorarium, far from a *Balwadi* teacher's wage, but recognition of the useful service to women of the community. And since all was under the 'benevolent' eye of the Pradhan, nobody protested, and things went smoothly. When the season was over mid-May, hectic work in the fields came to an end and we changed back to the conventional *Balwadi* timings. We approached the Delhi Social Welfare Board (DSWB) to recognise this is as one of their *Balwadis*, and they did, so she started getting a regular salary. But this *Balwadi*, unlike all others, continued to offer the seasonal day care service from February to May for many years.

It was a year full of varied learnings, some recorded in my daily notebook, entitled My Village Diary. Looking back, I realise how little I knew then about rural realities, especially of caste and class. Preoccupied as I was with children's education, I had not noticed, or even seen, the equally large numbers of Dalit women who also worked in the fields, and had to leave their children at home without care. No one mentioned them, and I asked no questions, nor reflected on the skewed patronage of the Pradhan. Later, I came to know that most of the *Balwadi* teachers were nominees, if not relatives, of the village Pradhans. The struggle to employ women from the stigmatised castes is still not over. My protected life had given me many skills, but not this knowledge!

Q. What about the family, home and children?
Did the women in the family make an impression on your life?

During these years, combining work with family was another dimension. Not only did I have to find time to be with my young children, but also keep in touch with my husband's large joint family. When I got married, I found the family I entered a big surprise—another world, quite different from mine. A huge extended rural family, with many branches, numbering perhaps 200-300 people. At that time, I was only surprised that they loved me in spite of the fact that I was so different! I too explored their lives, and we all became great friends. They told me interesting stories; for example, that my mother-in-law had, on hearing that my husband had decided to marry a girl who had been educated abroad, burst into tears, because she thought some monster was entering the home and she had no idea how to cope! But I was so eager to please and adjust, and she was warm and kind. Gradually, over a few years, I became her favourite daughter-in-law! It became a joke in the family, that she loved me more than the others and I too began to love and admire her. When I met her, she was about 45. Widowed at the age of 27, she had brought up her four children as part of the joint family, with much sacrifice and effort. Her husband, who died young, was not only a well-known surgeon and activist who rid the town of its mosquitoes, but a Gandhian, a member of the Congress Party, very active in the freedom struggle, and slated to join the Provincial Government in 1937, but for his untimely death. He had taken his wife to the Allahabad Congress, and travelled with her in north India. The whole family was Gandhian, spun yarn, wore only khadi made from it, learned Hindi by taking lessons, and tracked the national movement closely. Gandhiji stayed at their home whenever he visited the town, and the children remembered him because he asked for their gold ornaments! My husband wore only khadi when we first met. He no longer does so, but remains a Gandhian, moved by compassion. I am a staunch Leftie, fuelled by rage at injustice; yet we have remained close partners, accepting our differences, working for the same goals.

In 1971, when I was asked to contribute a chapter for a book on Indian women, I chose to write about her. The chapter, titled "Chellamma", a common Tamil nickname, referring to a loved person, described a cross between her and my grandmother, both of whom I loved and admired very much. This year the book has been republished and the new version is built entirely around her—a tribute to women of another generation, a model of what a woman of that time, place and social context could achieve.

This was also the period, until 1980, when we shuttled between Delhi and Kumbakonam, where the joint family still lived, every summer holiday, and that is how the children became bilingual. In those days, Tamil-speaking people faced great discrimination in north India. People would make fun of us, our language, our pronunciation, our food, everything. To protect them from such harassment in Delhi, I had seen to it that they were all fluent in Hindi. But the summer vacation? The train journey was about 36 hours, so as soon as we boarded the train at New Delhi station, I would start urging them "Don't speak Hindi, speak Tamil." By the time we got off at Madras they would slowly start suppressing the Hindi which came naturally to their lips, and speak in Tamil instead. On the return journey, when they got into the train at Madras Central, I would start urging the reverse; "Don't speak Tamil, speak Hindi" so by the time we reached Delhi they would start speaking in Hindi again.

III

The Mobile Crèches Years—The 1970s

Q. *How did you get involved with the Mobile Crèches (MC)? What did this experience signify?*

The 1970s, a rich and creative period in my life, were mostly the Mobile Crèches years. In 1969, I met J.P. Naik, former Secretary to the Kothari Commission, and my guide and mentor until his death in 1978. He was presiding over a debate where I passionately called for abolition of the so-called "public" schools, as a step towards the "neighbourhood schools" suggested in the Report, articulating the dream of universal, egalitarian education for all children. He laughed, but must have made some enquiries about me, because soon (in 1970), I found myself a member of the Central Advisory Board of Education (CABE) an august body of Central and State Education Ministers, high officials and a few specialists.

The Study Group on Preschool Education, set up by CABE, submitted its report in 1972, which, after being mulled over for two years by the bureaucracy, emerged as the Integrated Child

Development Services (ICDS), a far cry from what we had proposed. With neither political support nor awareness of the strategic importance of early childhood, combined with competition from earlier programmes like the *Balwadis* of Central Social Welfare Board (CSWB), ICDS has remained a set of hand-outs, especially of food, instead of growing into a rounded programme for child development.

At the same time as ICDS was announced, in 1974, Meera Mahadevan succeeded in getting the scheme of Crèches for the children of working and ailing mothers approved by the CSWB, through her contact with the then Minister for Social Welfare. Meera focused on the funding, while I worked in the field. 'Doing something' still meant only individual effort with state support. It was difficult to get either political leaders or bureaucrats interested in day care for the children of working mothers. It seemed to go deep against conventional Indian thinking about women and motherhood—I remember that Morarji Desai, then Prime Minister, who, when a delegation of women called on him to plead for crèches for working mothers, snapped back at us the unforgettable words: "A Bharatiya Nari will never allow others to care for her children!" Our request seemed to have attacked the very basis of Indian civilisation, and we were condemned as "Westernised" and disloyal!

At Mobile Crèches, I continued to delve deep into ECE from a practical angle—working with the children of the poorest; first, those of migrant construction workers living in makeshift huts on the construction site, and later in urban slums built at the edges of Delhi during the displacement led by Sanjay Gandhi.

Q. The challenges for MC?

It was to be more than just another charity, the challenge was that of offering the best quality programmes for the poorest, part of my rage against injustice. The key person was the teacher, or caregiver. We could not attract qualified teachers; the few who came were appalled by the work environment and conditions and left at once. So we recruited lower middle-class women and girls, themselves desperately seeking opportunity to better their lives. They were thrown into the worksite crèche, and asked to start working under the guidance of those already there. If they survived the first few days, they stayed on and gradually developed into good workers—if not, they left the next day.

Q. What response did the MC give?

The challenge was to build up an environment for child development—not only of nutrition, healthcare, immunisation and other basic needs, but also of stimulating play activities fostering the child's cognitive, social and emotional growth. The first task was to set up a few working centres as models, improving them step-by-step; next, to develop a cadre of skilled workers, who would not only care for the children with love and affection, but also be their teachers, playmates, nurses and caregivers—a tall order. Thus was born the unique system of "on-the-job" training for which Mobile Crèches is now famous—an innovative response to a desperate situation. In a nutshell, practice came first, theory later, and it worked. Most of those who worked with the youngest age group—below three—had little education and did not respond to visual materials like charts or notes. So we hit upon the idea of composing the key messages, into songs, each with a tuneful melody. They quickly memorised the songs and became masters of their trade.

I coined the term "experiential" for this kind of training—nowadays its called 'hands-on'. Over time, it became codified and systematic, with its own curriculum and a variety of materials to support it. At its core, it was what Paolo Freire summarised as "experience—reflect—do". When I came across his work, I was delighted to find that an unknown person far away in Latin America had arrived at the same method to help adults learn.

The training was backed by the design and development of low-cost play and learning materials, often using things that are easily found on a construction site—like bricks, wood, stones, pebbles, and easily picked–up scrap. The teachers also learnt to make a variety of dolls, toys and playthings using materials like used paper, pieces of cloth, and straw. Mobile Crèches then developed a band of volunteers who excelled in collecting such materials from homes and offices, and soon set up a regular supply chain. Ironically, among the poor, there is no waste—everything is used and reused until it falls apart. It was the 'waste' generated by the rich that was used for the benefit of the poor—in addition, well-off women felt they were making a useful contribution!

Q. How did you get involved with adult literacy?

Mobile Crèches had to deal with children up to the age of 12 (by which time they entered the workforce), along with their parents. The focus was on early literacy leading to school entry, achieved by efforts to enrol the children in local schools, to ensure that they stayed there for as long as possible. This was a difficult task in the case of migrant labour, but easier in urban slums.

The adult education effort began with literacy classes for both men and women held in the late evenings in the shacks of the families, lit by kerosene lamps. Conventional literacy materials were remote from the concerns of the people. So I developed a new set of primers, based on the everyday life experiences of men and women labourers on construction sites, selecting both topics and vocabulary on that basis. Another major innovation was gender equality. All the available literacy material had separate primers for men and women. The men learnt about the world as a whole, while the women's primers were confined to home and hearth, children and cooking! I developed a gender-neutral and linguistically more suitable primer.

Q. How did you develop the theatre in education medium?

Realising that literacy was a slow route to the destination, we began using other communication tools, like drama. Starting with simple skits on literacy, intended to entertain as well as attract the labourers to the literacy classes, we gradually developed a small theatre unit consisting of staff members, men and women with some talents and skills, and eager to participate. The group called itself *Lok Doot*, or People's Messenger.

Developed, in collaboration with the artist Jolly Rohatagi, this group produced effective and polished dramas on themes of concern to the community we were playing to, embedded in folk forms—using their literary idiom, music and story, to bring it closer to the audience. We introduced puppets, and other traditional aids to storytelling and the folk idiom enriched the process, leading to dialogue with the community. Soon we became skilled enough to do participatory plays, using alternative endings, parallel stories and other theatrical strategies. A memorable one was on the theme of gender equality, taking the role differences between the men and women on the construction site as its base. We did it in traditional idiom, structuring it as a series of alternatives, asking the audience each time to suggest what turn the story should take and what decision the character should make. This was perhaps one of the culminating experiences of *Lok Doot*.

Q. Did the State or government support your Initiatives?

I also worked continuously with and through the IAPE, a body with which I engaged for 30 years, serving first as Editor of its journal, then Secretary, and finally, much later, President. The journal *Balak*, or Child, was co-edited by me and Rosalind Wilson. Working for IAPE, I was transformed into a teacher educator.

At this time, both the NDMC[3] and the Municipal Corporation of Delhi (MCD) started nursery classes for 3–5 year-olds in all their schools. Both IAPE as a body and I as a member were deeply involved in this effort, visiting schools, organising workshops and interacting with both teachers and officials, working to improve the quality of education. Since then until now, Delhi continues to host the only two municipal authorities in the country steadfastly sponsoring ECE, a matter for congratulation.

Q. You said you were a leftie? What did you mean by that and how did that come about?

As I said, theoretically, I was a Socialist from my teens. But let me highlight on my sudden political 'growing up'. The latter half of the 1970s saw shocking events which abruptly aroused us from the golden dream of Gandhian socialism in which we had been living—the Emergency brought us harshly back to a fascist reality we were least prepared for. I can never forget the tale of horrors which I

3. New Delhi Municipal Committee.

witnessed on the streets and schools of Delhi and I was changed forever.

Two incidents particularly stand out in my memory—the first was the rounding up of hundreds of young men, many unmarried, most engaged in manual labour, on 19 April 1976, to be loaded into trucks and taken to sterilisation camps. This happened in front of my eyes in Sadar Bazaar, a market which I regularly visited to buy cheap play equipment in bulk. The second was on 26 September when a sudden rumour spread in the lanes around the Municipal school I was in, that young girls were being taken away to be sterilised by some mysterious "injection" (an impossibility!). Within minutes, mothers had appeared out of nowhere and snatched all the girls away home. Both the mechanism and its speed were astounding. During the following days, we learnt that the same incidents had taken place in most MCD schools (1800 of them) at the same time on that day—it was the underground opposition, the Rashtriya Swayamsevak Sangh (RSS), showing its muscle—perhaps in preparation for the coming elections. It was the first time I learnt the power of this invisible organisation, who again showed their strength a few years later with the mysterious "drinking of milk" by Ganesha idols in several cities. The religious imagery was powerful, adding black clouds of communal hatred.

This was a time of hardship for many sections of the people. We were witness to huge translocations of population from congested urban slums, uprooted overnight and thrown out into the far-flung outer parts of the city with no housing, water, facilities of any kind, and above all no transport to take them back to the city which was their only source of livelihood. We were also witness to other extremities of the sterilisation campaigns, with children in Class I obliged to bring certificates of sterilisation from their parents, little knowing what they were asking for, in order to be promoted to the next grade! Fear and anxiety added to the enormous difficulties already faced by the poorest sectors of the population.

In my youth I had been a theoretical Marxist and later on a Socialist. But it was the emergency which politicised me. It made me aware that far from being on the road to realising the dreams that we had in 1947, all the well-intentioned hard work of many, was being cut away at the roots by a despotic government interested only in the welfare of a few, not of the mass of its citizens. Henceforth, I decided that I would work not for the country but for its people.

Q. *When did you become aware of gender as an issue?*

Of the many from whom I learnt much, I can only single out Vina Mazumdar, who changed many lives, including mine, with that extraordinary report, 'Towards Equality', brought out by a team of women led by Vina *di* herself, opening our eyes to the true position of women in India. It broke the comfortable middle-class world in which we were living, and made us aware of the real situation of the millions of our countrywomen.

I had earlier known Vina *di* as the teacher of her two rebellious teenage girls whom I had taught in St. Thomas School. But now I began working with her. By the end of the decade, she had set up the Centre for Women's Development Studies, with me as one of its founding members. Not surprisingly, I was the first to perceive the link between women and children, and was instrumental in putting childcare on the agenda of the women's movement. (Earlier, the women's movement, had been hesitant to be clubbed with children, mostly because they feared losing their new-found recognition as 'persons', and being pushed backwards to the status of only 'mothers'). This changed in the 1980s further, when the stalwart woman Labour leader Ela Bhatt, also put childcare on the women's agenda, and led by developing crèches for the women workers who made up her organisation, Self-Employed Women's Association (SEWA). Not only that, she saw childcare workers not as mere employees, as elsewhere, but also as "self-employed women" in their own right, they formed cooperatives to run the crèches and raised their own funds. This was a unique experiment in marrying the cooperative movement with a service like childcare.

IV

Free Fall

Q. How did you find time for writing?

The 1980s can best be described as a free fall—cut off from all I knew—home, job, even house (we had lived only in government housing), friends, family, and above all, country. In the end, I came to terms with it, and reset my goals to accomplish something. I see now, I was forced to extend myself beyond my boundaries, but at that time it was dizzying. From quality improvement, I had to begin imagining, then developing, new possibilities, to think on a larger and more systemic scale.

It started on the day M.S. Swaminathan (MSS) decided to accept the job of Director-General of the International Rice Research Institute (IRRI) in the Philippines. No stranger to campus life, I was horrified by the social constrictions of the small and exclusive enclave of expatriates where we lived, cut off from both the Philippines and its people. With a well-equipped house and staff, I could hardly settle down as a 'homemaker' either, lacking interest, as I did, in that department. A diplomatic passport prevented me from looking for a job. Breaking out in new directions, in fact, led to new solutions.

For starters, I decided to transform myself into a writer, recording my rich experience, promising myself I would write five books in five years. In reality, I managed to write three! It was not so difficult, as I had been writing for years and had even published a fair amount.

The first was a manual/guidebook for teachers of young children aged between 3-6 based on my teaching and training experiences until then. First published in 1984 by United Nation Children's Fund (UNICEF), it was altered, revised, and rewritten, together with my partner Prema Daniel, and is today, the standard guidebook for teachers on early childhood education, published by the National Book Trust in English and Hindi. The second was the study on day care in India which I wrote for Centre for Women Development Studies (CWDS), for the Third World Women's Conference in Nairobi in 1985, still the only Indian study on the subject. To develop the case study, I travelled to Dhanbad to study the statutory crèches in the mining sector, and was shocked to find how unimportant the subject was in the eyes of the officials I met. None could even remember where the crèches were or whom I should meet! It took two days of running from pillar to post to locate somebody, who could guide me. But I got to see a few and met many women workers, crèche workers and supervisory staff from whom I gleaned information, to complete the report. At the Conference, it was a proof that the women's movement then was a strong advocate for childcare services. The third and last, published by United Nations Educational, Scientific and Cultural Organisation (UNESCO) in 1989, was a manual for those working with children below the age of three. Based on my experiences in Vietnam, it was intended to improve the skills of childcare workers working with the below-threes.

Q. Philippines was in turmoil, so how did you manage to explore anything?

Side by side, I began exploring the Philippines. To learn the language, I found a young schoolteacher to help me, but she did not quite know how to teach me her language! I had to help her, giving instructions and planning the lessons. I then got a set of audio tapes and began practising them with whoever I could. But my teacher became a good friend and we spent time talking together. She and her husband, a rural extension worker, took me to a village at the top of the mountain, where I met a family. I began to visit them often, living with them in their stilt house with the animals below, crawling up the ladder to reach the living room, using the outdoor toilet—a hole in the ground—going to the stream to wash clothes, playing with the children, and watching how my hostess caught a chicken for dinner. They became my adopted family in the Philippines, and I the godmother of their youngest child, born the following year.

In the village, I met the priest and the midwife, making friends and visiting people. Rural Catholic priests often supported the insurgency and protected the insurgents, I learnt later. The more I tried to practice the Filipino language, the more people tried to practice their English on me! We all learnt something, and I gradually improved. In a few months I was confident enough to start travelling around on my own across the country, using local transport. After the major earthquake in Mount Mayon, I visited the area to observe the relief activities. I found that the best, most organised group was the Church, in which people had great faith, while representatives of the government were hardly to be seen. When travelling, two favourite bits of advice from fellow travellers were—one, never get into a military vehicle even if you want a ride—you will be shot; and two, always stay with the nuns for safety. I followed both rules, even travelling to places like Mindanao, where there was constant insurgency.

At that time, at the height of Marcos' dictatorship, public discussion steered clear of anything political. Censored newspapers carried no news, only advertisements and bland stories; while TV had only "soaps", film and music. Innocently, I used to comment to Filipino friends about the difference between the Filipino press and our lively Indian press. They maintained a polite silence, only later, after Marcos was overthrown, I learnt many of the those people had relatives and friends 'in the mountains', the expression referring to those supporting the insurgency.

I also came to know about different forms of folk theatre in the Philippines and began visiting them regularly in various places. There were many forms, the most popular being the *sinaculo*, the local version of the Passion Play which would be acted out by the village people in the days preceding Easter, concluding with a solemn ritual on the Sunday. As in ritual theatre in India, like the *Ram Lila,* particular families in each village kept the costumes and had the right to play a particular character in the play. The Sunday early morning procession included tiny little girls dressed as angels, and strapped to long sticks held high in the sky. I also joined the Philippine Educational Theatre Association (PETA) and learnt about street theatre, revolutionary theatre and other modern forms, attending their conferences, workshops and festivals. I was sometimes viewed with suspicion by radical groups, but my knowledge of the language usually protected me.

The acme of my rich and varied experience of Filipino culture came when I was permitted to join in a sacred pilgrimage. It gave me the experience of all pilgrimages—the journey, the way people help each other, pray together, share everything, and jointly struggle to reach the goal. Rituals and observances of pilgrimage in every religion, however diverse, are basically similar—they provide the liminal experience—which I have documented in depth elsewhere.

Q. What did you learn from your work on early childhood development in South East Asia?

In 1983, UNESCO invited me to visit Vietnam, to study crèches and nursery schools and propose ways to improve them. In Bangkok, at UNESCO headquarters, I met my counterpart, J. Ratnaike, a Sri Lankan, a brilliant and thoughtful person who not only provided a window into Southeast Asia, but also into my role. In Hanoi, I was to stay at a beautiful old hotel in the French part of the city. But I soon found that it was a broken shell—beautiful tubs in the bathroom, but neither the faucets nor flush worked and the taps dripped all night! Everything was falling to pieces and no repairs were done. The old French villas had also been preserved exactly as they were; but each house had been parcelled out for about 10 or 12 families to live in, each in one or two rooms. That was post-war Hanoi—completely destroyed by the war and yet putting up a brave front. Again, they refused to remove the shot-down American planes from the airport. The reason? So that the young would never forget the war and its aftermath.

The crèches had been a response to the war, when all the men were at the battlefront and women had to manage both fields and home. Group care of young children was the only answer to free women for work—while a few took care of the children. The crèches were housed in simple but clean community shelters, the food being rice soup with bits of fish floating in it—not much else could be afforded. The village put together funds to provide two eggs and two bananas per child a week, and vegetables two or three times. Even to do this, adults had to sacrifice their share. In Hanoi, the crèches were often in the homes of elderly couples who volunteered to take care of 8 or 10 children there. The old man was often a retired soldier, watchman or gardener; between them the old couple managed the babies the whole day, and for this got, in addition to the pension, a small amount. It was like managing a family, except that there were no older children to help. It is surprising that in spite of our admiration and close contacts with Socialist countries, we never tried to emulate them in either childcare, or education—perhaps our attachment to the English language was a barrier?

In both village and town, basic needs were met. Although conditions were hard, care was warm and affectionate. But there was no place for developmental activities of any kind. This was the task I was called upon to do with little or no resources and materials. Just emerging from the war, the country was in an economic crisis, its people struggling for survival, often not knowing where the next meal would come from. What resources could I demand for play materials? I decided that I would not ask for anything not readily available in the market. To my horror, I could find none of the simple cheap things that one could easily pick up in any Indian market (for instance, one could not get paper, plastic or cloth bags—everyone brought their own; when I bought fruit, I had to carry it back in the *pallu* of my sari, since I did not own a cloth bag!). So, I learnt to improvise, and taught everyone to use whatever was available to fulfil developmental needs. It were such experiences that went into my manual for the under-threes—the Vietnamese later adapted it in their own way for use.

A painful aspect of the system in a country which I greatly admired was the extent of inequality in it. I was taken to visit several "model" nursery schools and "model" crèches—perfect in every respect, but reserved for the use of the lucky few—the *apparatchiks*—while common people had to make do with the common facilities. I remember my guide, Ratnaike laughing when I cried with disappointment about this. "Haven't you seen inequality in India?," he asked, mockingly, "Why the tears now?" "Its painful to see it in a Communist country," I replied. By the 1980s, of course, there was enough documentary evidence about such matters, but coming face-to-face with it was hard to take, and brought an end to any remaining illusions about Communist states.

Surprisingly, I managed to cultivate a few personal friendships. Relationships with foreigners were forbidden to officials, and the first time I approached someone, I knew I might be putting her at risk. But although she had to report it, she was not taken to task; perhaps since India was respected due to our support during the war. My closest friendship was with my interpreter, a delightful man who knew French, English and Russian, and introduced me to folk and modern theatre, cuisine, literature and more. Except politics, we talked of everything during our dinners together!

Between 1983 and 1988, I made six visits to Vietnam, one each to Cambodia (conditions there were heartrending) and Malaysia (to study the situation of the children of Tamil indentured labour on plantations) and short trips to Thailand.

All that I achieved, learnt and experienced in the Philippines and in Southeast Asia were only a part of my life. The rest was in India, continuing the professional life I had left behind. Strangely, the double life did not affect me seriously now—the two enriched and brought new energy to each other.

Q. *How did you enter the realm of policy discourse, formulation, and advocacy?*

Between 1983 and 1986, I was involved, through Anil Bordia, then Secretary in the Ministry of Education, in extensive discussions organised by the Ministry across the country—involving teachers, parents, academics, administrators, teacher educators, and others. The outcome was the New Education Policy (NEP) 1986, in which I drafted the chapter on ECCE while Vina *di* wrote the chapter on Education for Women's Equality. There was much debate over the policy and strong opinions from various quarters, including political parties. Two years later, GoI announced a review committee chaired by Acharya Ramamoorthy, a distinguished Gandhian educationist. In late 1988, my friend Anil Sadgopal, with my support (we were both part of that group), forcefully pleaded that Article 45 should be interpreted as meaning that the right to education applied from birth, and not from entry to school as many supposed (UNESCO's Jomtien declaration, 1985, which opened with the famous words

"Learning begins at birth" became our motto). We argued that early childhood education should be considered an integral part of the entire educational process. Sadly, this led to a backlash, and in 1999 the government moved the 86th Constitutional Amendment to prevent such a move, bringing in Article 21A which would confine education to the age group of 6 to 14.

This is how the Right to Education (RTE) Act was framed, when a country for the first time disenfranchised its own children! We conducted a campaign against it, meeting the Members of Parliament and holding public rallies, but the early childhood movement was politically too weak to bring the needed pressure and in 2002, the amendment was passed.

Q. *In what other ways did you take forward the Agenda of Childcare?*

The third major strand of work was the formation of Forum for Crèche and Childcare Services (FORCES) in 1989, initiated by me with the support of both Mobile Crèches and CWDS. In the first few years, FORCES was able to exert enough pressure on the government to get the National Crèche Fund set up, largely due to the leadership of Vina *di*.

V

The MSSRF[4] Years

Q. *You have seen a lot of changes and shifts in location. How have these shaped your life?*

This period, 1989 to the present, covers more than 25 years. Upheaval, change and new challenges surfaced in each new period in my life. Once again I was compelled to rethink, and start afresh—I see now that this repeated process, leading to new horizons, fuelled my own growth and kept me alive. It seems I'm a problem-solver—no problems, and I get bored and withdraw, going into depression.

4. MS Swaminathan Research Foundation.

When I came back to India for good, I made a big celebration of my post-menopausal status, because in India it really gives you freedom—I could travel without discomfort, anywhere anytime; I could (and did) sleep on railway platforms, often chaperoning a bunch of younger women; there was no more fear of being alone in a strange or dark place; one could interact freely and mingle with men friends without attracting disapproval; and above all, talk about it—in India for a woman its the best time to be alive!

Q. *What has the move to Chennai meant to you?*

The early period of adjustment was the most trying. I kept myself busy with various kinds of training workshops in ECCE, just filling time. My husband, after retirement from government, set up the MSSRF, and requested me to join him and take up whatever activity I wanted to. I was reluctant to do so, because of my long habit of keeping our work separate, when he was in government. He assured me it was no longer relevant.

The second problem, surprisingly, was language. Although Tamil is my mother tongue, and I can read and write it, it was a dialect for home and social use, rather than a working language. I was constantly breaking out into Hindi whenever at a loss for words, to the irritation or amusement of my colleagues. It took me a few years to learn to speak the standard public language, and become fluent enough to make public speeches and conduct trainings.

The biggest problem was working with scientists. The young scientists at MSSRF did not know what to make of me—not realising that I was well-qualified, or in what, they presumed, unscientifically, that I was unqualified! They respected me only for my age, and position as wife, and could not understand why I found that galling! I have struggled for years with this and still have not found the right way to deal with it.

Q. *How have you taken your primary agenda of ECD (early childhood development) forward in your new location?*

I started with an ECD project called ACCESS (Action for Child Care Education Strategies and Services), funded by the Bernard van

Leer foundation, which aimed to work with existing institutions in four directions—capacity building, advocacy, networking, and communication. I visualised working with the system to push for systemic change. We worked with the private and NGO sector as well as the public sector, that is, ICDS, but were successful with the latter only in the area of capacity building.

Capacity Building

The capacity building included travelling to more than 20 towns, conducting workshops for teachers, heads of institutions and parents, often co-sponsored by local institutions like teacher training colleges, or home science colleges. With ICDS, we began by training about 35 trainers, developing them into "master trainers" who could work down the system to the bottom. At the time, ICDS in Tamil Nadu had an unique training system, dispensing with the Anganwadi Workers Training Centre (AWTC), and developing mobile training teams which went from district to district, conducting trainings on the spot. This system worked well, but later got eroded, as no documentation was developed for permanent availability of all the learning materials.

Communication and Advocacy

We developed about 20 video films on different aspects of ECD, from advocacy for breastfeeding, to training for teachers of 3-6 year-olds. The short films—1-3 minutes long—a set of 22 now known as Messages that Move marked our entry into the world of communication. In the second half of the 1990s we made the maximum use of television, thanks to the support of Doordarshan. For several years the short messages on gender and early childhood were regularly screened as fillers on Doordarshan. Satellite television made it too expensive and we had to stop: now they are all on YouTube.

We also developed audio communication messages, producing a set of songs, on gender and on early childhood, composed by members of our team along with staff of ICDS, then set to music and recorded with the help of leading music directors. Cassettes were distributed widely, through all stakeholders, including to paediatric doctors, suggesting that they played these tapes in their waiting rooms so that parents waiting there could listen to them.

All these materials were to be discussed, distributed, and used by the network, which was conceived of as the Tamil Nadu (TN) branch of FORCES, and named TN-FORCES. We enrolled all the stakeholders with some interest in young children, both individuals and associations, to bring them together and advocate for the cause of children below six. They included medical doctors, professional societies like the Indian Academy of Pediatrics (IAP), Indian Military Academy (IMA), FGO, women's organisations like National Federation of Indian Women (NFIW) and All India Democratic Women's Association (AIDWA), trade unions like Centre of Indian Trade Unions (CITU) and All India Trade Union Congress (AITUC), the Anganwadi Worker (AWW) and Village Health Nurse (VHN) unions, schools, training institutions, University departments and teachers' associations like Indian Association for Preschool Education (IAPE) and many more. At its height, TN-FORCES was a vibrant body with an active membership; many meetings were held to promote policies and activities for young children.

Another interesting element was the successful involvement of both the print and electronic media, in providing more space for discussion of issues about young children, as well as innovative measures like theme-based competitions in writing stories, and photography, for writers, journalists, and photographers. The Tamil press and several writers and film-makers became supporters of the movement.

Networking

However, progress was uneven, because interests were diverse. For example, AITUC played a big role in getting crèches started for the women working in small factories in the Industrial Estate. On the other hand, the private schools and NGOs were interested only in teacher training and quality improvement, at no cost to themselves. The AWW and VHN unions though very cooperative, wanted support for their own demands. On the issue of sex-selective abortion, the medical profession was divided, with paediatricians and gynaecologists (often married to each other) on opposite sides! There was hardly any issue on which the whole group made a specific proposal to the state government, which was quite unenthusiastic about responding to demands of NGOs, who had no electoral clout. So the network was ineffective as far as its main purpose was concerned, since we did not know how to draw on and use the public opinion we had created.

Q. How has Chennai offered other/newer opportunities?

In 1993, new opportunities came my way, with no planning. A chance meeting with Mangai, built rapport and we did a few workshops together. At her suggestion, we set up a unit in MSSRF for 'women's theatre' headed by her, a part-time worker and anchored by me. It was to be called Voicing Silence, a title also chosen by Mangai, to give expression to women's voices through theatre.

The programme included: a) The development and performance of a variety of plays on diverse themes from a feminist perspective; b) The organisation of five major women's theatre festivals, named Kulavai, at the level of state, region and nation, in various languages and forms, which disseminated ideas and forms; c) conducting workshops and developing plays with women belonging to different categories, such as women traditional performers and transgenders, often in partnership with different groups.

Working with transgenders in developing plays and learning about their stigmatised lives and difficulties gave me insights into their lives and struggles, and we helped them in their struggle for rights with the tool of theatre. Today, I continue to help this highly marginalised and discriminated transgender as a patron of the LGBT (lesbian, gay, bisexual and transgender) movement. Ten years ago, I would have been appalled by such a thought—activism then meant struggle, action, sweat and toil as part of a movement—not using a personally advantaged position as a tool. But now I realise I can only use what I have.

Q. Apart from sexuality issues, has Chennai drawn your attention to any other type of social inequality?

Through my constant travel and meetings with different social groups, I have come to know and feel the meaning of caste in Indian society. That is something which was impossible in Delhi, where it is underplayed and ignored until it almost vanishes. But nearer the margins, one sees its hold over society, starting with the issue of cooks and helpers in ICDS!

Q. Have you found support for your ideas and interventions? Who have been your allies?

Gender and the Challenge of UDRC

In 1993, MSSRF received a large donation from a leading company headed by a woman. The only guideline was that the programme should be named in honour of her mother and should do something for women. So we started the Uttara Devi Research Centre for Gender and Development. Since MSSRF was a research institute, the next step was to interact with scientists, and see how the scientific programmes, both research-oriented and field-based, could be made more women-friendly. This is where the problems started. For example, in the case of a study on rice farming, the questionnaire was aimed at only male respondents. Innocently, I asked why women could not be included. Irritated, the elderly scientist in charge abruptly answered, "Because they know nothing." This seemed to me logically impossible—if both men and women were engaged in certain operations, obviously they would both know something about it, even though perhaps they might have different knowledge. I thought the scientists were prejudiced against women; they must've thought I was ignorant as well as obstinate.

It was not until Sumi Krishna entered the picture that the way opened. Sumi was as much or more of a feminist than I; but had a much better understanding of both science and scientists and had already done a lot of work in this field. She knew how to go about it and I tried to follow her and learnt a lot. The biggest problem in our institutions of higher education, which I was learning about for the first time, is that of hierarchy, especially of disciplines.

Most of the scientists had very limited exposure to social issues, and could not understand the relevance of gender to their work. Trying to convince them that women play a major role not only in agriculture, but also in biodiversity, informal sector, and other activities, and were capable of even more, proved to be very difficult. Yet today, for example, most of those producing and selling bio-pesticides and bio-fertilisers, and other scientific innovations introduced by MSSRF, are women! Some men even vocally protested that we were interfering in their programmes in the name of women!

Luckily, we soon started getting support from Food and Agriculture Organisation's (FAO) regional office in Bangkok, Thailand, where the gender programme was headed by a dynamic Indian woman, Revathi Balakrishnan. We organised a number of research studies, projects, seminars and workshops, and published on gender-related topics. These publications gave us a good reputation and slowly, internal attitudes began to change. In 2007, we developed an internal gender policy, with special reference to women employees, called the Gender Code. This was a landmark achievement, among Indian institutions.

However, real change began in 2009, when Revathi, now retired and settled in the United Satates (US), conducted a workshop for the Directors where she underlined the importance of mainstreaming gender in the institution from a funding perspective, since international donors expected it. Soon afterwards, a small staff cadre named GIM (Gender and Institutional Mainstreaming) was set up. To begin with, they lacked training and knowledge, and were not clear about either purpose or method. However, in late 2011, we were able to organise a workshop with the help of IFAD in order to train them to handle their responsibilities with skill. And this process has continued.

In January 2012, a new programme area on Gender and Grass Roots Institutions was started with cross-cutting concerns in all other programme areas. I can see that the 20 year struggle has been fruitful, and recently some gender orientation has also been provided for the Directors.

Staying Alive

The most exciting and worthwhile outcome has been the continuous learning, led by younger role models, colleagues and partners in work, both men and women. I cannot name all, but each is a treasure, starting from L.S. Saraswati, only a few years my junior and hence my contemporary, to Sumi Krishna at first, and then to a host of young people at least 25-30 years younger than me. It has been a joy working with them—they were full of new ideas and approaches, energy and passion, yet applying critical thought, enjoying their work and charting new directions. I had to run to keep pace with them. And this was what I enjoyed the most—the stimulus of debate and discussion which went on and on, and kept minds challenged and mine young.

Section I

Early Childhood: Learning and Wellbeing

2

ADARSH SHARMA

Supportive ECCE Practices for Optimal Brain Development

Introduction

There is substantial evidence available to reinforce that the process of brain development has implications for adopting positive caring practices during early years (Bos *et al.*, 2009; Shonkoff and Garner, 2012; Anderson *et al.*, 2010; Walker *et al.*, 2005; Gerhardt, 2004). The information can facilitate avoidance of life-long consequences, threatening the health and well-being of the growing child (Anderson, *et al.*, 2009). Scientists have been able to conceive of critical periods when neural pathways are established in the developing brain. The process needs enabling environment and positive experiences, and it is difficult to change many of these neurological pathways beyond critical periods and in the later stages of life.

We now understand better than ever before, how experience-based brain and biological development in the early years (conception to age six years) affect sensory nerve cell functions in the brain, that in turn impact neural pathways connected to various parts of the brain involved in emotions, response to stress, physical movements, language, cognition that determine individual's social emotional health and well-being (Mustard, 2007).

In order to comprehend the process of brain development, the paper describes the process of brain, growth of its structures, factors that affect its development, and how can one ensure its optimal development in utero and during the early years. Why is the growing brain of a young child more vulnerable to adversity and deprivation? Are these effects permanent or reversible, and which areas of the brain are more responsive to interventions due to the plasticity of the young brain? Attempt has been made, in the following sections, to seek answers to these questions based on the knowledge of neuroscience and possible implications it has for early childhood care and education (ECCE) practices (Nutbrown, 2011).

The Developing Brain

Human brain is the most effective living structure on earth and it contributes to all aspects of our lives. Even then, most of us are unaware as to how this part of our body grows and works. The Functional Magnetic Resonance Imaging (FMRI) and Position Emission Tomography (PET) techniques have, lately, enabled neuroscientists to measure activity in the brain and map its growth. The process of brain development begins in the third week of gestation and continues into early adulthood. The formation of the neural tube initiates the formation of the brain and the spinal cord. The brain cells called neurons and their supporting cells are produced in the neural tube, and from there they migrate to form major parts of the brain, growing at an astounding rate of 250,000 cells per minute.

Synaptic Connections

The formation of functional circuits starts in the third trimester and continues after birth. Human brain at birth has about 100 billion neurons that have not yet been connected to functional networks. Coordinated neural activity changes the shape of the brain and creates patterns, that enables the child to do complex activities, and impacts quality of learning in later life. Over production of neurons ensures that the young brain will be able to cope and meet demands of the body within a particular environment in which child is born, and this is referred to as tuning of network. Also, there is a programmed cell death, and this pruning makes space for new connections.

Describing the influence of stimulation on the process of wiring and sculpting of the brain, Hebb as early as in 1949 said, "neurons that fire together, wire together". The long-lasting synaptic connection is dependent on frequency of the stimulation received by neurons (Hebb, 1949). Stimulation activates genetic pathways in the brain which produces protein that strengthens the synapses. Scientists have confirmed that both biological and psycho-social environment, known as epigenetic, directly affect expression of genes that control development of brain and nervous system.

This intricate process of brain development is influenced by a variety of endogenous and exogenous factors, from the expression of genes to environmental conditions (Stiles and Jernigan, 2010). The genetic framework provides basic foundation for building of the brain, however, the ever-changing environment influences the development of growing brain and its functioning. The neuro-developmental events and their timing is crucial for determining the extent of the impact of environmental conditions.

Developing Brain

Prenatal Stage

During foetal life, the brain cells proliferate in large numbers, migrate and aggregate under a robust genetic influence, providing a framework for the developing brain. The on-going biochemical processes are not only influenced by genes but also by the environment of the womb. Changes in the environment of the womb can wreck the clockwork precision of neural assembly line. Placenta and brain development are linked and prenatal stress induced placental changes affect foetal development adversely (Walker *et al.*, 2011; Schneider *et al.*, 1999; King and Laplante, 2005).

Some important factors that aversely affect foetal brain development are: maternal nutrition and nutrients, impaired maternal thyroid function, depression, infections, alcohol intake and exposure to toxins. The outcomes of these are determined by the timing, extent, duration and nature of the adversity. Any significant insult, during early brain development, interferes with the process of production of neurons or their migration (Eunson, 2006). This may result in major malformation of the brain with consequent severe disability in the child. It is believed that, if insult happens at a later stage, it may still affect white matter tracts (early third trimester) or the cortical grey matter (late third trimester) resulting in spastic cerebral palsy, and other learning and cognitive difficulties or developmental delays, and even hearing and visual impairment (Singhi, 2014).

It is evident from the above description that the prenatal period is critical for early brain development. Hence the pregnant mother requires appropriate quality care in the prenatal period to ensure normal and optimal brain development of the foetus. It is imperative, therefore, that prenatal interventions comprising antenatal care, immunisation, nutritional supplementation, regular health check-up, provisions of safe delivery, social and emotional security, support and counselling are made available, to deal with adverse affects of intrauterine insults and to ensure birth of a healthy baby.

Postnatal and Early Years

After birth, new connections turn into circuits only if relevant sensory experiences are available in the surrounding environment. Synaptogenesis and myelination occur at different rates as and when different regions with particular function develop. Motor reflexes and sensory abilities, including hearing and vision, are fairly well developed at birth and undergo rapid maturation during the first six months of life. The synapses in the visual and auditory cortexes peak at about the age of three months and then pruning begins. If experiences that stimulate the development of synaptic connections do not happen within a certain time window, pruning can cause potential functions to be lost. An example worth quoting here is, if a child is born with cataracts, and it is not surgically removed by the age of two, the vision does not develop as the unused synapses in the visual cortex are pruned away resulting in blindness, even if the cataracts are removed at later stage (Davies, 2011).

The role of exposure/experience on pruning of brain circuitry related to language and communication in case of infants has reported a rather longer pruning process, and has interesting context for learning multiple languages as also the rationale of using familiar cultural language during early years for communication. The circuits that control the ability to understand and communicate through language continue to be overproduced until the end of the first year.

However, there is evidence that pruning has already been occurring at an early stage. A three-month old has the capacity to distinguish between full range of sounds in human languages; by age one, the capacity to recognise sounds becomes increasingly restricted to phonetic units in the language/languages that the infant has regularly been hearing. A study of brain imaging has reported that brain circuitry related to language makes a "neural commitment" to the language of child's culture by age one (Kuhal and Rivera-Gxiola, 2008). However, the window on sound recognition remains open, though dormant, into middle childhood, as evident by the school-age child's ability to learn and speak another language without an accent and difficulty (Cheour *et al.*, 1998).

From the above description and the well-acknowledged role of stimulating experiences in the environment on development, it may be inferred that well-timed stimulation, that is supportive to the on-going functioning brain, strengthens brain circuits, and ultimately the specific developmental capacities. It is essential at this stage to have a consensus about what we mean by stimulation when it comes to care-giving practices during early years.

Based on the comprehensive understanding drawn from allied disciplines of child development, we may operationally define stimulation in our context. It comprises active, responsive, age appropriate sensory experiences, joyful, playful interactions and attuned care-giving to meet the needs of the young child by sensitive, consistent and trusting adults in the environment of the child (conception to 6 years). The challenge lies in providing secure stimulating environment for using the fertile connections and networks for child's future proficiencies and abilities and optimal brain development (Figure 2.1).

Genes and Brain Stimulation

> In the dance of life, genes and environment are absolutely inextricable partners. Genes supply the rough blue print for the brain, then stimulation from the environment, whether it's the light impinging on the retina or a mother's voice on the auditory nerve, turns genes on and off, fine tuning those brain structures both before and after birth (Hayman, 1999).

Figure 2.1

Dance of Life Begins at Third Week of Gestation

Source: *http://www.urngarden.com/image/cache/data/companionurns/dance-of-life-double-urn-400x400.jpg*

It is generally accepted that there is a reduction in the plasticity of the circuits after the sensitive period has ended. Interestingly in a detailed analysis of neurons and their connections, it was found that, at birth, the axons and dendrites and synapses in the brain are not large or extensive. But at the age of six years, the neuron connections and synapses are extensive, and by the age of 14 years the synapses are observed to be less extensive (Figure 2.2). Frequent stimulation leads to activation of genetic pathways in the brain which produce proteins that strengthen synapses (Mustard, 2007). It clearly points to the significance as also vulnerability of the first six years, for the development of synapsis and their getting organised into circuits in the brain of the growing child. Needless to emphasise, this process is determined by the environment that surrounds a child.

Brain Structure: An Architectural Marvel

The process of brain development could be described as moulding of a living sculpture. First neurons and synapses are overproduced; the process of cell death and synaptic pruning sculpts away excess material and shapes the brain, and helps it mature. The resulting structure influenced by genetically programmed events and

Figure 2.2

Mapping Stages of Synapses Formation

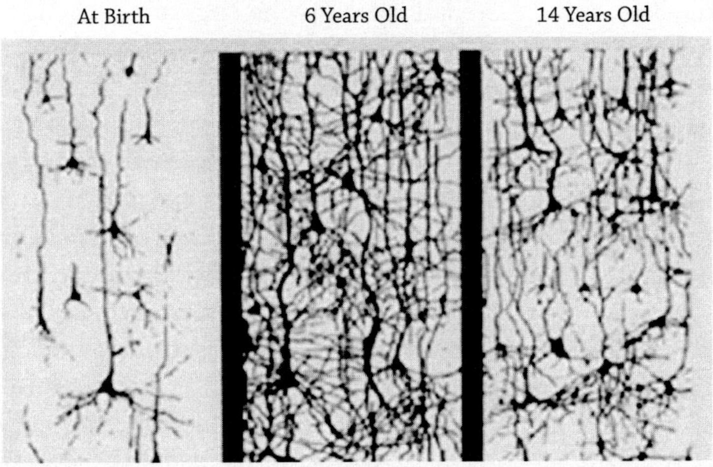

Source: Conel (1959).

environmental experiences has interconnected regions, each with an ability to perform a specific function. The structurally complex and competent centres are associated with sensory impulses (vision, hearing, taste, smell and touch), motor movements, balance, speech, language, emotional regulation and higher cognitive functions (Figure 2.3).

Figure 2.3

Brain Architecture

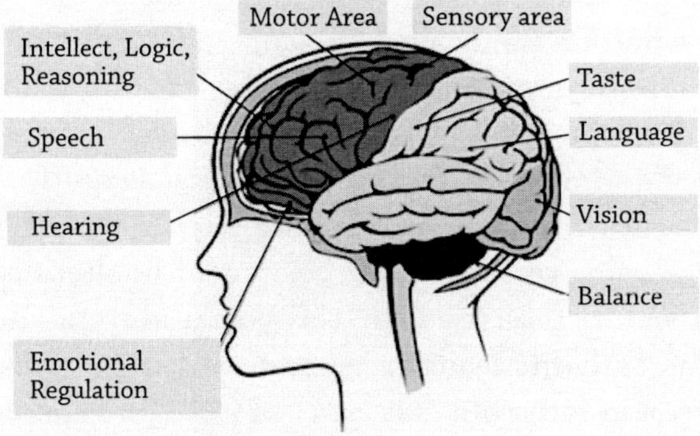

Source: http://www.zerotothree.org/baby-brain-map.html

Brain structures located at the top of spinal cord follow a sequence of growth beginning with central stem, cerebellum, limbic and cerebral cortex. Cerebral cortex is the largest and the last brain structure to appear. It is particularly sensitive to environmental influences for a far longer time than any other part of the brain. The two sides of the cerebral cortex are called hemispheres—left and right and both of these have clearly assigned roles, once sensations are received. Left is associated with verbal abilities and positive emotions and finer details, while right is for spatial abilities, negative emotions and integrates all sensations in a holistic way. However, these two parts are connected and often are engaged simultaneously to permit wider array of effective functioning. Specialisation of hemispheres is called lateralisation and the process begins even before birth. Acquiring of motor, cognitive and language skills promotes further the process of lateralisation. Preference of handedness is also an issue in this context, but the notion of right-brained or left brained person is an oversimplification and need not be given credence as far as acquiring of these competencies is concerned.

Environmental Adversity: Brain Plasticity

Evidence has confirmed that risk factors in the environment such as poor nutrition, infections, environmental neurotoxins, substance abuse, chronic mental stress, trauma, and family violence impose heavy burden and harm the developing brain during early years, as well as later in life (NSCDC, 2005). The above section has clearly indicated that the quality of environment and stimulation determines whether the brain will achieve its optimal growth or not. The window of opportunity is a term used to refer to the prime times when development is occurring in particular areas of brain and requires specific stimulation and environmental support.

Brain disruption or insult during such a sensitive time is detrimental, causing cessation of development or altering its course. It has been well established for the visual system where visual deprivation in early life leads to permanent loss of vision, but this does not occur in later life (Bedny *et al.*, 2010). Whereas, in case of motor system, functions of the damaged motor area is taken over by the undamaged area of the brain through the process of reorganisation of neural networks. Such compensation is almost unlikely to occur in adult years; for example, if in an accident of an adult, the head injury involves the motor centre, the specific body movements are lost forever. It is well acknowledged that the age at which a child sustains brain insult will influence his/her development and mastery of neuro-behavioural skills, although the relationship is not a simple one (Anderson *et al.*, 2009).

The Stress Pathway

Stress and stressful experiences during early years can adversely influence brain development. In the discussion on stress response, the role of limbic system and hypothalamus-pituitary-adrenal (HPA) pathway is considered important. The hypothalamus stimulates pituitary gland to produce adrenocorticotropic hormone, which stimulates adrenal gland to produce cortisol (ACTH). The slower acting HPA stress pathways result in release of cortisol, which affects functions of cells in different parts of the body, including brain, and has a longer lasting effect than epinephrine, which is released by autonomic nervous system having a quick action in response to fearful and threatening situations, resulting in increased heart rate, hearing, breathing and enhanced sensory awareness.

Cortisol when released on the other hand can affect gene activation in different organs including the brain. These can change brain programming, and permanently alter its structure and function (Barker *et al.*, 1989). Overproduction of cortisol can influence both behaviour and health such as antisocial behaviour, depression, type II diabetes, cardiovascular diseases, memory and cognitive functioning, immune system and addiction to alcohol and drugs. Underproduction is associated with chronic fatigue syndrome, fibromyalgia, autoimmune disorders, rheumatoid arthritis, allergy and asthma (Mustard, 2007). Research studies reveal that prolonged stress arising out of deprivation, lack of bonding and loving care influences the neural connection under formation and affects both learning and memory of the child due to high levels of cortisol (Hackman *et al.*, 2010; Juhasz *et al.*, 2006; Pollak *et al.*, 2010).

Caregivers play an important role in regulating stress hormone production during early years. Quality of care is of utmost importance, which comprises warm responsive interaction, time and skill in meeting needs of the child and providing stimulating experiences to ensure optimal sensory development to facilitate communication, language skills and cognitive functioning of the children. MRI-based studies have demonstrated that institutionalised children have decreased metabolism in areas of learning and memory-prefrontal cortex, amygdale, and delayed maturation of frontal brain circuits and reduced functional connectivity with other brain regions, reduced synaptic density and dendritic branching and overall reduction in the size of neurons as compared to normal children (Juhasz *et al.*, 2006; Pollak *et al.*, 2010).

Brain Plasticity

Despite the evidence related to the consequences of environmental risks, the good news is that the brain has a unique property termed plasticity. It can be defined as the brain's ability to change in response to an experience, whether it is a positive or negative one (Johnston, 2004). It is a very important feature that allows the brain to acquire skills of retaining information, related to the reorganisation of neural networks in response to environmental stimulation or threat and enables the organism to recover from brain damage or spinal cord injury. Brain is more plastic during first few years than it will ever be again in life. This points to the vulnerability of the early years and promises hope for effective recovery through appropriate enrichment of the environment. The advocacy message of 'catch them young' used in ECCE captures the rationale very aptly.

The findings related to adoption of institutional children into warm loving homes, or receiving high quality foster care before the age of two years has demonstrated that the brain activity can be restored and can reverse the adverse effects of maltreatment to a large extent (Zeanah *et al.*, 2003) Available evidence indicates that the reversibility of the negative effects of deprivation and insults after appropriate interventions is also possible (Morrone, 2010; Rosenbaum, 2011; Grantham-McGregor *et al.*, 1991). However, it may also be appreciated that reversibility is influenced by factors, such as timing, extent and severity of insult, level of development of particular function/capability and other environmental factors. Brain lateralisation has also given insights about brain plasticity as mentioned earlier that cerebral cortex areas, which are yet not committed to specific functions, can take over tasks that were to be handled by damaged part of the cortex. It is noteworthy that if lateralisation has taken place, it is then difficult to restore fully or easily the functions of that region or part.

Scaffolding Brain Development

If children are born with innate tendencies, it is important that adults harness and support these competencies/skills by providing an enabling environment to promote optimal development. Enrichment of environment enhances the very process by which learning takes place. Stimulation produces large neurons, which are large in size, exhibiting increased dendritic length with more complex branching, thereby enabling them to make more connections (Figure 2.4).

Figure 2.4

Neurons in Deprived and Enriched Environment

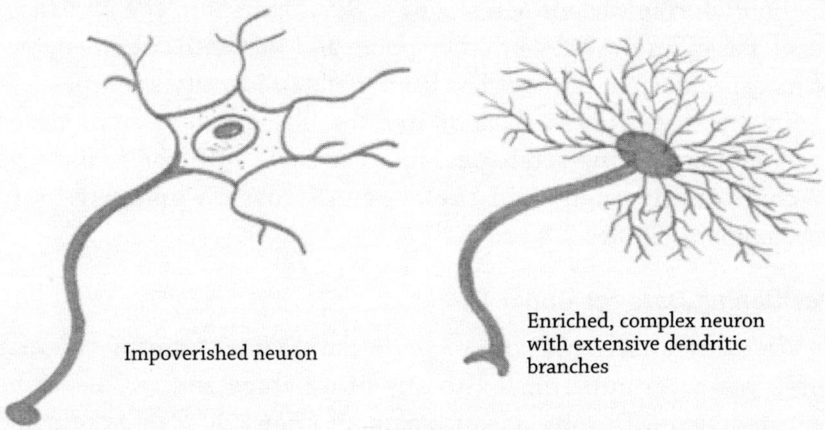

Source: Centre for Early Childhood Education and Development (CECED). ECED Brief 3 April 2014, p. 18. Delhi: Ambedkar University.

The increased connectivity and mapping is central to cognition as it results in heightened responsiveness and effective learning (Diamond, 2001; Singhi, 2014). Brain thrives on variety; the 'habituation' theory, thus confirms the importance of providing babies with novelty in their environment, as monotony in the objects and toys is soon disregarded by the brain (Brierley, 1994; Gopnik *et al.*, 1999).

Birth—Three Years: Unpacking Care

First three years are the magic years, due to rapid growth in sensory abilities of babies. During these years, the brain grows to almost 80 per cent of the adult size. The ongoing process is influenced significantly by the quality of interaction with primary caregivers. The care-giving routine provides a myriad of visual, auditory, sensory, and socio-emotional opportunities that allow the baby to interact with caregivers. The way in which caregivers respond to a young child, shapes his/her development. Connecting with the child in a responsive manner, ensuring safe environment, and providing a range of appropriate stimulating experiences are the kind of caring practices that can support 'windows of opportunity'. This can strengthen ongoing development, while the brain is still growing. There is a very clear pattern in emergence of various capacities of the brain during various sub-stages of development in the first three years. Based on the baby brain mapping and the status of emergence of its capacities, an attempt has been made to identify a few positive caring practices from birth to 36 months. These have been proposed as supportive caring strategies, in accordance with the knowledge of child development and the above discussion on early brain development (Tables 2.1 and 2.2).

Positioning Care for Under Threes

The pace and complexity of brain development during the first three years are unparalleled to any other stage and will never be repeated again. Despite advancement in knowledge, we are unable to use this one chance available to us for providing caring conditions congenial for the development of a child. All around the world and in developing countries, in particular, children are growing up in contexts of poverty, violence, food insecurity and deprivation. Deficit in family care and institutional care is so marked in terms of inadequate quantitative and poor quality provisions for under threes, threatening their optimal development and learning potential. The need of aggressive advocacy cannot be underscored to understand the limited understanding about brain functioning during first two years, the crucial stage when myelination and white matter is under formation that supports cognitive functioning—memory, thinking and planning process. The fact that by three years of age, child's brain is twice as active as an adult brain and has implications for caring practices and designing interventions, both caregivers/providers need to be informed of the potential role they can play to support the process.

Tables, 2.1 and 2.2, in the column 'What can we do', have identified elements, with a premise that these have to be integrated in early care. However, further elaboration is required to convert these into actions at various levels. Just to illustrate, it will comprise counselling for raising awareness and knowledge, up-scaling good quality institutional day care services for working women, designing technically sound training for care providers, maternal benefits in kind and cash, appropriate policies, allocation of adequate funds and good governance. Even if we turn to common sense for unpacking care, it implies—harbour care and love for the child, feed him/her adequately and appropriately, make sure he/she does not get hurt, play with him/her and provide enriched experiences (Alliance for Right to ECCD, 2012).

Children Age Three Plus: Optimising on the Growing Brain

We are aware that all babies are ordinarily exposed to varied sensory, social and emotional experiences in the environment that surrounds them. These encounters enable the brain to grow optimally and organise itself according to predetermined programme. It is called experience-expectant brain growth. If in addition to natural and routine experiences, specifically planned enriched learning experiences are organised, it then helps in refinement of established brain structures and in acquiring specific learning competencies such

Table 2.1

Baby Brain Mapping: Supporting Environment (Birth-18 Months)

Age in months	*Brain capacity: Status*	*What needs to be done*
Birth-2		*Ensure back and forth interaction*
Crying	• Means of communication	• Proactive response to crying
Touch	• First sensation to develop	• Cuddling, stroking, tender massaging
Feeding	• Promotes brain weight	• Opt for breastfeeding: close body contact
Hearing	• Hears rhythmic sounds/voice	• Soft and rhythmic voice in routine care
Vision	• Vision range 9-12 inches	• Keep visual contact within range
2-6		*Watching progress and delays*
Movement	• Holding head, turning, moving arms and legs	• Opportunity to move body in all directions
Touch	• Touch sensory nourishment	• Holding warmly for security & bonding
Language	• Cooing and uttering sounds	• Expose to sounds, talk and interact
Vision	• Fine tunes brain connections	• Attractive objects, focus on eye contact
Hearing	• Music is soothing for brain connections	• Variety of exposure, soothing music and lullabies
		• Early identification of disabilities and interventions
6-18		*Enriched, secure and safe environment*
Cognition and Learning	• Uses senses, learns from environment through repetition & deferred imitation	• Safe sensory exposure and experience, freedom to explore and create knowledge
Movement	• Gross motor movements become coordinated and refined	• Opportunity to exercise and practice—do not rush through; follow pace of neuromuscular development
	• As motor pathways improve trunk and limb muscles become stronger	• Onset of walking is a milestone and needs to be encouraged in a playful manner
Language	• Able to differentiate sounds, responsive to familiar sounds of native language	• Link sound to words, talk and expose to native language—receptive language
	• Process speech, enhanced understanding of sounds and words	• More you talk, the more they speak
Social Emotional	• Frontal lobe development—onset of attachment/bonding	• Be sensitive to their needs
	• Touch, tender care gives trust	• Help them express emotions & feelings
	• Unable to control emotions and behaviour	• Avoid harsh and punitive interaction

Source: Zero to Three (2007).

as reading, writing, singing, dancing, playing musical instruments, swimming and several other culture-specific behaviours and actions. Such learning continues throughout life and is referred as experienced-based brain growth. Much evidence confirms that after the age of three, brain is sponge-like ready to acquire new skills easily and quickly (Greenough and Black, 1992).

Table 2.2

Baby Brain Mapping: Supporting Environment (18-36 months)

Age in months	*Brain Capacity : status*	*What needs to be done*
18-36		*Encourage exploration, experimentation and explanation*
Cognitive Learning	• Can recall and memorise, analyse and solve simple problems	• Experiential learning to create knowledge. Follow pace of development and child's level in promoting and encouraging learning
Movement	• Gross motor movements strengthened and coordinated	• Provide opportunities and variety of material to develop finer muscles and their coordination.
Gross and fine	• Myelin becomes dense and allows neurons to receive messages faster • Brain circuits enable to control and coordinate finer movements effectively	• Manipulative activities to grasp, hold, pull, squeeze, and scoop, etc., through toys or play material
Language	• Variations in use of language due to environmental factors • Uses vocabulary of around 50, understands context. Presence of multilingual learning potential	• Encourage receptive learning of language • Use variety of ways to promote language learning
Social Emotional	• Unable to control aggression and other behaviours • Cannot understand perspective of others and are self-centred with a few social adaptive skills	• Anticipate behavioural outbursts; try to control these ahead of time • Encourage social and adaptive behaviours • Help them discover their feelings and relate to actions. • Accept them and encourage social adaptive behaviour development

Source: Zero to Three (2007).

The brain, during 3-6 years, is devoted to forming connections to ensure mastery of skills. The rear base of the cerebellum responsible for controlling body control and motor movements enables the preschooler to engage in well-coordinated play activities and then to finer motor coordination required for early literacy of reading and writing. The inner brain structure, hippocampus, undergoes maturation and establishes connections with the frontal lobe progressively to store information and enhance spatial understanding. The two hemisphere connections are strengthened by increased myelination. Production of synapses of the corpus callosum is at its peak during 3-6 years of the two hemispheres, facilitating complex integration of perception, attention, memory, language, problem-solving and other aspects of thinking (Thompson *et al.*, 2000). Preschool children have brains, which are more connected, and flexible than that of an adult. The young child is 'literally an alien genius' (Box 2.1) (Gopnik *et al.*, 1999).

The information from neuroscience has steadily grown in the last few years, and is being used properly and sometimes improperly; it is imperative that the burgeoning knowledge is translated into practical actions so as to deliver accurate messages for caretakers and teachers. In a recently edited volume by Wasserman and Zambo (2013), judicious views have been presented for linking cutting-edge research of neuroscience to early childhood education. Blending research, theory and practice of both disciplines, contributing authors have covered a range of issues related to strategies of effective learning and enriched environment that can be used by educators and caregivers for ensuring optimal brain development. The preface, by Layne Kalbfleish, has pointed out that neuroscience can be insightful and useful to educators, if applied ethically and with care.

Acknowledging the role of both heredity and environment, the book has come up with illustrative supporting practices which could be used for promoting optimal brain development of children during the early childhood years (3-6 years). These can serve as advocacy messages for parents, caretakers, service providers, ECE practitioners and policymakers in order to ensure that provision of quality services is made for all children as a right. While looking at these implications, it is fascinating to note that many of the ECE practices that originated long ago are in line with the research evidence and understanding provided by neuroscience. The syntheses of these learnings, as reported at this juncture, are to optimise on the evidence from neuroscience. It will be reassuring for the ECE community to reinforce existing technically sound practices and further refine the pedagogical approaches being used.

Box 2.1

Musings from Brain Research

Experience—everything that goes around the young child changes the brain growth—before birth and in early childhood

Everything that the baby sees, hears, touches and smells, influences the connections and networks of brain cells

Interaction with people plays a critical role in brain development

Babies and young children have powerful learning capacities

Babies and young children actually participate in building their own brain

Radically deprived environments may have negative influence on brain development

Source: BERAEYSIG (2003: 19)

Illustrative Supportive Practices

a. Due to the important relationship between movement and brain development, freedom to explore a safe and engaging environment need to be provided to young children. Ample opportunities to practice development of skills should be given for finer muscles, so that manual dexterity is accomplished.
b. Music also provides a vehicle for brain development and needs to be an integral part of young children's life and ECCE curriculum.

c. Moderate stimulation needs to be the norm for all sensory impulses. Too much stimulation is as undesirable and inappropriate as no stimulation. It is a cautionary note for caregivers and care-providers to keep this in mind while organising interventions, activities and the enriched environment for the young child.
d. Teaching the mother tongue in early years is to be promoted for optimal development of cognition and subsequent learning because the language centres respond to familiar sounds and learning, and use of language gradually becomes efficient for communication and learning.
e. Foster quality relationships through low teacher-child ratios, primary caregiving experiences, and interactive experiences that include responding, talking and cuddling, so as to ensure bonding that enhances brain development.
f. Following of a Developmentally Appropriate Curriculum (DAP) for effective learning, in line with the stages and maturation or development of the brain is endorsed. Scaffolding of the early learning by adults is imperative; this involves motivation, encouragement, engaging in cognitive challenges and is based on sustained and shared thinking.
g. Make learning a joyful experience through use of interesting teaching aids and play material as positive emotions enhance memory and cognition.
h. Play is an important experience for growing children; it comes naturally to most children, and needs to be supported by adults to make it a meaningful experience. Despite its importance, both parents and teachers do not have the skills and ability to make children's play an integral part of their life and utilise it for learning. Play and exploration lead to learning through experience, adult involvement, and adequate space and time to indulge in indoor and outdoor play. Verbal communication in play activities promotes language development and positive interaction with peers and adults and stimulates learning. The imaginative play promotes creativity and is also considered therapeutic

for children to express feelings. Play-based learning if designed properly is one of the best strategies to stimulate brain and promote learning. It is, therefore, endorsed as a positive practice to be followed with young children for their development

i. Good nutrition activates brain development; thus children should be given good quality nutritious food, appropriate to their age and growing needs. Breastfeeding for example has been linked to development of immune system, bonding, security and well-being of the baby. Similarly, the positive role of taking protein, micronutrients, trace elements and adequate calories in the diet must be kept in mind for facilitating development of the brain and cognition during prenatal and early childhood.

j. Prolonged exposure to stress, trauma and non-responsive care jeopardises young children's mental health due to excessive stress hormones that not only impact growth of brain, but later learning as well. It must be ensured that young children are protected from such situations. Loving care and nurturance is the hallmark of optimal and normal development during early years.

Linking Neuroscience and ECCE Practices: A Cautionary Note

There is no doubt that the developments in neuroscience, over the last few years, have led to an enhanced understanding of the process of growth and functioning of the human brain. It has generated extensive interest amongst the social scientists from various disciplines and educationists. The possible implications of the newly accumulated knowledge in promoting optimal development, healthy social emotional behaviour, learning and realisation of inherent potential have been a matter of exploration and extensive discussion. However, in our context, there has been considerable debate surrounding the implications of neuroscientific research for education and care in early years (BERA EYSIG, 2003).

This has led to a number of misconceptions and 'neuromyths'. Bruer (1997) for example argued that drawing link between cognitive neuroscience and education is 'a bridge too far'; it is felt by many that the potential use of neuroscience for education is unrealistic. The use of technology to study learning and cognition at most can complement, rather than replace the traditional methods of educational enquiry. Review of the work of 16 leading researchers in cognitive science came up with conclusions that learning changes the structure of the brain; learning organises and replaces traditional organisation of the brain; and different parts of the brain may be ready to learn at different times. Although, there are prime times for certain types of learning, the brain also has a remarkable capacity to change (Bransford *et al.*, 2000). British Educational Research Association Early Years Special Interest Group (BERA EYSIG), in 2003, summarised evidence from a brain research, given in the above section of the article, which interestingly matches with the psychological research conducted by Bureau of Applied Research in Anthropology (BARA). In fact many of the practices promoted and being used since long are consistent with current understandings from the field of neuroscience.

The argument used by Bruer (1997) for inability to link neuroscience with ECCE practices emerges from the fact that available understanding does not provide any direct links between brain structures and cognitive functions and instructional goals or its outcomes.

It is true that neuroscience has discovered a great deal about the growing brain, neurons and synapses, yet not enough in context of the educational practices. Cognitive psychologists, in particular, have raised both practical and ethical concerns about teachers using neuroscience based curriculum. It is believed by behavioural scientists that social science and cognitive research has already provided rich information about teaching, learning and cognitive development; therefore, we need to be sceptical about brain-based educational practices. It is further argued that brain research has little to offer when it comes to child's holistic development. Childhood outcomes are complex and cannot be solely attributed to biochemical explanations. We need a multi-dimensional/interdisciplinary approach to understand the process of child's development, factors that impact the process and the solutions to help them grow optimally. Neuroscience has a narrow interpretation of learning windows which has critical implications for teachers, caregivers and policymakers. We need to use the knowledge judiciously to fine tune practices to improve child's learning and brain functioning, and not give credence to the claims because it has been invoked by neuroscience.

Alfrink and Dougan (2010), despite being critical, have made an optimistic observation that neuroscience does have much to say about developing brain and how it learns. In order to make a bridge, educational practices need to be intertwined with neuroscience. This can be accomplished by a clearer understanding of the science of early childhood development and the underlying neurobiology.

Nonetheless, the author is convinced that there is a need to foster more accurate understanding of neuroscience research amongst all concerned with young children; only then, the chances of using its potential for application will emerge properly. We need brain savvy teachers/caretakers, who are inspired, competent and understand brain development and windows of opportunity within the brain and support realisation of the potential of young children. It requires strategic capacity building for providing supportive care that makes the brain grow optimally (Hurby, 2013). The concluding comments thus make a case for underpinning supportive ECCE practices on understanding of neuroscience.

Conclusion

It may be concluded that advanced technology has facilitated our understanding of the structure and functioning of the brain. Further, the scientific study has shed new light on the process of brain development, challenging the long-accepted belief that brain's potential is fixed and determined at birth. Eric Kandel, a psychologist and neuroscientist argued that the purpose served by neuroscience was to understand what happens in the brain. He wrote:

> The task of neuroscience is to explain behaviour in terms of activities of brain; how brain marshals its millions of individual nerve cells to produce behaviour and how these cells are influenced by

> environment—the ultimate challenge is to understand the biological basis of consciousness and mental process by which we perceive, act, learn and remember (Kandel, 2006).

Neuroscience has given us the confidence that rapid development which is taking place is fuelled by nature, and is supported and extended by environment and relationships in which children are nurtured. The research findings from neuroscience seem to have provided sufficient evidence to reinforce the need for having an enriched, stimulating environment and sensitive adult support in early years of life. "Children can take advantage of an innately determined foundation, powerful learning abilities and implicit tuition from other people" (Gopnik *et al.*, 1999: 186).

The enhanced insights into the linkages of brain and process of early development have made us aware of the potential role we can play as adults. It suggests use of supportive caring practices and making provision of a congenial environment that ensures health and well-being, and optimises on the learning capacities of a growing child. It has cautioned us, as to how to protect them from experiences that have serious lifelong consequences. Knowledge of the plasticity of the brain has entrusted an added responsibility to take concerted measures for intervening at various levels during the sub-stages of early childhood with effective programmes/services to reverse the effects of adversity and deprivations. Let us hope, it makes all of us affirm that we will use the accumulated wisdom and evidence to give children the best they deserve for realising their potential.

References

Anderson, V., R. Jacobs, L. Coleman, P. Anderson, J. Williams *et al.* (2009). "Does Early Age at Brain Insult Predict Worse Outcome? Neuropsychological Implications", *J. Pediatr. Psychol.* Advance Access published, doi: 10.1093/ jpepsy /jsp100.

Anderson, V., L. Coleman, P. Anderson, J. William and M. Greenham (2010). "Children's Executive Functions: Are they Poorer after very Early Brain Insult", *Neuropsychologia* 48(7): 2041-50.

Alferink, L.A. and V.F. Dougan (2010). "Brain-(not) Based Education: Dangers of Misunderstanding & Misapplication of Neuroscience Research", *Exceptionality* 18: 42-52.

Alliance for Right to Early Childhood Care & Development (ECCD) (2012). *Importance of a Comprehensive Policy for Early Childhood Care and Development*. New Delhi: Mobile Crèches.

Barker, D.J., P.D. Winter, C. Osmond, B. Margetts and S.J. Simmonds (1989). "Weights in Infancy and Death from Ischemic Heart Disease", *Lancet.* 2 (8663): 577-80.

Bedny, M., T. Konkle, R. Saxe and A. Leone (2010). "Sensitive Period for a Multi-modal Response in Human Visual Motion Areas MT/MST", *Curr. Biol.* 20(21): 1900-06.

Bos, K.J., N. Fox, C.H. Zeanah and C.A. Nelson (2009). "Effects of Early Psychosocial Deprivation on the Development of Memory and Executive Function", *Front Behav. Neurosci.* 3:16.

Bransford, J., A.L. Brown, and R.R. Cocking (eds.) (2000). *How People Learn: Brain, Mind, Experience and School.* Washington D.C. National Academy Press.

Brierley, J. (1994). Give me a Child Until he is Seven. *Brain Studies & Early Childhood Education.* 2nd edn. London: Falmer Press.

British Educational Research Association Early Years Special Interest Group (BERA EYSIG) (2003). *Early Years Research: Pedagogy; Curriculum and Adult Roles, Training and Professionalism.* Nottingham: BERA.

Bruer, J. (1997). "Education and the Brain: A Bridge too Far", *Educ. Research* 26(8): 4-16.

Centre for Early Childhood Education and Development (CECED) (2012). *Unpacking Care: Protecting Early Childhood.* ECED Brief-1. Delhi: CECED, Ambedkar University and CARE.

Cheour, M., R. Ceponiene, A. Lhtokoski, A. Luuk, J. Allik, K. Alho and R. Naatanen (1998). "Development of Language Specific Phonemes Representations in the Infant Brain", *Nature Neuroscience* 1: 351-53, doi: 10.1038/1561.

Conel, J.L. (1959). *The Postnatal Development of the Human Cerebral Cortex.* Cambridge, Mass: Harvard University Press.

Davies, D. and N.B. Webb (Series Editor's Note) (2011). *Child Development: A Practioner's Guide.* New York, London: The Guildford Press. pp.38-40.

Diamond, M.C. (2001). "Response of the Brain to Enrichment", *An Acad. Bras. Cienc.* 73(2): 211 -20.

Eunson, P. (2006). "Placental Pathology, Intrauterine Growth Restriction, and Subsequent Child Development", in P. Baker, C. Sibley (eds.), *The Placenta and Neurodisability.* London: McKeith Press. pp.70-87.

Fletcher, Janice (2004). *Making Connections: Helping Children Build Their Brains.* Storrs, CT: National Network for Childcare at the University of Connecticut Cooperative Extension System.

Gerhardt, S. (2004). *Why Love Matters. How Affection Shapes a Baby's Brain.* Hove: Bruner Routledge. pp.461-77. *http://goo. gl/87cMA.*

Gopnik, A., A. Meltzoff and P. Kuhl (1999). *How Babies Think.* London: Weindenfeld & Nicholson.

Grantham-McGregor, S.M., C.A. Powell, S.P. Walker and J.H. Himes (1991). "Nutritional Supplementation, Psychosocial Stimulation, and Mental Development of Stunted Children: The Jamaican Study", *Lancet.* 338(8758): 1-5.

Greenough, W.T, and J.E. Black (1992). "Induction of Brain Structure by Experience: Substrates for Cognitive Development", in M.R. Gunnar and C.A. Nelson (eds.), *Developmental Behaviour Neuroscience* (Minnesota Symposia on Child Psychology 24: 155 -200). Hillsdale, NJ: Erlbaum.

Gunnar, M.R. and C.A. Nelson (eds.) (1992). *Developmental Behaviour Neuroscience* (Minnesota Symposia on Child Psychology 24: 155 -200). Hillsdale, NJ: Erlbaum.

Hackman, D.A., M.J. Farah *et al.* (2010). "Socioeconomic Status and the Brain: Mechanistic Insights from Human and Animal Research", *Nat. Rev. Neurosci.* 11(9): 651-59.

Hayman, S. (1999). *States of Mind.* John Wiley

Hebb, D.O. (1949). *The Organization of Behaviour*. New York: Wiley.

Hielkema, T., C.H. Blauw-Hospers, T. Dirks, M. Drijver-Messelink, A.F. Bos and M. Hadders-Algra (2011). "Does Physiotherapeutic Intervention Affect Motor Outcome in High-risk Infants? An Approach Combining a Randomized Controlled Trial and Process Evaluation", *Dev. Med. Child Neurol.* 53(3): 8-15.

Hurby, George (2013). "Metaphors of Developmental Process for Brain Savvy Teachers in Wasserman", in L. Hailey (ed.), *Early Childhood Neuroscience: Links to Development and Learning.* Springer

Johnston, M.V. (2004). "Clinical Disorders of Brain Plasticity", *Brain Dev*. 26(2): 73-80.

Jalongo, M.R. (2008). *Exploring Young Role in Early Childhood Education.* 4th edition. Pearson

Joseph, S., T. Craig and Ramey L. Sharon (2006). *The Abecedarian Experience*.

Juhasz, C, O. Muzik, M. Maqbool *et al.* (2006). "Abnormal Brain Connectivity in Children after Early Severe Socio Emotional Deprivation: A Diffusion Tensor Imaging Study", *Pediatrics* 117(6): 2093-100.

Kandel, E.R. (2006). "In Search of Memory: The Emergence of a New Science of Mind", *FASEB Journal* 20(8): 1043-44.

Kuhal, P. and Rievera-Gaxiola (2008). "Neural Substrates of Language Acquisition", *Ann. Rev. Neurosci.* 31: 511-34.

King, S. and D.P. Laplante (2005). "The Effects of Prenatal Maternal Stress on Children's Cognitive Development: Project Ice Storm", *Stress.* 8(1): 35-45.

Mustard, J.F. (2007). "Scientific Underpinning of the Importance of ECD in a Global World", in Mary Eming Young with Linda M. Richardson (eds.), *Measurement to Action 2007.* Washington DC, The World Bank. pp.48-84.

Morrone, M.C. (2010). "Brain Development: Critical Periods for Cross-sensory Plasticity", *Curr. Biol.* 20(21): R934-6.

National Scientific Council on the Developing Child (NSCDC) (2005). "Excessive Stress Disrupts the Architecture of the Developing Brain", *Working Paper* No. 3. Retrieved from *www.developingchild.harvard.edu*

Nutbrown, C. (2011). *Key Concepts in Early Childhood Education and Care*. Los Angeles/London/New Delhi/Singapore/Washington DC: SAGE.

Pollak, S.D., C.A. Nelson, M.F. Schlaak, B.J. Roeber, S.S. Wewerka, K.L. Wiik *et al.* (2010). "Neurodevelopmental Effects of Early Deprivation in Postinstitutionalized Children", *Child Dev*. 81(1): 224-36.

Rosenbaum, P. (2011). "Family and Quality of Life: Key Elements in Intervention in Children with Cerebral Palsy". *Dev. Med. Child Neurol.* 53(Suppl. 4): 68-70.

Schneider, M.L., E.C. Roughton, A.J. Koehler, G.R. Lubach (1999). "Growth Development Following Prenatal Stress Exposure in Primates: An Examination of Ontogenetic Vulnerability", *Child Dev*. 70(2): 263-74.

Stiles, J. and T.L. Jernigan (2010). "The Basics of Brain Development", *Neuropsychol. Rev.* 20(4): 327-48.

Shonkoff, J.P. and A.S. Garner (2012). "The Lifelong Effects of Early Childhood Adversity and Toxic Stress", *Pediatrics* 129(1): e232-46.

Singhi, P. (2014). *Brain Development in Early Childhood: The Critical Years.* ECED Brief-3. Delhi: Centre for Early Childhood Care and Education (CECED), Ambedkar University and CARE.

Swaminathan, M. (2006). *Early Years Education: Policy and Practice in Early Education & Care.* Vol 3. p.107. http://goo.gl/T7pmO.

Thompson, P.M., J.N. Giedd, R.P. Woods, D. MacDonald, A.C. Evans, A.W. Toga (2000). *Growth Patterns in the Developing Brain Detected by Using Continuum Mechanical Tensor Maps* 404 (6774): 190-3. Retrieved from *http://www.ncbi.nlm.nih.gov/pubmed/10724172*

Walker, S.P., S.M. Chang, C.A. Powell *et al.* (2005). "Effects of Early Childhood Psychosocial Stimulation and Nutritional Supplementation on Cognition and Education in Growth Stunted Jamaican Children: Prospective cohort study", *Lancet*. 366(9499): 1804-07.

Walker, S.P., T.D. Wachs, S. Grantham-McGregor, M.M. Black, C.A. Nelson, S.L. Huffman *et al.* (2011). "Inequality in Early Childhood: Risk and Protective Factors for Early Child Development", *Lancet*. 378(9799): 1325-38.

Waller, T. (Ed.). (2008). *An Introduction to Early Childhood: A Multidisciplinary Approach.* 2nd edition.

Wasserman, Haley, L. and Debby Zambo (ed.). (2013). "Early Childhood and Neuroscience: Links to Development and Learning Series: Educating the Young Child", *Springer* 7.

Young, M.E. (ed.). (1997). *ECD: Investing in our Children's Future*. Amsterdam: Elsevier.

Zeanah, C.H., C.A. Nelson, N.A. Fox, A.T. Smyke, P. Marshall and S.W. Parker (2003). "Designing Research to Study the Effects of Institutionalisation on Brain and Behavioural Development: The Bucharest Early Intervention Project", *Dev. Psychopathol.* 15(4): 885-907.

Zero to Three (2009). *Creating Healthy Connections: Nurturing Brain Development from Birth to Three.* Retrieved from *http://www.zerotothree.org/about-us/funded-projects/parenting-resources/podcast/creating-healthy-connections.html*

———. (2007). *Baby Brain Map*. Retrieved from *http://www.zerotothree.org/baby-brain-map.html*

Acknowledgements: The paper has been written by the author in her individual capacity and does not represent the views of any organisation.The author acknowledges the inputs given by Ms. Swati Bawa, Government Reforms & Infrastructure Development, PwC, in reviewing and formatting the document.

3

REKHA SHARMA SEN

Literacy in Pre-Primary and Class 1

Processes of Teaching and Learning in a Trilingual Environment[1]

Introduction

The selection of this topic for research was guided by the well-known situation with respect to reading achievements of young children in a large number of Indian schools. The findings from Annual Survey of Education Report (ASER) (2013) show that only 40.2 per cent of children in Std. III can read first standard level paragraph, and 47 per cent of the children in Std. V can read Std. III text. Many of those who are able to read and write, do so without understanding the meaning. The ASER 2007 survey collected data on children's reading comprehension, which was judged on the basis of the children's ability to read and orally answer questions based on the text. Of the children in age group 6-10 years, 19.3 per cent could read Std. I level text and, of these, 66 per cent could answer text-based oral questions. For a large number of children, learning to read and write are stressful experiences.

In order to gain some insight into what leads to this situation, I decided to study reading and writing as introduced to children in the early grades in a particular school. In the school that I had selected, formal instruction in learning to read and write began in the pre-primary section where children were admitted at the age of four plus. Although this case study (idiographic) approach, describing practices in a specific school, hinders generalisations, in many ways

1. I gratefully acknowledge the guidance given by Dr Maxine Berntsen, (Professor Emerita in the Azim Premji School of Education, Tata Institute of Social Sciences, Hyderabad), during this study.

the ethos, culture and pedagogy practices evident in the school were 'typical' of many ordinary schools in various parts of the country. A detailed description of the school setting is provided in the section on 'Methodology' and the teaching practices are described under 'Findings'.

Objectives

The study was undertaken with the following objectives:

a. To examine the nature of literacy pedagogy in the first two years of schooling—pre-primary and Class 1, in this case;
b. To find out teachers' beliefs about how children learn to read; and
c. To examine children's competencies in reading, writing and meaning-making.

This paper makes a unique contribution by providing 'thick' descriptions of teachers' practices and children's learning behaviours when they are formally introduced to three languages at the same time during the pre-primary years, and adds to the qualitative research on processes of literacy acquisition in the earliest years of schooling.

Development of Early Literacy in Children: Theoretical Frameworks and Pedagogical Approaches

In this section, four theoretical perspectives that have currency in the field of early literacy and which guided this qualitative enquiry have been elaborated. Further, the chief approaches to teaching the ways to read have been discussed, which formed the background for examining teaching processes in the classroom.

Socio-cultural Theory of Learning

The socio-cultural theory of learning, pioneered by Vygotsky (1978), sees the child as embedded within various social and cultural contexts—ranging from the micro context of the family and the school to the larger neighbourhood, the community and society. Learning takes place as people interact with the child since birth and mediate the world for children, making it accessible to them.

Therefore, the socio-economic status of the family, its gender profile, their religion, ethnicity and access to resources, the education history of the family members, the socio-political status of the community and the cultural group to which the family belongs, the languages to which the child is exposed to—all these become some of the critical socio-cultural descriptors forming the context for the growing child.

Literacy and non-literacy in the home environment is a critical component of the child's socio-cultural environment, and has the effect of creating cultures which influence cognition and acquisition of reading and writing in school (Purcell-Gates, 1995). Thus, a culture of literacy serves two purposes: that of helping children to perceive written language as meaningful and purposeful as well as enabling children to accumulate a fund of recognisable material that will help them make sense of what is written when they begin reading and writing in school.

The socio-cultural theory of learning also sensitises us to the fact that the classroom is socio-culturally framed and the teacher has a large role to play in creating the socio-cultural ethos therein. When this ethos is at variance with the child's experiences in the family and the community, this may act as a hindrance in the achievement of literacy by the child. What is considered as knowledge and literacy in the classroom, what are the teacher's beliefs regarding the child as a learner, the value placed by the teacher on experiences and prior learning that the child brings into the classroom, the attitude of the teacher towards the child's language—all shape the way meanings are created in the classroom, which contributes towards whether the classroom experience is perceived by the child as relevant or not. Often when children do not belong to dominant groups in the community, they may perceive the schooling experience to be alien (Kumar, 1989; Talib, 1997) and may not succeed in school-related tasks.

Emergent Literacy Framework

The concept of emergent literacy introduced by Marie Clay in 1966 describes learning to read and write as a continuum of growth of knowledge about print literacy such that there are continuities between early literacy behaviours and those displayed once children are able to read independently. Emergent literacy perspective holds that learning to read and write is natural in a literate society and literate abilities and stances emerge developmentally. As children are introduced to literacy through holistic experiences in the everyday contexts of home and community, they begin to learn about reading and writing even before they begin formal instruction. As they see literacy being used for real life activities in order to "get things done", they begin to perceive reading and writing as purposeful (Teale and Sulzby, 1992).

Thus this stance is different from the traditional reading and writing readiness approach, which holds that children begin to learn to read and write only when they are introduced to formal literacy instruction in school and that teaching of reading and writing has to be through readiness activities that develop skills in the child part by part, wherein children love visual and auditory discrimination skills and writing patterns leading to formation of letter shapes. However, while phonological awareness, recognition of letters and understanding letter-sound correspondence (all aspects of reading readiness instruction) are necessary components of learning to read, these are not the only measure of beginning to read. Knowledge about directionality, the ability to distinguish print from other graphic forms, understanding the function of print and that print has meaning, reading print in context, pretend or invented reading, scribbling, drawing and invented writing, shared reading and writing—all these constitute aspects of early literacy development of children within the emergent literacy framework (Mason and Sinha, 1992).

The emergent literacy framework envisions that children learn language through active engagement with their world and lends itself to a Vygotskian model of learning. Children interact socially with adults in reading and writing situations; they explore print on their own and they learn as adults model literacy behaviours. Adults actively introduce children to literacy as they scaffold learning during formats and routines, such as during the routine of reading a story, to enable the child to participate at the level at which he/she is capable of (Bruner, 1983; 1990). In this way, the new language is brought within the child's zone of proximal development; the child is able to make sense of it and starts the process of internalising it. Children coming from environments with little exposure to print, find it difficult to cope with and make sense of literacy instruction in school as compared to those who come from homes where they are exposed to print. Thus literacy and non-literacy in the home environment has the effect of creating cultures which influence cognition and acquisition of reading and writing in school (Purcell-Gates, 1995).

Reading and Writing as Meaning-making

Approaching the process of learning to read and write as meaning-making, rather than simply learning a set of strategies for decoding, has its origin in Piagetian conception of the child as a sense-maker (Cameron, 2001). Piagetian view of the child as an active learner and thinker, who constructs his or her knowledge from working with ideas and objects, emphasises that children seek out intentions and purposes in their experiences, and bring their prior knowledge to bear upon the experience or the situation in order to make sense of it. The implication for literacy is that children are likely to master reading and writing fairly comfortably when they experience these activities as meaningful. Reading is a constructive development wherein the meaning is constructed by the learners through a process of integration of the written text with their prior background knowledge. Children are not passive learners who have to be taught reading, but are naturally motivated to make sense of the written texts they encounter, provided these have a meaning for them. Further, the meaning-making perspective does not isolate affective aspects from the cognitive aspects of learning to read (Rosenblatt, 1980; Sinha, 2009).

The work of many researchers—both in India and outside—has been inspired by this perspective. Thus, while it is important to focus on the methods of teaching how to read, these are not more important than the need to make meaning. Of course, children will need to learn to decode skills but these are to be taught within the context of reading as a meaningful activity (Stahl, 1992). Ashton-

Warner (1963) pioneered in approaching reading and writing as 'organic' activities wherein she began with teaching children words that they wanted to learn and used this 'key vocabulary' to introduce children to writing and reading.

Literacy in Multilingual Context

It is also important to bear in mind that most children in our country are exposed to more than one language as they grow and that they learn to read and write in multilingual contexts. Thus, while mother tongue is the medium of communication at home, in the community they are likely to be exposed to the standard state language, other Indian languages and English.

In most schools, the child is taught at least two languages—the standard state language as the first language and English, as the second language. In schools where the mother tongue is the basis of education, the child would learn three languages. There is a lot of variation in the way and the ages in which these languages are introduced in the school. Many language education researchers recommend mother tongue based (L1) education when the child begins schooling (in pre-primary or class 1) with the gradual and successive introduction of second (L2, standard state language) and third (L3, usually English) language in the subsequent classes, beginning with the spoken form of the language followed by the script (Malone, 2007; Mohanty, 1990). When introducing a new language, the learners should experience literacy development as integrated within the spoken language development. Rather than seeing oral skills as simply one aspect of language learning, the spoken form acts as the prime source and site of language learning. However, the reality in the schools is quite different.

While some schools may use the mother tongue as the means of communication in the initial months/years of schooling and then introduce the standard state language followed by English, in many schools, mother tongue is not a part of the formal instructional system. In fact, children may be barred from using their mother tongue in the school. Most often, English is given priority over the state language. Further, reading and writing in English or state language is introduced without adequate development of oracy. Since children vary in the extent of exposure they have had to English or state language before joining school, they are likely to experience different degrees of success in handling the instruction. Many simply rote memorise the content being taught in school without understanding its meaning. While introduction of the standard state language may also pose difficulties in the absence of use of mother tongue based education as a bridge, yet the difficulty in learning to read and write the standard state language may be somewhat less than English, since the mother tongue of the child may be quite similar to it. For example, while the languages spoken in different regions of northern India are different from standard Hindi, they bear considerable similarity to it, making it possible for children to understand what is being transacted in the school.

Pedagogical Approaches

The debate in literacy instruction has been between the whole language approach and the skills-based phonics approach, which symbolise two different philosophies regarding what it means to learn to read and write in a language (Krashen, 2002).

The comprehension hypothesis is a central part of whole language approach and holds that we learn to read by understanding meaning on the page and by expressing meaning in writing. The emphasis in pedagogy here is on appropriate children's literature, constructivist meaning-centred whole to part to whole learning process where phonics are taught contextually as "embedded" phonics. Whole language practitioners teach the grapho-phonic, syntactic, semantic and pragmatic aspects of language by immersing the child in the language experience and allowing skills to emerge. Thus reading and writing for real purposes, reading aloud, shared reading, guided reading and independent reading; modelled writing, shared writing, interactive writing and independent writing are some aspects of the curriculum. There is focus on motivational aspects of literacy, emphasising the love of books and engaging reading materials.

The skills-based approach holds that literacy is developed from the bottom up—that the child learns to read by first learning letter-sound correspondences. Explicit direct instruction is provided in developing this grapho-phonemic association through repeated practice and correction. Once this association is in place, the child is taught to sound out words and ultimately, he/she uses this ability to read larger texts, as the knowledge of sound-spelling correspondences becomes automatic.

It is now being increasingly accepted that subscribing to one approach of teaching reading rather than the other is an outdated view of how language learning occurs and that there is need to focus both on skills and meaning while teaching to read (Jayaram, 2011; Nag, 2005). There is evidence that children taught *via* the skills-based/direct phonics instruction approach tend to improve in their rate of word reading and word recognition (Nag-Arulmani, 2003). However research also shows that a singular focus on phonics develops in the child a mechanistic view of reading, where the child focuses solely on decoding, regardless of understanding what is being read. Sinha's (2000) analysis of NCERT's[2] Hindi textbooks is illustrative of the meaninglessness that can characterise reading when it is seen simply as teaching of decoding skills based on the use of phonics.

The use of whole language approach to teaching reading promotes a positive attitude to reading, a broader vision of language, its nuances and layers of meaning (Clay, 1991). The recently completed Mathura Pilot Project of the NCERT (2012-13) shows that where intervention was carried out with students in grades 1 and 2 using the whole language approach, 57 per cent of the children by the time they were in grade 3, were conventional writers as compared to 38 per cent at the time of baseline survey, and 35 per cent were confident readers and could comprehend one or both the stories of the assessment tool they read as compared to 3 per cent at the time of baseline survey. At the time of the baseline survey, it was observed that the teachers taught children using the standard

2. National Council of Educational Research and Training.

practice of phonic identification. Children's confidence/risk-taking behaviour *vis-à-vis* reading also showed a remarkable improvement with 54 per cent of the children, as opposed to 9 per cent at the time of baseline survey, were willing to take risks and attempted to read using illustrations or prediction. While all children, except 2 per cent who had not picked up any literacy skills, were somewhere on the continuum of learning to read and write by grade 3, one wonders if the organic language experience approach used during intervention had been coupled with systematically developing in the children phonemic and phonological awareness and alphabetic knowledge, the figure of 70 per cent of the students not being able to read in grade 3 may have been reduced considerably. (Of course, other factors could have also been responsible for this gap such as the extent to which the teachers actually implemented the intervention approaches in the classroom). Berntsen (2009) emphasises that even though the child unconsciously acquires the phonemes of a language in learning to speak, this unconscious knowledge must become conscious as a preparation for learning to read. In her own strategy of teaching reading in Marathi (called the Pragat Shikshan Sansthan approach), she has combined systematic teaching of phonemic awareness and letter-sound correspondences (decoding) with language experience and organic reading approaches, which involve writing down experiences narrated by children and helping them read the written accounts.

The components of a balanced early reading programme include explicit instructions about letter-sound linkages, reading aloud, shared reading, guided reading and independent reading, modelled writing, shared writing, interactive writing and independent writing, use of authentic texts and personally meaningful language experiences, and all this embedded in a lot of speaking and listening activities (Jayaram, forthcoming; Nag, 2005). Thus the focus is both on developing an awareness of sound segments (phonemes, syllables, onsets and rimes) and letter-sound correspondence as well as comprehension, vocabulary and spelling. In the Indian context, the approaches developed by Berntsen (refer above) and Jayaram's (2008) *varna samooha* approach for teaching Hindi facilitate word recognition through both phonological processing and processes of meaning construction. Describing a micro study evaluating differences in performance of children from intervention classes practicing *varna samooha* approach with those in non-intervention classes following the typical *varna mala* approach based solely on phonics instruction, Jayaram reported significant difference in the performance of children in favour of the intervention group. Qualitatively, while the children from the intervention class created words by manipulating syllables in various ways, quite a few children from the non-intervention classes wrote memorised words.

Method

My study was an exploratory qualitative enquiry, constructivist in nature, where I entered the field with a few *a priori* assumptions and did not use any structured pre-formulated tools to collect data. Rather, the research was guided by the grounded theory approach, wherein the process of data collection is controlled by the emerging theory (Kuzel, 1999). Thus the research process was iterative and evolving, rather than linear and fixed. The research questions, methodology and sample categories evolved and were modified as the fieldwork unfolded while the interpretive process occurred spontaneously and informally, along with data collection and data gathering. Data analysis and theory construction occurred concurrently, as is usual in constructivist enquiry (Addison, 1999; Miller and Crabtree, 1999a; 1999b).

Field Site

A self-financingschool, charging a fees of about ₹1200/- per month located in a Muslim populated area in Delhi was the field site. English was the medium of instruction in the school. However, the medium of conversation among teachers and children was dominantly Hindi and Urdu during most teaching periods. Hindi, Urdu and English were formally taught as languages right from the pre-primary class. Textbooks for all subjects were introduced in pre-primary class. The school had one section of pre-primary with 60 children, four years of age. Class 1 onwards, there were two sections per class, with about 50 children per class.

The community catered to by the school belonged to middle and lower middle SES (socio-economic status). Urdu was the mother tongue of the community; they were fluent in Hindi as well, there being not much difference between spoken Hindi and Urdu. English was rarely spoken in the community. For the children, introduction to English was chiefly through formal instruction in the school.

Sample

The only pre-primary class of the school and one section of Class 1 comprised the sample. The classes were studied as a unit for a total of 32 Teaching Events, involving eight different teachers. Of the 32 Teaching Events sampled, 21 were in pre-primary, and 11 in Class 1.

Additionally, I interacted with 30 children individually to know their competencies in reading and writing as well as with five teachers, teaching Hindi and English, to know their beliefs about how children learn to read.

Tools and Procedure of Data Collection

Data was collected over a period of 20 days. Non-participant observation was used to make a detailed record of 32 Teaching Events in pre-primary and Class 1. These were later transcribed. Some teaching events were recorded on video.

In order to find out what children were comprehending and learning, I interacted with individual children, asked them specific questions and observed their written work in notebooks.

Semi-structured interviews were carried out with five teachers teaching Hindi and English to know their beliefs regarding how children learn to read.

Analysis

Content analysis of the Teaching Events, children's written work, their verbal responses as well as the responses of teachers to the interview was carried out to determine the features of the process of teaching children reading and writing and the efficacy of the process in enabling students to learn.

Findings

Analysis of the Teaching Events showed that teaching children to read and write was carried out using a strikingly similar pedagogy by the eight teachers who taught the two classes and the three languages. While their individual styles varied somewhat, their basic approach was largely similar. The teachers had conceptualised learning to read essentially as a process of decoding, learnt sequentially in three stages. The stages were—letter recognition and naming, learning to read words, learning to read sentences/text. Meaning-making during learning to read was largely relegated to the background. The detailed findings have been presented further under three sections:

a. Literacy pedagogy
b. Children's competencies
c. Teachers' beliefs about how children learn to read

Literacy Pedagogy

The process of teaching reading and writing has been analysed with respect to five aspects:

- Teaching decoding
- Opportunities for oral expression
- Meaning-making
- Written work
- Other features of the process

Teaching Decoding

i) Teaching Letter Recognition

Teaching decoding began by teaching children to recognise letters by naming them. When children were taught letter names, I did not observe letter-sound correspondence, or phonics, being deliberately taught in any of the three languages, except in the case of English vowels. While in Hindi the letter name corresponds with the letter sound, this is not the case in English or Urdu. When children name words or hear the teacher name words beginning with a letter, it is likely that they may associate the letter name with its sound. However, this cannot be assumed to happen each time by itself, and certainly not in case of all children.

In fact, interaction with the children revealed that many had not made this association spontaneously. They could not state the sound of the particular letter upon hearing a word beginning with that letter, which shows that the extrapolation of this principle cannot be left to the child. A striking proof that children may completely miss the connection between letter sound and word-initial sound was provided when a child replaced the word 'lion' with 'tiger' with ease, when he was shown the picture of a lion and asked "L for...?" This happened because while on one hand the child did not see the lion and the tiger as visually distinct from each other, he had not made the connection between the sound of letter L and the word-initial sound in 'lion', nor realised that the sound of the letter L was not the same as the word-initial sound in 'tiger'.

Further, interaction with the children brought out that even in case of Hindi, where the letter name and letter sound are in complete fit, children may still need to be guided to deliberately focus their attention on the sound of the letter and the initial sound of the word beginning with that letter. In the absence of this deliberate training, children may make faulty and arbitrary associations between letter sound and word-initial sound. In fact, children did do so (refer to section on Children's Competencies which provides evidence for these conclusions).

Use of Pictures for Letter Recognition

When letter names were introduced, teachers drew pictures of objects with names starting with that letter and named the object. The pedagogical intent of this activity was to help the child make the association between the letter sound and word-initial sound and thus practice letter-sound correspondence. It was expected that when children say 'a' for 'apple' on seeing the picture of an apple, they will learn to associate the sound of letter 'a' with the letter name 'a'. Interaction with children however, revealed that this objective was not being achieved and many of them seemed to miss the point. For them, the word-initial sound in the name of the object and the letter sound had no relation. The picture served the purpose of helping children recall the name of the object and state it without them understanding the reason why a particular picture was drawn for a particular letter. That children seemed oblivious of the phonetic association was evident from their substituting the English name of the object with the Hindi name or an English word with another related English word. Thus, children provided 'g' for *angoor*, 'l' for *seedhi*, 'k' for *chabi*, forgetting the English names 'grapes', 'ladder' and 'key', respectively. A child interchanged 'lion' with 'tiger' as stated above. Thus the picture only served the purpose of object identification and in a way hindered phonetic associations. Since children did not focus on phonetic associations, they arbitrarily associated a picture with a particular letter. Thus, when I asked the child to name the letter she had written under her drawings of 'ladder' and 'man', she said the name 'm' while pointing at the letter 'l' and vice-versa.

This happened in case of Hindi and Urdu as well. The teacher drew a 'thermos' to represent the Hindi letter *tha*. A child named the drawing as *botal* (bottle) and provided *tha se botal* because for her, the picture of the thermos looked like that of a bottle. In case of Urdu, the teacher had provided *za se zakhira*. *Zakhira* means treasure and the teacher drew a round-ish bag, colouring it orange-ish red. The child drew it in her copy and later on my asking what stood for letter *za*, stated *za se tamatar* (tomato!), forgetting the word zakhira, because that is what the picture looked like to her.

While the above discussion is critical of children's abilities to make phonetic associations, especially in terms of substituting Hindi names for English letters ('g' for *angoor*), one can interpret children's response more favourably as their attempt to make meaning as best as they could. Since English was not part of children's environment, other than for the limited period of formal instruction in school, they did not own the English words. But since they needed to make meaning of their experience, they did the next best thing that they could. They provided the Hindi name for the picture they recognised.

Gradually, as they become familiar with English, they would perhaps provide English names too. However, the larger issue here is about how languages—both the familiar ones and the not-so-familiar ones —could have been introduced to children more meaningfully. This has been elaborated upon in the section 5 i.e., Conclusion.

It also seemed to me that one could not always be sure that the teacher herself consciously understood that the purpose of naming the object in the picture was to associate the letter sound with the word-initial sound. The teachers focused on the letter name rather than the letter sound while naming the picture. For example, the teacher said, "p for pencil; *bolo* pencil; 'p' *ki aawaz aa rahi hai*?" (p for pencil; say pencil; Can you hear the sound of 'p'?). The teacher used the name and not the sound of the letter 'p' as 'pa' in the above sentence.

ii) Teaching Reading Words and Sentences

The next step in teaching using the decoding strategy was reading words and sentences. I did not observe this process for Urdu, since I was not familiar with the script. The approach to teaching reading English and Hindi words and text was spelling based, using what I have named as the 'spell-reading aloud-recite-repeat' method. In case of English, the teacher spelled a particular word by naming the individual letters and read it out aloud; the children recited the spelling after her and this process was repeated 4-5 times for a particular word. In class 1, where the children were expected to read text, the teacher read out a line in parts and the children repeated the line after her. This 'read aloud-repeat' was done 3-4 times for a line (or a portion of it, if the line was a long one) and then the teacher moved on to the next line (or the next portion of the line), following the same process. If while reading a line, the teacher encountered a 'difficult' word, she spelled out the word and the children recited the spelling after her. After 3-4 repetitions of the spelling of this word, the teacher resumed reading out the rest of the line. Sometimes, a big word was not spelled in one go—the word was split and the spelling and reciting of a part was repeated 2-3 times and then the remaining part of the word was spelt and recited in the same way and following that, the word was recited as a whole. Thus, the reading of a line was not always continuous; the big ones were 'broken' for reading in the following way—a part of the line was read, then a big word in the middle of the line was spelled and read out loud (sometimes by breaking the word into parts) and then the remaining part of the line was read.

The 'spell-reading aloud-recite-repeat' method was a natural consequence of teaching letter recognition by letter naming, without teaching letter-sound correspondence. Since letter sounds had not been introduced to children, except for English vowels, phonics could not be used as a strategy for reading words.

In Hindi, using the spelling-based approach, the letters and *matras* were spelled and taught individually instead of treating them together as a unit. It is known that such a strategy puts load on the child's working memory and hinders efficient and quick processing of words.

The consequence of the spelling-based approach to reading is that the child has to learn to read each word individually and remember the word. Repeated drilling to spell the word, as was happening in this school, may enable the child to identify the commonly occurring words as whole words/sight words after a while. But the point is that the spelling-based strategy does not enable children to process words quickly or to see pattern in words. Of course, one could argue that when the child spells and then speaks the word, he/she is also hearing the letter sounds during utterance of the words. But as described earlier, when phonics is not deliberately taught, then one cannot really be sure that the child has extrapolated the letter sounds. Interaction with children showed that this was indeed true, as described further in the paper.

Moreover, given the way the 'reading aloud and recite' method was carried out, it appeared doubtful whether children were really learning to get familiar with the appearance of the words and whether they could really use them as sight words. As children recited after the teacher, they were expected to keep their fingers at the word they were reading. But many while reciting simply looked at the teacher, keeping their finger arbitrarily anywhere on the page. They did not connect the printed (visual) stimulus with what they were reciting. Later, interaction showed that many children had memorised the text and so could recite the text but did not know where the words, which they were 'reading', were.

Depending on memorisation as the chief learning strategy made children's learning context-bound. Firstly, some children were able to read the words only when they were in the same layout in which they had learnt them—for example, the child was able to read words written in the copy but could not read them in the book. Secondly, there were children who could read the text transacted in the class very fluently but not a fresh text from the same textbook, being unable to recognise letters and *matras* in the fresh text. This showed that they had simply memorised the transacted text due to several repetitions at home and the school, and had not really learnt to decode.

The teachers' focus was on correct performance. If a child volunteered to read or spell a word but could not do so, the child was not helped to read—instead he/she was reprimanded, and others were asked to volunteer to 'read'.

Oral Expression

Encouraging children's oral expression is the cornerstone of a language classroom facilitating both reading and writing. However, during the duration of my observation, children never got an opportunity for oral expression in any class. Teachers did not converse with children and neither encouraged them to express themselves. Singing of rhymes, reciting of poems or free conversation were not used as strategies for oral expression. During the study period, two poems in English were recited in pre-primary class but these were prescribed poems in the textbook, transacted as drill and were not used as a means of oral expression.

In class 1, I observed a Hindi period which was meant to be specifically devoted to oral expression. The teacher was expected to encourage children's oral expression using the given illustration in the NCERT class 1 textbook, which depicted children going out for the day in a bus. However, what happened was the exact opposite.

The entire imagination and description was that of the teacher's. He decided the places that would be 'visited' and gave their realistic descriptions and imagined for the children what they would do there! Since children had not visited these places, they could not contribute to the description. The teacher owned the content of the oral expression, and the children tried to live the teacher's imagination. Children's participation was reduced to answering the few mundane close-ended questions which the teacher posed to them—such as "what will you eat there?", "what will you buy to get inside the monument?"

Oral expression in English was problematic because children did not understand the meanings. Equally, children did not understand meanings because they did not have adequate exposure to spoken English and opportunities for self-expression. This became a vicious cycle.

During the school hours, other than reading the English text, the teachers largely spoke with the children in Hindi, with a couple of teachers occasionally translating the Hindi sentence into English or vice versa. Children's spoken English in pre-primary and class 1 was confined to two memorised sentences: "Ma'am, may I go to the washroom?" and "Ma'am, may I come in?" Many children spoke the sentence as one long word—as "Ma'ammayIgotothewashroom"— and perhaps did not even know the individual words that comprised the sentence.

Meaning-making

Meaning-making was compromised in several ways in this entire process. The fragmented way in which reading (whether of individual words in pre-primary or of text in class 1) was being done using the 'spell-reading aloud-recite-repeat' approach prevented the children from gaining a holistic experience of what it meant to read. They encountered the text as strings of letters or words. Once I observed the teacher reading out the entire chapter before beginning with the 'spell-read aloud-recite-repeat' approach. But since children neither knew the meaning of words nor could recognise those, this reading held no relevance for them.

Learning to read was completely textbook bound. There were no children's storybooks and no other teaching-learning material. Children's own vocabulary was not used as a resource for teaching reading, which could have been done for Hindi and Urdu. This would have made the reading 'organic' and meaningful.

An obvious thing for the teacher to do in order to help children to perceive reading as a meaningful activity, is to explain to them the meaning of what they are reading. In pre-primary and class 1, this was the exception. Even when the teachers did tell meanings, there were limitations in the way in which they did so:

- Explaining meaning was done as a onetime activity, with no attempt at finding out later on whether or not the children have understood and remembered the meanings.
- Pictures were drawn to explain the meanings of words. While some pictures were unambiguous, in case of others children extracted meanings quite different from the ones intended (see *zakhira* example above).
- It is doubtful whether children connected the meaning with the word because they were reciting while looking at the teacher and did not know where the word whose meaning was being told was on the page.
- The teacher referred to the meaning in a very indirect manner, leaving it to the children to infer what was meant.
- In case of English text in Class 1, the holistic meaning of the text was told in Hindi after it was read and recited. Consequently, the children were able to paraphrase the story broadly and briefly in Hindi, but were unable to explain meanings of specific sentences or words. Thus they could not understand or answer specific text-based questions.
- Meaning was explained by using another English word, the meaning of which may or may not be known to the child.
- The meaning given by the teacher was one of the right meanings but not the one in context.
- The teacher provided an explanation but not the meaning.

Although teachers relegated meaning-making to the background, the children needed to make meaning of what they are doing. So based on their experience, they constructed meaning as best as they could. Children understood the Hindi text simply because of their everyday familiarity with the language. In case of English text, many did not understand the meaning of what they read. Many constructed wrong meaning, as will be described in the section on children's competencies and one wonders how to clear their misconceptions.

Written Work

Since developing decoding skills as well as making meaning were compromised, writing on the board became the chief pedagogic tool as it was important that children copy correctly in their notebooks to memorise and reproduce later.

Further, writing in the copy was taken as evidence of understanding. However, this was often not the case as many children simply copied without understanding what they were writing and were unable to read or explain the same. The time taken for the children to get their copies corrected individually, could have been used by the teacher to interact with each one to know what had been understood. I did not see the teachers making use of this opportunity.

Other Features of the Process

The teaching process was teacher-centred. The teachers' objective was to complete a certain amount of content from the textbook on a particular day. They did not seem to have set any objective with reference to the children—in terms of expanding their thinking, enabling them to understand and comprehend, to read, to make connections between experiences, between content taught on the previous day and that being transacted presently. The performance of the group was taken as evidence of the performance of individual children.

Children's Competencies in Reading, Writing and Meaning-making

I interacted with the children to find out their ability to recognise letters, provide letter-sound correspondence, read words and sentences and explain meaning. There was a large variation in children's competencies. The gaps in children's learning seemed to be singularly the consequence of the teaching process.

Competencies in Letter Recognition and Letter-Sound Correspondence

In the pre-primary class, there were children who could correctly name letters and provide words beginning with the letter in all three languages. But, for many of these children, naming words beginning with a particular letter was a memorised action. Only a few children could identify letter sounds and provide more than one word beginning with the letter. Many children experienced difficulties in letter recognition and letter-sound correspondence as described further, with an example each.

i) Incorrect Letter Naming but Correct Letter-Sound Correspondence

A child identified the Hindi letter *chha* as *ja* and provided *ja se jahaaz*.

ii) Incorrect Letter Naming and Incorrect Letter-Sound Correspondence

On seeing the Hindi letter *tha* (as in thermos), the child could not recognise it; then on seeing the picture of the *thermos* that he had drawn, he named the letter *tha* as *ta* (as in *tarbooz*) and provided the word *botal* for thermos stating *ta se botal*. The word *botal* means *bottle*—to the child the thermos drawn appeared like a bottle. The letter name/sound and the word for the picture resided as two separate categories in the child's mind, unrelated to each other. Therefore the child found nothing amiss in stating *ta se botal*.

iii) Confusion Between Similar Sounding Consonants

Certain sound groups were confusing for children—such as the Hindi sound group *ta*, *Ta*, *tha* and *Tha* (as in *tarbooz*, *tamatar*, *tharmas* and t*hathera,* respectively) and *da*, *Dha* and *Da* (as in *dawaat*, *dhakkan* and *damroo*, respectively).

I pointed to picture of *damroo* and asked for its name. The child replied correctly. On asking, "What does Damroo begin with?", the child replied, *da se* (as in *dawaat*) and on being asked to show the letter, pointed to *Dha* (as in *dhakkan*), written on the same page.

A little later, the letter *Dha* (as in *dhakkan*) was named as *da* (as in dawaat).

iv) Correct Letter Naming But No Awareness of Its Sound

This largely happened in the case of English letters. Many children could name the letters. Many among them could also name words beginning with the letter. But when asked the sound of the letter, they were unable to do so. In case of sound of the letter (for example, a question like: "*m ki awaaz kya hai*?"; what is the sound of the letter 'm'?), they would state its sound as 'a' or any other sound. It was this lack of awareness regarding sound of a letter that made a child say with certainty 'l for tiger' on seeing the letter 'l' and the picture of a lion (which probably appeared to him to be not much different from a tiger).

v) Confusion Because of Similar Formation of Letters

A child, for example, found the written Hindi letter *tha* (as in thermos) to be confusing with *gha* (as in *ghar*) because of the way the teacher wrote both the letters, with a loop at the beginning of formation of the both.

vi) Use of Picture to Recall the Memorised Letter and Word

Many children could not identify the letter and/or provide the word beginning with the letter without the picture. For example, a child could not recognise the English letter 'p' when the researcher wrote it on a page, but on seeing the letter in the primer where a picture of the related word was drawn, stated "p for parrot."

vii) Providing Memorised Tag Word for the Letter Irrespective of Alternate Picture

This was quite common. For example, a child had drawn the picture of a man to represent the word beginning with the letter 'm'. When I pointed to letter 'm' he had written in the notebook, and asked what it was, the child immediately stated "m for monkey' and not "m for man", since the former word is more typically associated with the letter 'm' in primers and it was this that the child had memorised. These instances showed that although the children had been told these English words by the teacher, they did not own them yet.

viii) Disconnect Between Meaning Intended by Teacher Through the Picture and that Extrapolated by Children

The example from the Urdu language, described earlier, of the picture of *zakhira* being identified as *Tamatar* and the child providing '*za se Tamatar*' explains this point.

ix) Providing Hindi name for objects when asked for English words with particular word initial sounds

Children on being asked 'l for...?' provided *seedi* (ladder); for 'g' provided *angoor* (grapes), for 'k' provided *chaabi* (key), for 'z' provided '*chain*' (implying zip); for 'r' provided *khargosh* (rabbit). These instances reflect that children had not grasped the phonetic rationale for naming a word beginning with a particular letter sound.

Competencies in Making Meaning

As the preceding descriptions bring out, teachers were not able to make learning to read a meaningful activity for children. This itself made learning a challenge for children. Added to this were the challenges of unfamiliarity with English language and learning three languages simultaneously in the school. Making sense is the foremost need of the human mind. Within this scenario, the children valiantly tried to construct meanings using whatever 'clues' they could get.

i) Meaning Construction in Hindi

Meaning construction was more accurate in case of Hindi and Urdu words because children's familiarity with the language was a big 'clue'. Each child knew the meanings of a fair number of words, though not all. Often when children knew meanings, they knew near approximations which showed that the children had constructed these meanings themselves and had not been formally told the meanings by the teacher. In some cases, the meanings had been told by the parents.

ii) Meaning Construction in English

Meaning construction was more difficult in English. With respect to many English words, not having been told meanings, several children simply did not know what they meant. They said as much or simply kept quiet when asked the meanings of words.

Whenever they could, however, children constructed meanings of English words. When the picture was present along with the word, the children provided meanings by looking at the picture. Sometimes these meanings were correct. Sometimes the picture evoked associations which were related to the picture, but were not the meaning of the word. While the meanings thus constructed were not the correct ones, they represented valiant efforts on part of the children to make sense. For example, associating 'nest' with birds, the child provided its meaning as *chidia* (bird); in another case the picture led a child to infer the meaning of 'queen' as *ladki* (girl).

It has been stated earlier in the discussion that sometimes the children of pre-primary could not recall the English word beginning with the particular letter. In such cases, upon seeing the picture, they provided the Hindi name for the object (see examples l *se seedi*; k se *chabi*; g for *angoor*; m for *aadmi*, described earlier). Such responses of the children can be looked at in two ways. One can take the view that children had completely missed the phonetic association between letter sound and word-initial sound and therefore did not hesitate to provide the Hindi word. This was indeed true for some children. But some of them showed the awareness that they were not stating the appropriate word by providing the Hindi name. In case of these children, mention of the Hindi name may be seen as a forward step in their learning. Not being familiar with English, they did the next best thing to create meaning in the situation and provided the Hindi word.

There is a view that correct pronunciation of words should not be rigidly insisted upon. However, I found that incorrect pronunciation of English words was often the cause of incorrect meanings generated by children. If not corrected, this would make the child's writing and speech incomprehensible to others. For example, the meaning of 'pan' was explained by a child as *kalam* (pen). This was confusing for me but I soon realised that this happened because the word 'pen' was pronounced with an extended 'e' sound (sounding like 'pain') and the word 'pan' was also similarly pronounced.

Sometimes, the picture in the textbook contributed to incorrect meaning-making, becoming a liability instead of a resource for learning to read. This happened because the teacher did not connect the depiction with meaning of the word. Perhaps the teacher did not consider the picture to be necessary in understanding meanings; perhaps she thought that the children would make the connections themselves. For example, the word 'fell' had been explained through a picture of a tree with apples falling from it. On asking the meaning of the word, a child said *pedh* (tree). The tree was what was prominent in the picture and this is what the child focused upon, deducing that the word 'fell' represented the most dominant object in the picture. Given the child's need to make meaning of his/her experience, and having nothing else to rely on, it was the best that he/she could do.

iii) Making Phonetic Linkages Across Languages

Being exposed to three languages simultaneously enabled children to make intuitive inferences across languages, as the following discussion brings out:

Some children intuitively compared letter-sound correspondences across the three languages. For example, when asked to provide sound of the English letter 'b' and words beginning with it, the child responded, "b says ba; ba se *batakh* (duck), bat , ball". Similarly, when I asked for words with the Hindi letter 'ga' children provided *gamla*, *ganda*, *gaal*, *gadha*, *gaj*, *gajar*, *goli*, and also the English words 'gum', 'gun', 'girl'.

Children also intuitively transferred learning from Hindi to English. In Hindi, the letter name stands for the letter sound. In English, the letter name and letter sound are different but at times there is correspondence. A child seemed to have grasped this intuitively. She provided the sound of 'c' as 'sa', but gave words such as 'cat' and 'cup'. I asked her, "You said 'c' *ka* sound 'sa' *hota hai*, *par* 'cup' *mein to* 'c' ka sound 'ka' *hai*?" (you said the sound of 'c' is 'sa', but in 'cup' the sound of 'c' is 'ka'?). The child replied, *ka bhi ho sakta hai or sa bhi*" (it can be 'ka' and it can be 'sa' as well). There were children who read 'cap' as 'sap' and 'gap' as 'jap'—they were using the letter name as letter sound, transferring their learning from Hindi to English.

Competencies in Reading

Children were at different levels with respect to their ability to read. The details are as follows:

i) On the Road to Being Readers

Many children could recognise letters, and *matras* in case of Hindi words in class 1, and could successfully use the spelling approach to read the words correctly. In case of English, through repeated spelling and recitation, some children had intuitively grasped the letter-sound correspondence and used this to read the words fairly well. In case of Hindi, by class 1, some children had reached the stage of processing the letters and *matras* in the word as clusters, and did not need to sound out the individual letters and *matras*. This learning was intuitive as the teachers had never used this approach while teaching. Children seemed to have learnt decoding and seemed to be well on the road to reading.

ii) Using Prior Learning: Negotiating New Text by Self

When children did not have letter-sound correspondence in English, they used prior learning to negotiate new words. While the word was pronounced wrongly, yet it was a meaningful attempt on part of the child to negotiate a new experience on the basis of prior learning. The following examples drawn from Teaching Events in pre-primary class show the same.

Children had been exposed to three-letter words with the vowel 'a' sounded as in 'apple'. On the same page was another set of words with a different sound of letter 'a'. These words were: ball, wall, hall, call. Although the children had not been taught the words, a child identified the letters correctly and using the same sound for letter 'a' as in 'bat' and 'can', tried to sound these words. Another child began by pronouncing 'ball' with the 'a' sound as in bat, but on seeing the picture of a ball next to the word, she self-corrected to read the word rightly. She then applied this newly generated awareness about the different sound of letter 'a' and correctly read the other words in the series.

iii) Memorisation Rather than Reading

There were children who appeared to be good readers, but extended probing showed that they could only read the text that had been transacted in the class, negotiating it with fluency and speed. They could not read fresh text from the same textbook which had not been transacted in the class yet. This showed they were not reading but were reciting from memory. That children memorised text was evident in other ways too. A child who began reading by spelling the words painstakingly, after reading the first couple of words of the sentence correctly, recalled the entire sentence and then stated the sentence without actually reading it.

iv) Reading with Inappropriate Pronunciation

Some children read the English text with quite a different pronunciation, making it difficult for me to understand what the child meant, in the absence of the original text in front of me.

v) Difficulty in Combining Letters to Read Word

Some children could name individual letters in English words, but could not combine them to pronounce the word. In the absence of phonics, they needed to rely on the memorised name of the word. If the child did not remember, he/she could not say the word. In case of Hindi, while children could name individual letters and matra, they could not process these quick enough to read them together as a word. A child, for example, read the word *tikat* (ticket) by individually identifying the letters and the matra as "*ta, ta par ee ki matra, ka, ta.*" Then the child kept quiet. I asked her to say the word. The child replied "*kata*". She was unable to hold all the individual letters and *matra* in her memory, and so had simply constructed a word from whatever she could remember.

vi) Difficulty in Identifying Letters

Many children could not identify letters and so could not read. Indeed how could they when they had been reciting looking at the teacher.

vii) Learning Ineffective Strategies as a Consequence of Teaching

A teacher set a difficult task for the children in pre-primary—after reading a poem of four stanzas twice in the class, she wrote some words from the poem on the board. The children were expected to be able to read the words, locate them in the poem on their own and underline them. Children adopted different, ineffective strategies to cope with the situation, as described further:

Many children underlined many words, revealing that they only understood the mechanics of the activity. Also this was children's way of coping—not underlining anything would have isolated them from what was going on. In order to preserve the self, they carried out some action similar to what was expected.

Some children looked for the first letter of the word. Thus, a child trying to locate the word 'pretty' tried to locate the first letter. However, this strategy did not work when there was more than one word which began with the letter. This was because children did not have letter-sound correspondence to proceed to the next letter in the two words, which would have enabled them to differentiate which of the two words was the required word. They could have also matched the word in the book with that on the blackboard letter by letter, but they did not do so and this would have been tedious.

Competencies in Writing

Written work in both the pre-primary and class 1 involved copying from the board. Written work did not involve self-expression. Children did not construct any sentence or words on their own except as part of one chapter-end exercise where they had to create three-letter words by filling in the appropriate vowel.

The written work of many children in the two classes was fairly good, although some children did find it difficult to form letters, arbitrarily making shapes. However, good quality of written work was no indicator of children's conceptual understanding. When children wrote words, they copied letter by letter from the board, looking at their copies and the board alternatively. Errors crept in as they found it difficult to maintain eye-hand coordination.

Teachers' Beliefs About How Children Learn to Read

Interviews with teachers revealed that they saw the process of learning to read as an incremental stage-by-stage process beginning with letter recognition, then reading words (in isolation of the text), and then reading text. It was this approach to reading that guided their teaching strategy. The textbook for Hindi and English used in the pre-primary also revealed this pattern—it began with letter naming, followed by pages of three and four letter words with different vowel sounds, followed by pages of text using bigger words. Teachers did not mention other approaches to reading such as phonics, sight word or the whole word approach or the lesser known language experience and organic reading approaches. Since some teachers had introduced letter-sound correspondence in case of English vowels, during the interviews, I specifically asked about the phonics approach. Discussion showed that awareness and understanding about phonics varied among teachers. Those who did know about phonics were at a loss to explain why they had not introduced letter-sound correspondence for all letters of English alphabet.

Learning was seen as the process of memorisation through imitation and repetition, and children were seen as very good at being able to memorise. Memorisation held a positive value for the teachers and children's ability to memorise was seen as indicator of their intelligence. Thus they expected children to learn to read by memorising and their pedagogic practices of drilling, repetition and lack of focus on meaning-making synchronised with their beliefs.

To my amazement all teachers, except one, agreed that teaching rarely focused on meanings and that children rote memorised the text without understanding, especially English text. No teacher could provide a clear answer about why the teaching should be so. The one teacher who was the exception, was even more puzzling—she stated that it had never occurred to her that children did not understand meanings!

While agreeing that their method was teacher-centric, teachers also justified their pedagogical approaches, citing the large number of children in the class, the issues of discipline that would emerge if the class became participatory, and short periods as constraints that prevented them from employing anything other than didactic teaching-learning approaches.

Conclusion

The findings throw light on the challenges children face in becoming literate when literary experiences in multiple languages are introduced in school without due attention to children's socio-cultural context, using pedagogic practices that are teacher directed and do not privilege the centrality of the learner in the learning process. Although the languages—Urdu, Hindi and English—were at varying distances from the children in terms of their direct experience with these, they were expected to master them to the same level of competence through a teaching process that was largely similar across languages and did not take cognisance of the varying degrees of prior learning that children had in each of the languages because of differential exposure to these. This was one of the foremost limitations of the teachers' pedagogic practices within the emergent literacy framework (Kumar, 2000; Purcell-Gates, 1995). Further, while the onus of learning was on the children, their active agency and their need to make meaning while learning to read were repeatedly compromised, which were the two critical factors that could have enabled them to achieve literacy in the face of challenges. Literacy was introduced as a mechanical process of learning decoding skills with a severe compromise of meaning-making. The textbook dominated as the 'icon of sacred knowledge' (Kumar, 2005), right from the pre-primary. The decoding skills too were taught in a limited way as spellings, with no focus on phonics.

The examination of the Nali-Kali curriculum and pedagogic practices therein (Menon, 2013; 2014) carried out as part of the larger Literacy Research in Indian Languages (LiRIL) project shows striking similarity with the findings of this study. Like the curriculum and pedagogy evident in the school in this study, the Nali-Kali curriculum is tightly organised around the sequential introduction of letters, with decoding as the primary goal, then comprehension. Oral conversations are severely restricted, typically to the group action song at the start of each session, with little opportunity for the children to engage in extended/meaningful conversations with each other or the teacher or to bring in stories from their own lives outside school. Despite this emphasis on decoding, 79 per cent, 58 per cent and 33 per cent of the children in grades 1, 2 and 3 respectively had difficulty with decoding-level tasks and could not read the first level of word lists. Gee (2003) notes a similar challenge being faced by children from marginalised backgrounds in the US. Although they could handle complex symbols related to video games, children were unable to acquire the English alphabet year after year, since motivation was compromised in the learning situation.

The present study, and the others cited above, show that when skills based instruction using letter names, spelling and letter sounds is prioritised at the expense of other aspects of language awareness, relevance and meaning-making, learner success in learning to read is severely compromised. Further, the present study shows that when children's agency was compromised in the classroom, the language learning, which got the most affected, was the one that found least support in the home and community environment. The families had minimal exposure to English and could not compensate for lack of children's active engagement in the class while learning the language. Given children's almost complete unfamiliarity with spoken English, what they needed right at the outset were opportunities to hear and speak the language and be immersed in it for some months before initiating reading and writing. What was taking place in the classroom was the reverse, with the consequence that all that children knew of English was what they had rote memorised. Enforcing reading and writing in the absence of communicative competence in the language may lead to an abiding lack of motivation and interest in reading in the language, since the need to communicate is what drives the child to learn a language (Tomasello, 2003). My informal interactions with children studying in higher classes in the same school indicated that difficulties in understanding and speaking English plagued children all through the school years, causing them to resort to rote memorisation.

Since oral expression and familiarity with English was not fostered in the classroom, children did not own the English words the teacher introduced. As a result, they made errors in associating the letter with the word, provided Hindi names for English words, and could only speak the memorised sentences, unable to create their own. Teaching English by way of organic reading and writing as described by Aston-Warner (1963), would have perhaps made the process personally meaningful and motivating for children. Combined with judicious use of explicit phonics instruction, the children would have had the tools to make sense of print. Of course, the initial challenge in organic reading would be to locate words in English that would be meaningful for children, given their unfamiliarity with the language. Teachers' dialogue with the community may lead them to identify an initial set of words, for in the metropolis of Delhi it would be difficult for a community not to have some or the other contact with English, howsoever minimal. Freire and Macdeo (1987) too have emphasised the necessity of including people's words in the curriculum to enable true learning.

Hindi and Urdu were familiar languages for children, but the gains so achieved were compromised by the limited 'spell-read aloud-recite' approach adopted by teachers. Unfortunately, many children were memorising the Hindi text as well, when their greater ability to make meaning in Hindi and its one-to-one letter-sound correspondence should have enabled a large number of them to be well on the road to being independent learners. Learning a language, whether its oral or written form, is a process of learning how to mean (Rosenblatt, 1980), and this was being compromised across the teaching of all three languages. Cambourne (2000/01) postulates that the conditions under which children learn to talk, apply to the process of learning how to read and write. We could see that in the present study, nearly each of these conditions—immersion, demonstration, expectation, responsibility, approximation, employment and feedback—was comprised in the process of teaching the written form of the language, more so in case of teaching of English.

Taken together, the findings across the three languages being taught in the school suggest that using a balanced eclectic approach that draws from the skills-focused phonics instruction and the meaning oriented whole language approaches would likely to have enabled more children to become competent and confident readers. Use of authentic language activities, meaningful for children, guided by an organic approach to literacy pedagogy, may have enhanced student motivation and interest in learning. As Dyer (2008) notes in her study of literacy in primary classes, simple strategies like inviting children to contribute words to practice with, or jointly develop a story, would have helped them to relate how the words and sounds of their spoken language link with their written symbols. Combined with developing phonemic and phonological awareness, children would have had a strategy to bring the infinite number of words into a manageable pattern. In the case of Hindi, the teaching of phonics could use the strategy of teaching consonant and vowel clusters, leading to reading of meaningful words and sentences as followed in the Pragat Sikshan Sanstha's approach and the Varna Samooha approach developed by Berntsen (2009) and Jayaram (2008), respectively.

The findings raise other issues as well: Is it appropriate to start teaching of three languages at the same time, especially when children do not have an exposure to one of them in their natural environment? Children were intuitively trying to make meaning across the three languages as best as they could—comparing sounds and transferring learning across languages—yet the difficulties in meaning-making, understanding letter-sound correspondences and letter recognition were evident. Some of the issues could have been taken care of by a meaningful approach to teaching reading as has been discussed above, but the school needs to have a well-thought approach to introducing the three languages guided by the theory and practice of multilingual education (Agnihotri, 2007; Bedadur, 2012; Dwivedi, 2013; Mohanty, Panda, Phillipson and Skutnab-Kangas, 2009).

Having critiqued the process, it is also important to point out that the teachers' pedagogy was quite typical of Indian schools and was a consequence of our mechanical and behaviourstic model of teacher education (Govinda and Buch, 1990), where developing teachers' pedagogical content knowledge (Shulman, 1986) takes a backseat. The understanding that the socio-cultural context frames children's learning and that the classroom itself creates a socio-cultural context for learning is something which needs to be consciously imbibed and is difficult to occur intuitively to the teachers. Dyer and Choksi (cited in Dyer, 2008) studying literacy teaching and learning in government-run urban primary schools, note that overall initial teacher education does not address theory and practices of children's literacy learning substantially, and is in general weakly focused on pedagogy. My engagement with curricula for training of pre-primary teachers over the years shows that there is an absence of theoretical perspectives underpinning children's literacy learning because the dominant paradigm that informs teacher preparation for the pre-primary grades is the reading readiness paradigm wherein learning to read and write is expected to begin once the child enters primary school and the task at the pre-primary stage is seen as building the pre-reading and pre-writing skills of auditory discrimination, auditory memory, visual discrimination, visual memory, letter names and sounds, in a discrete manner. The focus on writing is interpreted narrowly as developing eye-hand coordination and learning to form letters—drawing is seen as an independent act in itself, a medium of self-expression and developing eye-hand coordination, but not as a form of writing. While stories are an integral part of the pre-primary curriculum, this is often limited to children listening to story narration. Talking about the story, when it takes place, is usually limited to a few factual questions which children answer and its dramatisation is assigned to a few selected children. Although storybooks are also curricular materials in pre-primary, children's literature and storytelling are not consciously linked to a theoretically grounded holistic strategy to foster early literacy. In all, the potential of story-telling as a pedagogical tool is not adequately exploited.

Teachers cited reasons such as class size, the division of the teaching day into short periods, the tension of maintaining discipline, the expectations of parents who emphasised performance (as written work) over process (in fact, what else could they do, having gone through the same system themselves), and the pressure of success in examination, which prevented them from creating a participatory culture in the classroom. Thus, as has been observed in other studies (Dyer, 2008), teachers consistently located explanations for difficulties within the social context, overlooking any pedagogical explanations for slow progress.

One concludes that while a web of factors influence achievement of literacy by children, the process of teaching learning in the school is the critical factor that can make all the difference. Every school needs to consciously select its strategy for teaching of languages, informed by the socio-cultural profile of the students, an evidence-based framework for introducing literacy and a balance between group-based and individualised pedagogical approaches, including regular appraisal of each child's learning needs instead of a generalised assessment of efficacy of pedagogical approaches based on performance of a few children who are able to make quick progress on the road to literacy.

References

Addison, R.B. (1999). "A Grounded Hermeneutic Editing Approach", in B.F. Crabtree and W.L. Miller (eds.), *Doing Qualitative Research.* 2nd ed. New Delhi: Sage. pp.145-62.

Agnihotri, R.K. (2007). "Towards a Pedagogical Paradigm Rooted in Multilinguality", *International Multilingual Research Journal* 1 (2): 1-10.

Annual Status of Education Report (Rural) (2013). New Delhi: ASER Centre.

———. (2007). New Delhi: ASER Centre.

Ashton-Warner, S. (1963). *Teacher*. New York: Bantam edition.

Bedadur, N.V. (2012). "Teaching in Class", *Language and Language Teaching* 1 (2): 23-25, July.

Berntsen, M. (2009). *Teaching Early Literacy in Indian Languages*. Learning Curve, XIII, October, pp.38-39.

Bruner, J.S. (1983). *Child's Talk: Learning to use Language*. Oxford: Oxford University.

———. (1990). *Acts of Meaning*. Cambridge Mass: Harvard University Press.

Cambourne, B. (2000/01). "Conditions for Literacy Learning", *The Reading Teacher* 54 (4): 414-17.

Cameron, L. (2001). *Teaching Languages to Young Children*. New York: Cambridge University Press.

Clay, M. M. (1991). *Becoming Literate: The Construction of Inner Control*. Portsmouth, NH: Heinemann.

Dwivedi, R. (2013). "In a Multilingual Class", *Language and Language Teaching* 1 (1): 10-11, January.

Dyer, C. (2008). "Early Years Literacy in Indian Urban Schools: Structural, Social and Pedagogical Issues", *Language in Education* 22(5): 237-53.

Friere, P. and D. Macdeo (1987). *Literacy: Reading the Word and Reading the World*. Santa Barbara, CA: Praeger.

Gee, J.P. (2003). *What video Games have to Teach Us About Learning and Literacy*. New York: Macmillan.

Govinda, R. and M.B. Buch (1990). "Indian Research in Teacher Education: A Review", in R. Tisher and M. Wideen (eds.), *Research in Teacher Education: International Perspectives*. Ney York: The Falmer Press. pp.141-16.

Jayaram, K. (2008). "Early Literacy Project-Explorations and Reflections Part 2: Intervention in Hindi Classroom", *Contemporary Education Dialogue* 5 (2): 175-212, Spring.

———. (2011). Report of the Consultation on Early Literacy. Sir Ratan Tata Trust and Navajbai Ratan Tata Trust. Retrieved 18.09.14. *http://www.srtt.org/institutional_grants/pdf/report_consultation_early_literacy.pdf*

———. (forthcoming). "Linguistic and Cultural Diversity and Language Teaching - with a specific focus on the Teaching of Reading and Writing", in R.K. Agnihotri, A.L. Khanna and A. Saxena (eds.), *Cotemporary Trends in Language Teaching*. New Delhi: Orient BlackSwan.

Krashen, S. (2002). "Defending Whole Language: The Limits of Phonics Instruction and the Efficacy of Whole Language Instruction", *Reading Improvement* 39(1): 32-42. *http://www.sdkrashen.com/content/articles/defending_whole_language.pdf.*

Kumar, K. (1989). "Learning to be Backward", in *Social Character of Learning*. New Delhi: Sage Publications.

———. (2000). *The Child's Language and the Teacher: A Handbook*. New Delhi: National Book Trust.

———. (2005). *The Political Agenda of Education* (second edition). New Delhi: Sage Publications.

Kuzel, A.J. (1999). "Sampling in Qualitative Enquiry", in B.F. Crabtree and W.L. Miller (eds.), *Doing Qualitative Research.* 2nd ed. New Delhi: Sage. pp.33-46.

Malone, S. (2007). "Mother Tongue-based Multilingual Education: Implications for Education Policy", Paper presented at the Seminar on *Education Policy and the Right to Education: Towards More Equitable Outcomes for South Asia's Children*, Kathmandu, 17-20 September. *http://www.sil.org/sites/default/files/files/mtbmle_implications_for_policy.pdf.* Retrieved 18.09.14

Mason, J.M. and S. Sinha (1992). "Emerging Literacy in the Early Childhood Years: Applying a Vygotskian Model of Learning and Development", in B. Spodek (ed.), *Handbook of Research on the Education of Young Children*. Macmillan: New York. pp.137-50.

Menon, S. (2013). "Learning of Early Language and Literacy in Nali Kali Classrooms", Paper presented at *National Conference on Early Learning*, Ambedkar University of Delhi, 25-27 September.

———. (2014). "Language and Literacy Learning in Early Years: What should It Look Like?" *Learning Curve: Early Childhood Education* XXII, May.

Miller, W.L. and B.F. Crabtree (1999a). "The Dance of Interpretation", in B.F. Crabtree and W.L. Miller (eds.), *Doing Qualitative Research.* 2nd ed. New Delhi: Sage. pp.127-44.

———. (1999b). "Depth Interviewing", in B.F. Crabtree and W.L. Miller (eds.), *Doing Qualitative Research.* 2nd ed. New Delhi: Sage. pp.89-108.

Mohanty, A.K. (1990). "Psychological Consequences of Mother Tongue Maintenance and Multilingualism in India", in D.P. Pattanayak (ed.), *Multilingualism in India.* Clevedon: Multilingual Matters. pp.54-66.

Mohanty, A., M. Panda, R. Phillipson and T. Skutnabb-Kangas (eds.) (2009). *Multilingual Education for Social Justice. Globalising the Local.* Delhi: Orient Blackswan.

Nag, S. (2005). *Language Attainments and Learning Opportunities: Pointers for a New Curriculum Framework.* National Focus Group: Teaching of English. New Delhi: NCERT. *http://www.thepromisefoundation.org/TPFLO.pdf.* Retrieved 18.09.14

Nag-Arulmani, S. (2003). "Reading Difficulties in Indian Languages", in N. Goulandris (ed.), *Dyslexia: A Cross-linguistic Perspective.* London: Whurr Publishers Ltd.

National Council for Educational Research and Training (2012-13). *End Term Survey Report: Mathura Pilot Project.* New Delhi: NCERT.

Purcell-Gates, V. (1995). *Other People's Worlds: The Cycle of Low Literacy.* Cambridge, MA: Harvard University Press.

Rosenblatt, L.M. (1980). "What Facts does this Poem Teach You?" *Language Arts* 57 (4): 386-94.

Shulman, L.E. (1986). "Those Who Understand: Knowledge Growth in Teaching", *Educational Researcher* 15 (2): 4-14.

Sinha, S. (2000). "Acquiring Literacy in Schools", *Seminar* 493: 38-42, September.

———. (2009). "Rosenblatt's Theory of Reading: Exploring Literature", *Contemporary Education Dialogue* 6 (2): 223-37.

Stahl, S.A. (1992). "Saying the 'p' Word: Nine Guidelines for Exemplary Phonics Instruction". Reprinted in R.D. Robinson, M.C. McKenna and J.M. Wedman (1996), *Issues and Trends in Literacy Education*. Boston: Allyn & Bacon. pp.52-56.

Mohanty, A.K., M. Panda, R. Phillipson and T. Skutnab-Kangas (2009). *Multilingual Education for Social Justice: Globalising the Local*. New Delhi: Orient Longman.

Talib, M. (1997). "Educating the Oppressed: Observations Form a School in a Working Class Settlement in Delhi", in S. Shukla and K. Kaul (eds.), *Education, Development and Underdevelopment*. New Delhi: Sage Publications. pp.199-209.

Teale, W. and E. Sulzby (1992). "Introduction", in W. Teale and E. Sulzby (eds.), *Emergent Literacy: Writing and Reading*. USA: Ablex Publishing Company.

Tomasello, M. (2003). *Constructing a Language: Ausage based Theory of Language Acquisition*. USA: Harvard University Press.

Vygotsky, L.S. (1978). "The Pre-history of Written Language", in M. Cole, V. John-Steiner, S. Scribner and E. Souberman (eds.), *Mind in Society: The Development of Higher Order Psychological Processes*. Cambridge: Harvard University Press. pp.105-19.

4

ARCHANA MEHENDALE

Right to Childcare in India

A Critical Review

The Central Question: Who Cares?

Let me start by drawing from Swaminathan (1985), a pioneering research aptly titled "Who Cares" which studied childcare facilities available to low-income working women in India. She argues that women and children should be not be seen in isolation and needs of the family should be seen as a whole. While she observes that the achievement in provision of day care, however small it may be, signifies "a triumph of progressive forces in the ongoing conflict between modernising and preserving forces", she simultaneously locates the lack of day care provisioning to the three social 'myths' (Swaminathan, 1985: 80-81) . These are: (a) the myth of 'invisible working woman' which is based on the belief that Indian women do not work, (b) the myth of the 'invisible nuclear family' which assumes that the Indian families can take care of their children adequately without any assistance, and (c) the myth of 'invisible skills' which considers that anyone or any woman can take care of the children. She argues that it is these 'myths' that have contributed to the inadequacy of childcare facilities for the low-income working women in general, and the women working in the unorganised and agricultural sector, in particular. Almost 30 years later, roughly equivalent to one generation, provision of childcare facilities remains extremely poor across India. This is a compelling reason for us to revisit Swaminathan's explanation of the title "Who Cares", which she observes could be interpreted both in a literal sense as well as an ironical expression made in despair. In this paper, I have attempted to answer both these interpretations. The literal interpretation is examined using available literature on status of childcare in India and the ironical interpretation is discussed critically by analysing how laws and policies relate to various dimensions of right to childcare in India.

Who Cares and Looks After the Young Children in India?

The first literal interpretation of "Who cares" pointedly inquires about the status of childcare facilities for young children in India. This is not too difficult to answer because the status of childcare provision has not changed much since Swaminathan (1985) raised this question. Young children are largely cared for in their own family setting, by parents, grandparents, relatives or older siblings. Families are sometimes unable to look after their young children due to demands of survival and work, or family distress in the form of illness, disability, or death. In such situations, children are looked after in non-family settings, which include institutional and non-institutional childcare arrangements. Institutional childcare could be either statutory, which means it could be provided by the employer in fulfilment of statutory requirements that are applicable to certain organised sectors or by voluntary agencies offering services to families in need, either for a payment or otherwise. In some cases, families hire informal paid services provided by non-family members. However, these arrangements are not always available and accessible to families, and paid services are beyond the financial capacities of low income households. In other words, the responsibility of caring for or organising childcare is primarily left to the family, which in turn is expected to negotiate these on their own with little assistance from the state.

Gill (1993) argues that childcare services in India have received apathetic treatment as a result of variety of historical and cultural factors. She points out that although the adoption of the National Policy for Children in 1974 gave the necessary impetus to programmes for the care of young children, the overall provision remains extremely inadequate. Available literature on the status of provision of childcare through different models presents a discouraging picture.

Creches Under Governmental Schemes

A recent evaluation of the implementation of the Rajiv Gandhi National Creche Scheme shows that there has been a decline in the number of crèches from 2006-07 to 2011-12 and significant fluctuations in the budgetary allocations made to the scheme between 2006-07 and 2012-13 (Supath Gramodyog Sansthan, 2013). Intra-state and inter-state disparities in the spread of crèches are also evident. Data on implementation available with the Ministry of Women and Child Development (MoWCD), which runs the scheme shows that in 2009, out of the total 31718 crèches across the country, Andhra Pradesh (AP) had the highest number of crèches (3102), followed by Madhya Pradesh (MP) (2815), while northeastern states and states like Jharkhand, Himachal Pradesh (HP) and Punjab had fewer number of crèches.[1] Swaminathan (n.d.) points out that crèches run under grant-in-aid scheme are restricted to urban and semi-urban areas, covering mainly children between two and six years, are extremely inadequate in their coverage, are poorly resourced and without the required degree of training and monitoring, which makes provision of quality care difficult. Moreover, the timings of the crèches do not coincide with the women's working hours, resulting in them seeking other options that meet their requirements.

The services provided under the Integrated Child Development Scheme (ICDS) do not include childcare facilities. Although the Plan of Action (PoA) of the National Policy on Education, 1992, stated that 25 per cent of the Anganwadis would be converted into Anganwadi-cum-crèches, only a fraction of the targeted number was met. According to Swaminathan (2000), instead of 100,000 Anganwadis, only 659 were converted into Anganwadi-cum-crèches by 1996, thereby leaving out childcare from the largest programme for the young child in the world. In fact, Swaminathan (n.d.) argues that ICDS actually takes no notice of the need of women for day care and views them solely in their role as mothers and not as working women.

1. Data on status of implementation retrieved from *http://wcd.nic.in/SchemeChildren/Rajiv%20Gandhi%20%28Creche%29release06-09.pdf* on 12 August 2013.

Statutory Crèches

Statutory crèches have been the oldest form of childcare provision in India and were introduced as part of labour welfare measures in the organised sector employing a stipulated minimum number of women.[2] Gill (1993) argues that by being applicable only to women working in the organised sector, it leaves out a large proportion of those working in agriculture and the unorganised sector. In her study of implementation of statutory crèches in the *beedi* sector, Swaminathan (2000) explained how it was being availed only where there were strong unions as the employers are otherwise disinterested in providing the facility. The statutory provisions mainly focus on provision of custodial care with a minimum required infrastructure and even this is only on paper (Swaminathan, 1991). Statutory crèches that operate for half day do not serve their purpose and working mothers have to find suitable alternatives to care for their children while they are away at work. Gill (1993) explains that provision of crèches is a low priority for the employers as well as labour department officials and inspectors. Even when statutory crèches are able to adhere to the legislative standards on care, they still fall short on early stimulation and development which is not stipulated in the legislation (Swaminathan, 1991). The maternity entitlements enjoyed by working mothers are also negligible. Wage protection at least at minimum wage level is required for women to be able to breastfeed. The National Food Security Act, 2013, which provides for ₹1,000 for nine months is not sufficient to support the increasing demands on the new mother-working woman and her family (Swaminathan, 2013).

Interestingly, statutory crèches are considered to be under the jurisdiction of the Ministry of Labour with the MoWCD having limited or no role to play. Swaminathan (n.d.) argues that none of

2. Statutory crèches are provided under the following labour legislation: Section 48 of The Factories Act, 1948; Section 12 of The Plantations Labour Act, 1951; Section 14 of The Beedi and Cigar Workers (Conditions of Employment) Act, 1964; Section 35 of The Buildings and other Construction Workers (Regulation of Employment and Conditions of Service) Act, 1996; The Inter-State Migrant Workmen (Regulation of Employment & Conditions of Service) Act, 1979; The Mines Creche Rules, 1966 and Section 55(1) of The National Rural Employment Guarantee Act, 2005.

the various economic programmes for women initiated by MoWCD itself or the government in general, makes any reference to provision for day care for the children of the women working in them, with the sole exception of the National Rural Employment Guarantee Act (NREGA), 2005. However, implementation of childcare provisions under NREGA is poor and a number of children, including those below three years, are left to look after themselves without any adult supervision (Narayanan, 2008).

Day Care Services

Paid day care is more common in urban areas than in rural areas and as Datta (2007) argues, is closely related to the scaling down of the state by way of reduced expenditures and closing down of programmes (such as those run by the Central Social Welfare Board on nutrition and Balwadi), as well as state outsourcing responsibility to voluntary organisations. Paid day care services emerging as a market is left largely unregulated for all kinds of service providers. Sriram (2007) observes that regulation is mainly limited to infrastructure and structural features but leaves out the programme and the caregiver-child interaction from its purview, which in fact holds the key to better quality outcomes. In fact, as Datta and Konantambigi (2007) show, government has not acted upon formulating or implementing quality standards in their own crèches or those provided by private actors. Palriwala and Neetha (2009) argue that lack of regulation of market solutions to care issues has been reinforced by neo-liberal paradigms where private players have entered into the field of institutional, non-domestic childcare, which remains largely outside public monitoring and accountability in terms of facilities provided and working conditions of employees.

Day care services and crèches run by voluntary organisations in India do not operate with a profit motive and hence are able to reach to the most needy families and communities. The services offered by them are more flexible and need-based, but their coverage is very limited based on availability of resources.

To summarise, the various models of childcare provision in India do not collectively fulfil the need for such services in the country, especially for the marginalised and disadvantaged communities. What is also evident is that there is no state intervention to ensure a basic minimum guarantee of childcare services, even to the most deserving sections of the society. One of the reasons for this is that legislation, policies and programmes for women and children have evolved in parallel and without taking into consideration the needs, interests, priorities and rights of the other constituency (Swaminathan, 1991). The need for convergence has been repeatedly recommended by various committees such as the Committee on Status of Women in India (1974), Working Group on Employment of Women (1978), National Commission on Self-Employed Women and Women in the Informal Sector (1988), but these have not translated into policy measures. Swaminathan (n.d.) suggests that this lack of convergence and failure to address the issue can be traced to lack of acceptance at the policy level of the inter-linkages between women's multiple roles and young children's developmental needs, and also because childcare work is simply not recognised and valued by society and also the state.

Is There a Right to Childcare in India?

The second interpretation of Mina Swaminathan's question "Who Cares" is an ironical 'taunt or a challenge' and that is somewhat difficult to address because it requires the question to be located within the larger framework that governs public and private decisions about women's roles and status, role of the state, the explicit and implicit assumptions that underlie gender relations, the institution of family and the demarcation between the public and private sphere.

In other words, such a question would seek to address the following five issues:

1. Is right to childcare really a right in India?
2. If so, what are the grounds for justification of the right?
3. Who enjoys the right/whose right is it?
4. Who are the duty bearers and what are their duties?
5. What are the implications or remedies if this right is violated?

Before getting into the first question—is right to childcare really a right in India, it would be important to understand some of the ideas about young children, particularly those prevailing in Western societies that seem to have influenced the idea of child rights as enunciated through the various international treaties. Woodhead (2005) summarises four competing ideas about young children and their moral status as right bearers:

- The young child is naturally wild and unregulated and thus development is about socialising children to take their place within society (e.g., as in the writings of Thomas Hobbes, 1588-1699)
- The young child is naturally innocent and thus development involves protecting their innocence and giving them the freedom to play, learn and mature (e.g., as in the book *Emile*, by Jean Jacques Rousseau, 1712-1778)
- The young child is a *tabula rasa*, a blank slate and thus development is a critical time for laying down the foundations that will enable children to achieve their potential (e.g., as argued by John Locke, 1632-1704)
- The young child is shaped by nature and nurture, and thus development is an interaction between potential and experience (e.g., linked to the philosophy of Emmanuel Kant, 1724-1804).

Some moral philosophers and legal scholars have argued that children, especially young children, cannot enjoy negative rights due to their immaturity and dependence on adults (Griffin, 2002; Brighouse, 2002), while others argue that young children lend themselves more readily to a positive rights regime. Their very dependence and capacity for growth call for a positive right to protection and to the means necessary for their development. Thus, the 'positive agenda' on child rights involves emphasising the fulfilment of positive rights of children with a focus on roles and obligation of adults and the state (Ezer, 2004).

International treaties such as the Convention on Elimination of all forms of Discrimination Against Women (CEDAW), 1979 and the United Nations Convention on Rights of the Child (UNCRC),

1989, embody the principles of both negative and positive rights. Given that childcare has been traditionally considered as the primary function of women, the CEDAW includes Article 11(2)(c) which recognises the need 'to encourage the provision of the necessary supporting social services to enable parents to combine family obligations with work responsibilities and participation in public life, in particular through promoting the establishment and development of a network of child-care facilities'. Thus, women's right to childcare facilities is not limited to 'working' women alone, and it is seen as an enabling right that the state is required to promote.

The Preamble to the UNCRC indicates that a family is seen as the fundamental group of society and the natural environment for growth and well-being of all its members and particularly children, and that the family should be afforded the necessary protection and assistance so that it can fully assume its responsibilities within the community. Article 18 specifically focuses on childcare and the duty of both the parents in childcare and child rearing. It imposes a duty on the state to render appropriate assistance to parents and legal guardians in the performance of their child-rearing responsibilities and to ensure the development of institutions, facilities and services for the care of children. Para 3 of Article 18 provides that states shall take all appropriate measures to ensure that children of working parents have the right to benefit from child-care services and facilities for which they are eligible. Even the General Comment 7 issued by the Committee on the UNCRC reiterates the primary role and right of the family in child rearing and assigns a secondary role to the state to provide the required assistance to the families (Mehendale, 2010). This right is conceived of as a universal right and not a targeted provision that is restricted to a particular category of families or children.

Thus, what clearly emerges from both CEDAW and UNCRC is an unequivocal universal right of families to receive assistance from the state in order to enable them to perform their child-rearing responsibilities so that women in particular are supported to work and participate in public life. The duty of the state, as recognised by both the binding treaties, includes development of appropriate institutions and offering a network of facilities and services for care of children.

India is under an obligation to bring these treaty provisions into effect by formulating/amending its domestic legislation, and creating institutions and services to realise this right. But these rights have not been incorporated in domestic law even after decades of ratifying the treaties. A beginning has been made with two new policy initiatives in the recent past: (a) National Policy on Children, 2013, pronouncing that the state shall 'provide universal and equitable access to quality Early Childhood Care and Education (ECCE) for optimal development and active learning capacity of all children below six years of age'; and (b) the National Early Childhood Care and Education Policy, 2013, expressing a vision that facilitates comprehensive childcare support, infrastructure and services aimed at holistic well-being of children and effectively responds to their needs based on continuum of care and universalisation of ECCE through inclusion. Although these policy pronouncements imply a universal, comprehensive and an inclusive focus on childcare, these are not translated into legally binding provisions, and hence remain at a persuasive if not at a rhetorical level. The Supreme Court directions on universalisation of ICDS Anganwadis in PUCL *versus* Union of India (Civil Writ Petition 196 of 2001) are again helpful in reinforcing the principle of universal provision, although ICDS by design does not include childcare as an integral component of service to be provided.

So while the international treaty provisions as well as recent developments on policy and case law have emphasised the importance of 'universalisation', right to childcare in legislation remains singularly targeted at women working in the organised sector. Such resistance to recognise a universal right to childcare in India is often justified by the caveat attached to socio-economic and cultural rights, of these being aspirational rights and meant to be realised only progressively, subject to maximum availability of state resources. This may be acceptable if the state intervenes by targeting the most deprived and marginalised sections of the society and upholds their right to childcare. However, as we saw in Section 2, childcare provisions are not made even minimally available to all those who belong to the deprived and marginalised section of the society. Palriwala and Neetha (2009) discuss how the welfare programmes meant to react to market and family failures did not provide assistance to "all members of any deserving group" and how the welfare regime in India had few "universal" components, and even those such as health and education that were supposed to be universal were "differentially, unevenly and minimally available". This is because of a flawed conceptualisation and a problematic rationale used to justify and restrict right to childcare, as we shall see in the next sections.

This takes us to the second question—what are the grounds for justification of the right? In this regard, it is pertinent to briefly examine the rationale critically discussed by Bussemaker (1998) in the context of childcare in The Netherlands as it has a wider relevance. She notes that childcare can be justified on primarily three grounds—'morality', whether government funding of universal childcare is morally justified and if it fits within the political hegemonic notion of good life where the mothers look after the young ones while fathers go out to work. Thus, appeals for a universal childcare for other reasons such as self-development, leisure or participation in public life that are related to women's autonomy are strongly resisted. Bussemaker concludes that the morality argument dominated Dutch childcare programmes during the 1970s, and childcare was seen to be superfluous and unnecessary in a welfare state.

The second rationale is that of 'interest' where childcare is represented as benefiting specific groups such as children benefited through social-emotional and cognitive outcomes, working mothers benefited through increased productive time, employers benefited by improved productivity of women workers, and so on. However, the 'interests' argument can be potentially distorted because it can be represented as conflicting interests between child and the mother, mother and the family, female worker and employers, depending on whose interests the right actually purports to uphold. It is from the standpoint of that particular interest that other auxiliary interests get negotiated or calibrated.

The third rationale is that of efficiency, wherein childcare facilities are seen to yield returns on investment and help the economy to become competitive. This is seen to stimulate labour market participation of women, and an instrument for enhancing economic productivity. This narrowly restricts the justification to economic criteria alone, while leaving out the possibility that the idea of care that is somewhat abstract could lead to social and cultural spin-offs as well.

Gromley Jr. (2007) argues that normative debates on ECCE are influenced by values significant to other policy domains such as equity, efficiency and choice. He asks whether disadvantaged children deserve "not just childcare but high-quality childcare, not just preschool but a high-quality preschool". Questions of efficiency, he says, focus on the value that childcare programmes bring to society as a whole and if society sees it benefiting from such investments. Efficiency debates ask if childcare subsidies meant to facilitate female employment are 'good' for society as a whole and if regulations help improve quality without adversely affecting the supply of childcare facilities. Debates over choice are concerned about that enjoyed by parents, and if it includes freedom to make bad choices such as letting their children be looked after by an indifferent relative or an ill-equipped childcare centre. He questions if poor parents can exercise any meaningful choice when government subsidies can only enable them to avail care services that are average or worse.

While the three rationales proposed by Bussemaker (1998), and then by Gromley Jr. (2007), may have played out during different phases and shifts in the welfare regimes, in India, one finds that these have been simultaneously advanced. The morality argument is evident in the Indian context where by default, childcare is considered to be a woman's responsibility, particularly so if she is not working outside her home. The justification of specific interests seems to be at play when state policy targets protection of interests of specific groups (working women in the organised sector) because of what it yields and produces for society at large, which is the efficiency argument. However, the equity argument is rarely advanced for justifying universal childcare because it tends to clash with competing justifications of efficiency and choice. Moreover, in a neo-liberal regime, rationale for childcare based on values of efficiency, interests and choice is more likely to be integrated than one based on value of equity. Thus, we find that provision of universal childcare as a right remains inadequately justified, and therefore facilities for childcare are restricted to certain sections of working, needy and ailing women based primarily on justification of interests and efficiency. It further reiterates the fact that childcare provision in India is still subjected to idea of morality and patriarchal gender relations within family and efficiency measured by economic benefits alone. This would have to be fundamentally challenged if childcare has to be recognised as a universal right in India.

The third question is who enjoys the right and whose right is it? International law sees childcare both as a right of a child and right of a 'working woman-mother'. In domestic legislation, historically, childcare has been under the purview of labour welfare legislation applicable only in the organised sectors and hence a right of a 'working woman-mother' alone and not that of a child. The new National Policy for Children, 2013, also recognises childcare to be provided to children of specific groups—working mothers, poor and ailing mothers and single parents. Unlike UNCRC which looks at childcare as a right of all children and that of families, domestic law and policy considers childcare as a right of working mothers alone. This precludes enjoyment of childcare facilities by men, women working in unorganised sector including agriculture, and self-employed women. Furthermore, the working mother enjoys this entitlement only with regards to young children, typically below six years. This implies that children who are of school-going age can look after themselves. While the UNCRC obligates states to provide assistance to families for growth and development of children, the underlying idea of childcare in Indian labour legislation is that of custodial care of the young ones. A review of the relevant provisions under the labour legislation shows that the central statutes provide only for rooms with adequate light, ventilation, and a hygienic space with a woman trained in the care of children.[3] The state governments

3. As specified in various labour legislations. See footnote 2.

are delegated the responsibility of framing rules on matters such as furniture and equipment required, feeding timings and provision of additional milk to infants. Thus, even the restricted right available to a small segment of working women emphasises mainly on space and basic care, and not on stimulation and play for children.

In other words, in domestic law, childcare is a right granted to working women in specific organised sectors of employment who have children below six years of age and care is restricted to primarily custodial care. Thus, it is not a child's right (as in independent of having a mother who works in specific sectors), it is not a right enjoyed by all working women, it is not a right enjoyed by men or families, and it cannot be enjoyed by women with children older than six years. This exclusionary nature of the entitlement is closely related to the notions of unpaid care work done by women.

Prasad (2007) points out the inadequacy of the Census process, which does not quantify women's participation in the economy and therefore makes it difficult to plan and support it. With more and more women being pushed into being self-employed, contractual and unorganised workers, less women workers are benefiting from maternal and childcare and social security benefits. Neetha (2010) has argued that national statistical paradigm is based on market bias, a male bias and a measurability bias. Unpaid care work is undertaken simultaneously with other activities and hence it may be difficult to estimate the time spent specifically on care work. Many women take their childcare work for granted and may hence fail to report. The complexities of care work are not fully understood in the activity-based work measurements. Thus despite the large presence of women in workforce, the unit of labour legislation remains the traditional family with man as a breadwinner and woman responsible for housekeeping, child rearing and child bearing. Psacharopoulos and Tzannatos (1989) explain that there is a "cultural reluctance" to admit that unpaid activities of women are of economic value. Moreover, labour legislation does not provide for complexity of the needs of triple role of women—worker, mother and home-maker (Arulraj and Samuel, 2007). These are closely linked to politics of recognising gender equality, and Mahon and Brennan (2012) argue that although the new politics clearly addresses women as wage earners as well as mothers, there is no guarantee that this recognition will be played out in ways that promote gender equality. Although there is increased participation of women in work, Palriwala and Neetha (2009) discuss how the focus remains on home-based work and self-employment because it allows flexible timings and enables women to combine paid work and domestic care. In this manner, they argue, the state's orientation reinforces simultaneously the idea of women in paid work who also remain familial workers.

What stands out in this critique is the continued association of women with their maternal duties of caring that gets normalised in state's narrow demarcation of who is the subject of the right and upon whom is the right bestowed. Women working in specific sectors alone stand to gain from a minimalist provision of the entitlement. This narrow specification of rights-holders does not align with international norms that look at care as a fundamentally parental right, without singling out the woman/mother and without associating her with her working status. Hence, right to childcare in India is not only limited, but also does not view the child or the parents as subjects of the right.

Following the question on right-holders is the fourth question—who are the duty bearers and what are their duties? In this regard, the idea of the 'care diamond' proposed by Razavi (2007), including family/household, markets, the public and the not-for-profit sectors (including voluntary and community provision), is relevant. She notes that the role of the state in the welfare architecture is of a qualitatively different kind, compared to, say, families or markets, because the state is not just a provider of welfare, but also a significant decision maker about the responsibilities to be assumed by the other three sets of institutions. In the Indian context, the state is not a direct duty bearer for provision of childcare.

Even when UNCRC recognises both parents as the primary duty bearers and state having the responsibility to assist the families, the domestic legislation primarily recognises the employers as duty bearers for providing crèches to women workers. The law does not obligate the government to provide childcare facilities itself, but mandates it with the task of monitoring and regulating childcare provisions in statutory crèches. The question that needs to be raised here is that—can we consider childcare as a right in India when only private duty bearers/employers are required by law to provide the same? In pursuance of its policy objectives, the government provides funds to voluntary organisations to run crèches for targeted groups, but this is discretionary and not universal. While there has been an increasing juridification of welfare rights, can childcare be seen as a right in India if it is not provided for by the state as a universal entitlement and is only implemented in a targeted manner? Moreover, the state only regulates and partially funds the private providers without donning the role of a provider itself. So, with the state being a limited provider-limited regulator-limited funder, there is no substance to right to childcare in India. While a mixed delivery system and public private partnership may be a worthwhile idea for organising childcare, the fact that this arrangement has come in the way of universal spread and access to childcare needs to be noted. In particular, it must be noted that the private sector has no incentive to reach the most deserving areas and hence the state itself needs to take the responsibility of provisioning such uncovered areas. But if the government has not reached (and is not under any obligation to reach) the unorganised sectors and geographical areas not covered by voluntary organisations, can we say that right to childcare is recognised in India? It must be also noted that parents are considered as primary duty bearers of young children's care, both in international and domestic frameworks, and there is still a great deal of ambiguity about the role of state in actually intervening in the private family sphere in order to determine or regulate standards of childcare within homes. The Juvenile Justice (Care and Protection) Act, 2000, which justifies state intervention when families are unable to care for their children is sparingly invoked, except in cases of worst forms of abuse of young children and infants. Even though the Act allows for such intervention of the state on the principle of *parens patriae*, it fundamentally holds the family to be the best place for children to grow.

Another implication of over-reliance on private duty bearers is that they are neither subject to regulation and monitoring at the domestic level, nor are they available for scrutiny under international treaty monitoring procedures because it is the governments that are parties to the treaty and not the private duty bearers. Thus, there is little that the governments can report on with regards to the extent to which private duty bearers (including the families and private agencies) perform their duties.

To summarise, if we go back to Razavi (2007), we find the 'care diamond' in the case of right to childcare looks lopsided, with the assumption that families are the primary duty bearers followed by the employers. The duty of the public sector to provision and fund is not stipulated under law, even though the duty to regulate has been historically present. Furthermore, the informal or not-for-profit sector which in practice provides the biggest network of childcare provision is outside the duty bearers recognised under the domestic law.

The fifth question is—what are the implications if the right is violated? In a way, this question offers the litmus test that can tell us if childcare in India is a right or a mere rhetoric. Two examples can explain this point. First is the case of two young children in Bangalore who were left unattended by their parents who left for work early morning. They were charred to death in a fire that gutted down their hut. Although the Karnataka State Commission for Protection of Child Rights (KSCPCR) took up the matter and convened a larger consultation on the need for crèches, this particular incident was considered as an accident. Who could have been held responsible for this under the current legal framework? The second example is that of poor implementation of provisions of statutory crèches. Despite the legal cover, the inspectoral system is heavily overburdened and lack of crèches rarely invokes reprimand or fines from the inspectors. Is right to childcare (even in its most restricted sense) really a right if it is only recognised at a normative level, without creating the institutions required to effectively realise and monitor the right meaningfully? From the above mentioned examples, it is clear that firstly there is ambiguity about the duty bearers (parents, state, or community) and their relative burden of responsibility, and secondly, even when there is clarity on duty bearers, there is political and administrative inertia against taking suitable deterrent action, thereby making it an incomplete right without an effective corresponding duty.

Way Forward

In the light of the discussions in the earlier sections, it is evident that a universal right to childcare is not recognised under Indian legislation and there are several issues related to the way in which the right is defined, the nature of justifications offered, the restricted view of right holders and duty bearers and the lack of remedies if the right is violated. However, in order to chart a way forward, it is important to note that early childhood rights, particularly right to childcare continues to straddle within the dichotomy of public and private. In order to resolve this dichotomy, it would be useful to draw upon the tripartite typology of obligations that was first introduced by Henry Shue as state obligations 'to avoid depriving', 'to protect from deprivation' and 'to aid the deprived', which was later developed by Asbjørn Eide, who acted as the UN's Special Rapporteur for Food during the early 1980s.[4] Eide's typology of obligations in context of early childhood rights and right to childcare would include obligation on the state to move from a passive to a more active obligation to:

- *Respect*: duty of the state not to violate right to childcare by its actions, by refraining from interfering directly or indirectly with the enjoyment of rights of young children and their families.
- *Protect*: duty of the state to prevent violations of right to childcare by others, by preventing third parties from interfering with or violating the same. This means adopting the necessary measures to regulate.
- *Fulfil*: duty of the state to act in order to ensure that rights can be enjoyed and exercised through adoption of appropriate legislative, administrative, budgetary, judicial, and other measures. This obligation to fulfill is often broken

4. Right to Food as a Human Right, UN Doc. E./CN.4/Sub.2/1987/23 of 7 July 1987.

down to include the obligations to facilitate; to provide; and to promote.

It is important that right to childcare is redefined with clear obligations on the state to perform all three functions—respect, protect and fulfill. Without such a normative foundation, right to childcare, even if it is recognised as a universal right, will remain merely on paper and the question "Who Cares" would remain unresolved.

References

Arulraj, M.R. and R.S. Samuel (2007). "Childcare Strategies of Women in the Unorganised Sector", in V. Datta and R. Konantambigi (eds.), *Day Care for Young Children in India: Issues and Prospects*. Delhi: Concept

Brighouse, H. (2002). "What Rights (if any) Do Children Have?", in D. Archard and C.M. Macleod (eds.), *The Moral and Political Status of Children*. Oxford: Oxford University Press.

Bussemaker, J. (1998). "Rationales of Care in Contemporary Welfare States: The Case of Childcare in the Netherlands", *Social Politics*, Spring Issue.

Datta, V. (2007). "Ensuring Quality in Child Care", in V. Datta and R. Konantambigi (eds.), *Day Care for Young Children in India: Issues and Prospects*. Delhi: Concept.

Datta, V. and R. Konantambigi (2007). "Future Perspectives", in V. Datta and R. Konantambigi (eds.), *Day Care for Young Children in India: Issues and Prospects*. Delhi: Concept

Ezer, T. (2004). "A Positive Right to Protection for Children", 7 *Yale Human Rights and Development Law Journal*.

Gill, S. (1993). *India in International Handbook Childcare Policies and Programs*. Edited by M. Cochran. Westport, CT: Greenwood Press

Gormley Jr, W.T. (2007). "Early Childhood Care and Education: Lessons and Puzzles", in *Journal of Policy Analysis and Management* 26(3): 622-71, Summer Issue.

Griffin, J. (2002). "Do Children have Rights", in D. Archard and C.M. Macleod (eds.), *The Moral and Political Status of Children*. Oxford: Oxford University Press.

Joshi, H. (2002). "Production, Reproduction, and Education: Women, Children, and Work in a British Perspective", in *Population and Development Review* 28(3): 445-74, September.

Mahon, R. and D. Brennan (2012). "Federalism and the 'New Politics' of Welfare Development: Childcare and Parental Leave in Australia and Canada", in *Publius: The Journal of Federalism* 43 (1): 90-108.

Mehendale, A. (2010). *Early Childhood Education & International Law*. Pune: ICICI Centre for Elementary Education.

Misra, J. and F. Akins (1998). "The Welfare State and Women: Structure, Agency, and Diversity", in *Social Politics*, Fall.

Mitchell, D. and G. Garrett (1996). "Women and the Welfare State in the Era of Global Markets", in *Social Politics*. Summer/Fall.

Narayanan, S. (2008). "Employment Guarantee, Women's Work and Childcare", *Economic & Political Weekly* 43(9): 10-13.

Neetha, N. (2010). "Estimating Unpaid Care Work: Methodological Issues in Time-use Surveys", in *Economic and Political Weekly* XLV(44): 73-80. 30 October.

Palriwala, R. and N. Neetha (2009). *The Care Diamond: State Social Policy and the Market*. India Research Report 3. Geneva: UNRISD

Prasad, V. (2007). "Socio Economic Context of Childcare in India", in V. Datta and R. Konantambigi (eds.), *Day Care for Young Children in India: Issues and Prospects*. Delhi: Concept

Psacharopoulos, G. and Z. Tzannatos (1989). "Female Labour Force Participation Rate: An International Perspective", in *Research Observer* 4(2), July. The World Bank and IBRD.

Razavi, S. (2007). *The Political and Social Economy of Care in a Development Context: Conceptual Issues, Research Questions and Policy Options*. Geneva: UNRISD.

Reese, E. (2001). "The Politics of Motherhood: The Restriction of Poor Mothers' Welfare Rights in the United States, 1949-1960", in *Social Politics*, Spring.

Shue, H. (1996). *Basic Rights: Subsistence, Affluence and US Foreign Policy*. Princeton: Princeton University Press

Simon-Kumar, R. (2011). "The Analytics of 'Gendering' the Post-Neoliberal State", in *Social Politics* 18(3).

Sriram, R. (2007). "Strengthening the Arms of Day Care: Networking and Advocacy", in V. Datta and R. Konantambigi (eds.), *Day Care for Young Children in India: Issues and Prospects*. Delhi: Concept.

Supath Gramodyog Sansthan (2013). *Performance of Rajiv Gandhi National Creche Scheme for Children of Working Mothers*. Sponsored by Planning Commission. Gujarat: Supath Gramodyog Sansthan. Retrieved from *file:///D:/ECCE/child%20care/ser_RGNCreche.pdf* on 3 March 2014.

Swaminathan, M. (1991). *Childcare for Children of Working Parents in India*. Delhi: ILO.

———. (2000). "Worker, Mother or Both: Maternity and Childcare Services for Women in the Unorganised Sector", in R. Jhabvala and R.K.A. Subrahmanya (ed.), *The Unorganised Sector: Work Security and Social Protection*. New Delhi: Sage.

———. (2013). "A Note on the Some Entitlements of Women and Young Children in the Draft Food Security Bill from Gender Perspective". Unpublished.

———. (n.d.). *Why Day Care?* Retrieved from *http://allforecd.org/Mina%20Swaminathan%20Why%20Day%20Care.pdf* on 28 April 2014

Woodhead, M. (2005). "Early Childhood Development: A Question of Rights", in *International Journal of Early Childhood* 37(3): 79-98, December.

Zylan, Y. (2000). "Maternalism Redefined: Gender, the State, and the Politics of Day Care, 1945-1962", in *Gender and Society* 14(5): 608-29, October.

5

RAJALAKSHMI SRIRAM

Harnessing Fathering Potential to Ensure Child Well-being

Women's Empowerment and Involved Fathering: Two Sides of the Coin

I begin the chapter on a personal note on how I started engaging with the theme of fathering in my research and action, as it also highlights the need to partner men for achieving gender equality. Since the mid-1980s I have been involved with issues of childcare and women's development/empowerment. I have explored these through research and participatory action. Along with my team from Mahila Samkhya, Gujarat (a programme of education for women's equality launched in selected states by Government of India [GoI]), I observed that the community based child care support services in villages where men/fathers participated were more successful as compared to villages where they did not participate as much. Women in such situations could come out more openly to discuss their concerns about how the centres were being run and to resolve conflicts amicably.

Simultaneously while engaging with students in teaching family, gender and parenting as part of course work in the Human Development department, we would have several debates on the current status of women and girl children; each discussion, irrespective of its contours, would end up with a conclusion that there are many changes in family and women's position, situation and roles at both the global and local levels, but parallel changes are yet to occur in the situation and roles of men. Further, all experiences with women (rural, the urban classroom and workshops), readings, and discussions made it very clear that even though there are genetic differences between men and women, gender is more a socially constructed phenomenon. If so, why does the same logic not hold true for men and women; if women have changed then why not men? This raised a question for us—are all men alike and have they not changed? It was time to reflect on individual experiences. This brought forth some alternative images of many men especially fathers/brothers, uncles, grandfathers (including my own family) who are supportive, sensitive, compassionate and understanding and involved in family life and in raising children. In these individual narratives one noticed that where fathers/husbands were supportive their daughters/wives were more successful and had a stronger sense of self-confidence and empowerment.

However when we look at global society (macro level), the dominant image of a man/father has been constructed quite differently: distant (a provider and an authority figure), not involved actively in child rearing, violent, abusive and often an alcoholic—someone better away from the family, than involved in making trouble for the family and the kids. Although this is a reality in many families and communities, our experiences do not permit us to consider it as universal.

At this time, I started thinking if parenting can act as an entry point for involving men positively and found our perspective on parenting rather skewed. Most studies conceptualised parenting by men and fathers on the same template as mothering; so they focused on basic care activities (for e.g., cooking, feeding, bathing, putting the child to sleep and participation in domestic activities) and time spent with the child. The conclusions from such studies focused on what men don't do and are labelled as the role-deficit perspective in literature. There is no doubt that such an understanding is important when we argue for domestic democracy and demand more involvement from men to reduce women's drudgery and add value to this unpaid work. However it does not help to initiate any change. Aiming to arrive at a more holistic conceptualisation of parenting, which is not just a list of activities but an investment a parent makes and includes mental, emotional and social components, I delved deeper into literature on parenting as a generative activity, which draws from the psychosocial theory of Erikson. I realised that the theory resonates with the basic principles of *Grihastashrama* (the stage of a man's life from 25 to 50 years of age considered that of a householder)—the second stage in *Ashrama Dharma* in Hindu philosophy, which accords importance to parenting and care of others as part of *Dharma* (a moral duty and obligation).

Simultaneously I studied the work of Snarey (1993), Dollahite and Hawkins (1997) and Palkovitz (1997), who worked on developing an expanded template of parenting that is more inclusive and comprises cognitive, affective and behavioural dimensions of parenting, and applied it to understanding fathering. Such a conceptualisation provides the scope to assess what men actually do and how they contribute to bringing up children. Thus was nurtured my interest in understanding academic literature in the field of men and fathering; I was also inspired to undertake primary research on fatherhood and fathering in India through the experiences of men, women and children. Research with middle class families in Vadodara, Mumbai (Navalkar, 2010; Saraff and Srivastava, 2010), Jaipur (Mathur and Mathur, 2006), Delhi (Roopnarine and Suppal, 2003) and Chennai indicate that in a changing context fathers are quite involved and contribute to their children's lives in many ways and try to maintain friendly relationships with them, which is quite different from just being providers or authoritarian patriarchs who discipline children.

We need to use a 'strength-and-capabilities based approach' to bring about change in gender role socialisation. Men are not to be solely blamed for their lack of participation, as masculinities and fathering are also products of the interplay of several factors that shape individual lives—including gender socialisation. Hence we need to understand that boys and men are also part of the same patriarchal structures. They need supportive interventions to break stereotypes and progress towards becoming men who are nurturing, supportive and equally involved in care work. As an off shoot, we began a dialogue with parents and teachers in preschools to promote involved fathering through the Shishu Palak Vrund (Child Care Association). These experiences reinforced the need to understand men as fathers and converse with various groups on the process of involved fathering. Positive involvement will not only ensure well-being of the child, but also contribute to gender equality. The first part of this paper focuses on the importance of fathering in the welfare of children and adults; the second dwells on interventions attempted across the globe to engage fathers. The last part highlights our approach to engaging with fathers. The paper concludes with opportunities that can be used to successfully unleash the fathering potential in the Indian context.

What is Fathering Potential: Why Should we Harness it?

From the time Michael Lamb (the father of fathering research) first acknowledged the role of fathers in child development through academic literature (from the West in 1976), we have come a long way to when the United Nations (UN) endorsed the importance to be accorded to men and fathers in families in its publication titled *Men in Families, and Family Policy in a Changing World* (Department of Economic and Social Affairs, United Nations, 2011).

First we should give some thought to how we make sense of fatherhood and fathering. By fatherhood we usually mean the social or legal status and by fathering we refer to the responsibilities, caring or nurturing activities that are often, though not inevitably, associated with it. As a corollary, rather than considering fatherhood as being only biologically determined, there is a recognition that it may vary widely depending on the circumstances in which the role is played out. Therefore all men who are supportive and play important roles in the lives of families are in some way fathering, thus acknowledging social fatherhood. Based on the responses of leading scholars and practitioners in the field, Beardshaw (2004) summarises four types of images of responsible fatherhood in view of fathers' status as they are interpreted across the globe now.

- *Biological fatherhood:* The ability to have one's own child, acknowledge paternity and thereby take responsibility for the welfare of children.
- *Caregiving fatherhood:* Being involved in the lives of children by care and direct relationship with the child, which can be done by any responsible adult concerned for the child's

well-being, inclusive of social fathers, like a grandfather, uncle, teacher or an elder sibling and the like. We also need to recognise that fathers who are away due to reasons of work can be involved with children through regular communication, guidance and support, despite physical absence.

- *Partnership*: Providing the partner with physical and emotional safety, and working with her to provide for the economic, emotional, educational and other developmental needs of children; this is applicable to a variety of family types.
- *Economic provision:* By making appropriate levels of economic resources available to the child applicable even where father and child do not live together due to family break up.

Our understanding of fathering and its impact has expanded enormously in the last three decades. The attitude that feminine and masculine cultures are opposites is also on the decline; there is a stronger tendency now to regard them as complementary. Although a parent's sex will definitely influence an infant's/child's development, there is no reason to believe that one sex automatically has a greater influence, or that the mother's influence is better than the father's. Fletcher (2013) summarises evidence which tells us that fathering in humans has evolved to ensure that our offspring survive and that fathers since the Ice Ages have the needed social skills to communicate and bond with others; the ability to be a father who cares for young children is hard wired into our genetic make-up. In humans, levels of 'nurturing hormones' are found to be the same in men and women exposed to 'infant stimuli' before their babies are born and when interacting with them afterwards (Fatherhood Institute Research Summary, 2014; Pruett 2000). The *Natya Shastra* too (a scientific treatise on Indian classical dance), recognises *Vatsalya* (parental love, especially paternal love) as an important constructive emotion in humans (cited in Sinha, 2013). Fletcher (2013: 178) reports that:

> We now understand that though DNA material that can make up genes can be changed only after many generations, many pieces of

> DNA can be switched off or on without changing the DNA code. In a single generation these DNA code switches can be tripped. Because sections of DNA control the activities of other parts, these switches can be changed, as a result of which the behaviours affected by DNA can also be altered.

Hence it is possible that now we can speed up this process and pass on good fathering to the next generation.

Expression of this ability begins from the time a person experiences fatherhood. It is reported (FI research summary, 2014) that within 15 minutes of holding a baby, men experience raised levels of hormones associated with tolerance/trust (oxytocin), sensitivity to infants (cortisol) and brooding/lactation/bonding (prolactin). Therefore, this is a good time to examine some of our long-standing notions about parenting, one of which is that children develop attachment only to mothers; that mothers are more nurturing and provide better care. In this section, we look at fathers' capabilities and see how they can benefit children and families based on academic knowledge and evidence from research. Research also indicates that a father's role changes in response to the changing needs of children at various ages. I hence use an age/developmental stage approach from infancy to adolescence.

I draw from published work on effects of fathers' involvement and studies from the Department of Human Development and Family Studies, in Baroda by me or under my guidance (a total 22 studies). Data were collected mostly from Hindu middle class intact families, on purposive samples of fathers, mothers and children that represented variations in gender and age of children, family type, mothers' and fathers' employment. Studies used an interpretive constructivist approach and construed father's involvement on an expanded template. Data were generated using free flowing in-depth interviews or interviews with semi-structured interview guides, on the chosen domain of study, and applied principles of triangulation to enhance validity or credibility. We also have used a self-constructed, validated scale to measure levels of fathers' participation. Studies that analysed the portrayal of the father in media (children's stories, television commercials and Bollywood movies) used qualitative and quantitative approaches to content analysis.

Fathering Role in Infancy/Toddlerhood: Bonding and its Impact

Becoming a father is a welcome event in India; it proclaims a man's ability to produce offspring, a sign of his virility. Many men, especially in low income families and communities, become fathers at a young age as there is high pressure to bear progeny. Scholars such as Raju (2001) and Verma *et al.* (2006) have argued that within Indian society the image of a real man is constructed as someone who takes care of his children, wife, parents, and siblings and assumes responsibility for the family. One can effectively draw on this sense of duty and responsibility towards family to start a dialogue on fathers' contributions to the well-being of children and women. Experiments by the Community Aids Sponsorship Programme in Delhi, Centre for Nutrition Education and Health Awareness in Ahmedabad in 1998 and by Finger and Barnett in the Philippines in 1994, as cited in Raju (2001), endorse this. The study of Sriram *et al.* (1998) conducted on a sample of hospital deliveries in government and private trust hospitals in the city of Vadodara, Gujarat, reported that about 15-30 per cent of husbands in their sample offered active support in antenatal and postpartum care and 30-50 per cent made decisions about treatment and care. However only about 10 per cent of fathers showed concern in decisions related to family planning. Education played an important role in fathers' levels of awareness and responsibility for antenatal care as well as conception (Sriram, 2003).

Western research reports no biological differences between the sexes in sensitivity to infants. Fathers' responsiveness seems to vary depending on the degree to which men assume responsibility for the care of their infants. A Vadodara city study by Shukla and Sriram (1998) on urban middle class dual earner households found that 80 per cent fathers were aware of common diseases and preventive measures, developmental milestones, and needs of infants. Around 30-50 per cent knew about appropriate feeding practices and home remedies, and three-fourth believed that fathers can be involved in all activities except breast-feeding. About 60-75 per cent fathers were always involved in food and healthcare matters, play, interaction, habit formation and discipline. However they were less frequently involved in regular routine activities of care such as changing, cleaning, or attending to the child at night. Fifty per cent clearly reported that they had never ever told a story or sung a lullaby, and did not feel the confidence to attend to a sick child. However images in Hindi films where the father is the caregiver, show a father being able to do everything for the child (Takwani and Sriram, 2014). As observed by Kakar (1996; 2010), middle class fathers have begun to provide early emotional access to the son, not only attenuating the overheated quality of the mother-son bond, but also laying the foundations for a less hierarchical and closer father-son relationship. Anthropological accounts have depicted Indian fathers as sensitive, loving and charged with feelings for their sons. This feature is also seen in affectionate play between fathers and their children, among middle class parents in Delhi (Roopnarine *et al.*, 1990). It is important to note that fathers' individual characteristics and the quantity of time given are less important and what matters are their warmth, sensitivity and response with individual children. A Canadian study with primary caregiving fathers by Doucet (2006) argues for the need to move beyond the debate of gender differences and similarities in parenting and highlights unique, positive masculine qualities they bring to parenting, by altering the meanings of these responsibilities. Since infants benefit from bonding with multiple caregivers, close bonding with father is beneficial to the child in many ways, some of which are enumerated here drawing from evidence (Burgess and Jones, 2012; FI Research Summary, 2014; Fletcher, 2013; ICRW and Pramundo, 2007; Russell, 2005).

Fathers are enthralled with their infants as much as mothers, irrespective of how they express it. When a close bond is formed, it affects the architecture of the brain. Therefore, children are more cognitively competent as babies and toddlers, laying strong foundation for emotional intelligence through secure attachment, and learning of relational social skills. Rough-and-tumble play with fathers can help children manage aggressive impulses and learn to control their emotions during physical activity. Girls can grow up strong and physically fit when fathers engage in rough play with them, leading to mental strength and self-esteem. Fathers can engage energetic children safely. With gentle children, father can help them develop strategies to stay out of trouble. Six-month-olds whose fathers are involved in their care score higher on tests of motor development. In addition, an involved father helps the mother receive better antenatal care and health care, ensures immunisation and hence improves survival. Breastfeeding rates can become higher when fathers are directly addressed on the benefits and mechanics of breastfeeding and support mothers in the same.

Fathering Role in Childhood: Focus on Cognitive, Social and Emotional Development

The elements of this care conceptualised on an expanded template (cognitive, affective and behavioural aspects of involvement) include routine care activities, planning and providing, communication, and availability and shared activities, practical and emotional support, disciplining, monitoring, guidance, support to extra-curricular activities, teaching and mentoring and the like. In a study by Sandhu and Sriram (2008) on a sample of 240 fathers drawn from schools catering to middle class children, about 65 per cent fathers displayed moderate levels of involvement, 18 per cent high involvement and about 17 per cent low involvement. Fathers consider children's social competence and achievement and making them good human beings to be important goals and therefore participated in related activities. Their involvement in providing and mentoring was the highest, followed by practical emotional support and teaching. They displayed slightly lower levels of involvement in communication, availability and shared activities. Sarkar and Sriram (2014) in their study on military families (cosmopolitan) in Vadodara, found that fathers who are forced to stay away were also actively involved in their children's lives and kept active communication with them.

Across all samples, family type, children's age, or woman's work status did not have any significant effect on overall involvement scores. However gender interacts with family type, reducing the involvement of fathers in girl's lives as they grow older in extended families. Singh and Sriram (2014) in their sample of postgraduate women students found that fathers supported and encouraged them in every way. Daughters mostly appreciated fathers' personal characteristics, the loving, caring, understanding and supportive nature. Daughters gave their fathers special recognition by adoration and hero worship. Studies conducted in the West (UK, Australia, USA) as reported by Allan and Daly (2007) and Fletcher (2013) highlight special benefits of such involvement. Fathers' parenting styles help children understand the world in different ways. Fathers also respond to children's emotions by a problem-solving approach. Quality father-and-child time increases self-esteem, confidence, social competence, emotional intelligence and life skills. Children are less likely to be depressed, and display fewer expressions of negative emotionality such as fear and guilt. Fathers are more likely to find new and unexpected ways to play with familiar toys, which expands their child's creative horizons. Fathers tend to use more "what and why" questions and more requests for clarification than mothers, both of which encourage conversation, thus developing verbal skills. School-aged children of involved fathers are also better academic achievers, which in turn impacts economic and educational achievement, career success, and occupational competence. Disadvantaged children gain even more from a strong father-child relationship than better-resource children; they suffer more when this is deficient. A positive and substantial father-child relationship can 'buffer' children from the negative effects of socio-economic and other disadvantages. Fathers' and mothers' involvement at age seven independently predicted educational attainment by age 20 for both sons and daughters.

Fathering in Adolescence: It's Potential for Reducing Negative and Risky Behaviours

As pointed out by Kakar (2010), the father-son relationship provides great emotional rewards for both.

In traditional India a son accompanies his father's work life in the natural course of events, first as a curious onlooker and then, more often than not, as an enthusiastic apprentice, be a weaver, trader or a shopkeeper, or a nomad. Nothing is more vital for developing a stable sense of masculine identity than emotional access to the father. By working alongside his father, a boy comes in contact with the most valuable part of his father's identity—his work.

The father's physical touch and guiding voice can be a powerful influence. Urban fathers of middle class school-going children were involved in supporting children in academic achievement, in school and college admissions and in career choices, irrespective of the child's gender. They also concerned themselves with monitoring their teenage child's friends, daily activities and studies. They were authoritative in their approach to parenting and also thought they could negotiate better with the outside world, and hence needed to assume an active role in linking their child with the world (Kumari and Sriram, 2008; Mathur and Mathur, 2006; Sarkar and Sriram, 2014; Shah and Kapadia, 2007; Sriram, 2011; Sriram and Sandhu, 2013).

Apart from continued impact on educational attainment, high levels of father involvement in childhood correlate with lower criminality, anti-social behaviour and substance abuse in adolescence. Adolescents who strongly identified with their fathers were 80 per cent less likely to have been in jail and 75 per cent less likely to become unwed parents (Allan and Daly, 2007). Fathers can act as gate-keepers as reported by Ahluwalia and Sriram (2009), and Singh and Sriram (2014) based on their sample of educated urban women. More than two-third of fathers held gender equal beliefs in education and career domain skill training, but imposed some restrictions on mobility and expected daughters to learn home management and domestic skills. When the father was supportive, and provided opportunities, it had a positive impact on their personality and self-worth; could break barriers in education, profession, and family life; and had more power to negotiate their gender roles. The restrictions or differential treatment resulted in a negative impact in terms of stress, frustration and loneliness, negative personal traits (lack of confidence, reserved, introvert, shy, etc.), a sense of neglect and inferiority, loss of fun and opportunities, discomfort with the opposite sex, lack of social skills (making friends) and dependence.

Father Involvement: Impact on Fathers and Mothers

A study by Kaur and Sriram (2011) with 30 involved urban educated middle class fathers shows that these men experienced changes in their personality (51% responses); they reported increase in generative traits (26% responses), changes in social relationships (11% responses), cognitive and practical skills (7% responses) and affective changes (4% responses). Ninety six per cent fathers noted that their self-esteem had increased because of fathering, as they felt confident to care for children and had acquired many more skills. Three-fourth felt that their commitment towards family had increased. Based on western evidence, Palkovitz (2003) noted that high involvement has a modest, positive impact on occupational mobility, work success, and societal generativity (leading, mentoring and contributing to strength and continuity of subsequent generations). Men's emotional involvement with their children was found to act as a safeguard against work-related stresses. There is a positive relationship between increased involvement of fathers and their subsequent hours of work and earning. Men who occupy many roles such as husbands, employees, and fathers reported higher well-being and lower distress, and were found to enjoy greater mental health. Fathers enjoy many bonuses such as better relationships with children and partners, and an overall feeling of positivity and well-being (reported in Allan and Daly, 2007).

As for gender division of roles, Sriram (2003) and Sriram, Ali and Karnik (2002), based on their sample of dual earner households, found many patterns as per practical circumstances. The father's gender ideology influenced sharing of parenting work. Both fathers and mothers took equal responsibility to monitor and determine the conduct of children, and to support their achievements and education. In making sacrifices, 90 per cent mothers accorded first priority to mothering against 40 per cent fathers, and felt that despite a desire to be involved they had to be more committed to work due to social expectations and financial needs. About a quarter of committed fathers altered their life course and made life decisions in the interest of their children. Holter *et al.* (2009: 239) opine that "like mothers' participation in the paid workforce, fathers' participation in caretaking is linked to greater equality in decision making which, in turn, is linked to lower rates of violence and physical punishment of children." It is difficult to prove causation, but evidence indicates that caring for a partner and/or children influences behaviour in biological (i.e., hormonal, neurological or physical) ways, leading to a reduced likelihood of angry or violent responses to stress (cited in FI Research Summary; 2014, ICRW and Instituto Pramundo, 2007). When involved fathers talk about gender, equality they take many perspectives based on their own thought and experiences. Some relate it to their role as a model for children; others talk of providing equal opportunities/freedom for children to do what they want rather than conforming to stereotypes, sharing tasks with their wives/partners and enjoying time with partners and children that reduces stress (White Ribbon Campaign, 2014; Kaur and Sriram, 2011).

Across studies we found that fathers wish to be more available to their children and to be more involved in teaching and extra-curricular activities. Practical considerations and personal factors did not allow fathers to be fully engaged as reported in workshops and research (Sriram and Navalkar, 2012). Time was a major barrier as fathers did not have any power to negotiate at their work places except senior government employees, or self-employed professionals. Fathers' personal incompetence like lack of knowledge, skills, and interest in dealing with children due to their own socialisation and the absence of role models in their society impeded fathers' involvement (gender playing out in an indirect way). Although gender and social norms are cited less as barriers to involvement, fathers emphasise that their success in professional careers carried greater value than their success as family men, and rationalised it saying "it is after all for the wellbeing of the family." It is quite obvious that fathers are in conflict and unable to create or choose conditions that enable a balance between work, family and children's requirements, and therefore need supportive interventions. Many programmes have been tried and tested across the globe to engage men and fathers in various contexts (with special focus on vulnerable groups) to enhance their contributions to child well-being, health of men and women (physical and mental), to reduce violence, abuse against women and children, and to promote gender equality. This forms the crux of the next section.

How to Harness Fathering Potential?: Paving the Path to Reach the Goal

We have a fair amount of evidence to believe that efforts to involve men and fathers are like an insurance which might yield positive results in our movement towards the goal of gender equality and child well-being. I say this for two reasons. First, we all know that if we want to change a system we must work with all its parts, in this case, all institutions and segments of society. Despite this, as a society we have focused more on working with women and mothers and other female functionaries; as a corollary, 'care' has become a women's issue instead of a societal one. Second, it is time to draw from the strengths we have in each culture, and nourish the generative potential, the duty bound moral consciousness and the sensitive side of men to create a win-win situation for all. To begin with, I present programme approaches from across the globe, followed by a description of what we have attempted in the local context.

Intervention with Fathers: A Glimpse into Approaches Across the Globe

An extensive review of programmes across the globe by McAlister and Burgess (2012) reveals that these programmes reaching out to fathers are broadly of three types. First, programmes that focus on enhancing fathers' capacities, making them more responsible towards the child improving their parenting skills, and nurturing co-parenting with partners, beginning with pregnancy to the later years. Canada has tried to implement a home visiting self-monitoring programme for new fathers; in Niger there are husband schools; and Papa schools are seen in Ukraine. For fathers of preschool children, there is Head Start in USA and Sure Start in UK which focuses on early childhood care and development (ECCD), and has a built in fathering component. Similar is the highly rated triple P-Positive Parenting

Programme of Australia, which helps in the parenting of children of all ages and those with special needs. Better parenting programmes (BPP) are implemented by United Nations Children's Fund (UNICEF) across many countries. The Father Support Programme in Turkey, and the 24/7 Dad Curriculum or *Siempre Papa* (Spanish Edition) developed by the US National Fatherhood Institute focus exclusively on fathers. LAS for Mej, Pappa (Read to me daddy), a Swedish programme for addressing family literacy initiated by IF Metall and three other national unions in Sweden, is a special programme for migrant fathers; and The Fathers in Action Project Proyecto Papa en Accion, Peru, is based on experiential learning for fathers. Although their curriculum and approaches are varied, they have special sessions (ranging from 5-18) for men to equip them with the skills needed to become involved and engaged fathers. The curriculum covers a wide range of topics related to masculinity and fatherhood, including what it means to be a man, power and control, disciplining and rewarding children and ways to form emotional bonds with children. In addition, some programmes especially for the disadvantaged, support development of work skills, financial self-sufficiency and improve employment, as it is seen that fulfilling the provider role is very important for a man to feel successful in most communities. Those who are unable to do so feel deficient and ashamed, which leads to engaging with negative behaviours. Qualitative results of most approaches indicate that fathers felt more connected to their children, used kinder means of discipline, engaged more with them, and responded better. They felt more involved in the family, learnt to respect family members, shared more of the domestic and caregiving work and learnt to refrain from using violence.

Second, programmes that focus on reducing child abuse, maltreatment, domestic violence against partners, re-defining masculinity, promoting sexual health and encouraging safe sexual behaviours including respect to women. These are directed towards perpetrators and try to reconstruct notions of masculinity and sexuality through reflective discourse. Some examples are Caring Dads, initiated in Canada, now implemented even in UK, 17-week intervention for fathers who have mistreated their children and/

or engaged in violence towards their partners. Programme-H by Pramundo in Brazil and Partners has two main elements: workshops dealing with relationship, sexual health and fatherhood issues; and 'social marketing campaigns' where sexual health messages are conveyed through 'cool' slogans encouraging men to have protected sex, assume caring roles and to respect women. Popular figures such as singers and sportsmen and branded merchandise are used to advocate active fatherhood and safe sex. Rozan in Islamabad engages with men and involves all stakeholders at the community level to bring attitudinal change through "father and couple groups". Similarly, Mobilising Men in India engages with universities, governments and the Dalit community to address gender-based violence as a public issue. All programmes have brought about positive results and attempt to partner sensitive men in the community to move forward.

A third kind of programme focuses on improving fathering in divorce, separation and incarceration situations. Safe Ground's 'Family Man' and 'Fathers Inside' programmes, UK, support incarcerated fathers to understand the importance of their role in family and how to engage with children through creative avenues to develop life skills. They also work with family members outside ending with a 'What Next' session linking the fathers, their families and children to post-release support resources. Small-scale evaluations indicate that participants value the course and it makes men more responsible for their own behaviour and relationships. Fathering Court, a federal government supported programme for fathers after divorce, that begun in Missouri, USA in 1998 (National Centre for Fathering, 2009), is designed to enhance provision of child support not only in the financial sense, but also in the family sense, by ongoing action and support in positive ways. It has proved to be a positive alternative to prosecution and incarceration. Dads for Life is considered a model programme that was developed to reduce risks of divorce for children, by working on father-child relationship, promoting fathers' parenting skills, reducing conflict and fostering co-parenting behaviours (Bronte-Tinkew *et al.*, 2007). All these have reduced conflict but there is no conclusive evidence for improved co-parenting yet.

Lessons from programmes across the globe tell us that we need to engage fathers early on and also generate their commitment to the fathering role. Programmes that work also choose staff that believe in the programme and train them, use targeted curricula and provide support materials. They also use a variety of interactive methods suitable to the population served and engage for sufficient periods of time. Staff had one-to-one interactions so that it is personalised to every father/participant (McAlister and Burgess, 2012; Tinkew *et al.*, 2007). Recommendations highlight the need for programmes in the global south to encourage men's involvement in child well-being using a multi-pronged approach. Hence sharing our initiatives and experience is valuable.

Constructing Images of Involved Fathering and Nurturing the Fathering Potential: The Local Experience

During discussions with participants and professionals as part of the research endeavour, we found that the theme generated a lot of interest, curiosity and enthusiasm. In a study where we collected perspectives of staff involved in healthcare and educational institutions, they opined that we should have programmes on involved fathering. We initiated our work in 2005, by organising an interactive panel discussion on the theme in a local school. The panel comprised a lady spiritual Guru who was highly respected, a doctor, I as a subject matter expert, and an involved father. The discussions brought forth multiple perspectives on involved fathering and the session ended with some thoughts on the importance of the father in a child's life. We implemented such sessions partnering with CSR (corporate social responsibility) units, the Department of Preventive and Social Medicine, and play centres and schools. On reflection, we strongly felt that one needs to engage not only with fathers, but mothers, professionals and communities too, in order to construct an image of an involved father and take them on a journey to see how to translate this image to practice. We would need to work at three levels—attitudes (an intra-personal component) relationships (an interpersonal component) and help people change what they actually do at behavioural level. With this goal, we have tried to reach out to:

- Individuals—parents, grandparents, professionals, students
- Early childhood and health professionals—teachers and frontline workers, through schools and NGOs (non-governmental organisations)
- Community and institutional events

Irrespective of the settings and activities, we found that there is a lot of value attached to the fathering role; however, the understanding of how fathers can contribute to child and family well-being is very limited. Our task was to give inputs so that people feel convinced of the need to unleash the fathering potential. We chose strategies that are culturally appropriate to help us embed fathering into the social context. For instance, the use of mythological stories or instances from epics, popular films, advertisements or children's stories are good starters to generate a participatory discussion about different types of fathers, their actions and results. I illustrate some approaches that have brought positive results.

Analysis Based on a Simple Question: "Can Father be like Mother? Why? Why Not?"

When we posed this question to the group, it helped unravel people's perceptions about fathers, mothers, parenting, its effects on children and the like. We moved this discussion forward connecting it to research about men's capabilities for caring and the contributions they can make as fathers. The next question was to connect this information to their lives. There would be very few willing or confident to open up. It is at this time we banked on previously identified involved father/s who could share some experiences and get the conversation going. Discussions on what prevents fathers' full involvement are rather smooth, where many barriers get identified, mostly limited time and lack of skills. We treated these two issues separately. With reference to skills, we focused on how parenting is a learnt behaviour. Although society expects that such training is a natural process, in reality new challenges in parenting and lack of any systematic training make both parents feel inadequate.

With reference to time, the focus was on the quality of time and interactions rather than the amount of time available or spent with the child. Sessions concluded with a presentation on ways in which fathers can be involved across domains (meals, communications, play, guidance, teaching, values and the like) and its impact on children. We also focused on negative behaviours that need to be avoided with stress on over-involvement, very high aspirations and expectations and harsh methods of control. If the group had elderly participants, there was an added focus on the role of grandparents in democratic family relations to encourage involved fathering through personal anecdotes, drama and the like. With mothers, we often discuss maternal gate-keeping, the intertwining of childcare and women's sense of self. Interesting discussions occur on how to open up family spaces so that fathers feel motivated to be involved without the fear of criticism of their inadequacies.

Assessing father friendliness in services is another approach we use with frontline workers and teachers. We provide a checklist to rate how father friendly their services are? There is much discussion about the items of the checklist which enlarges one's vision of the need for fathers' involvement, and how to reach out to them. The ratings are discussed in a group and then the group is encouraged to think about the advantages of reaching out to fathers, and creative options they can try out. The session ends with a discussion and presentations on possible options.

In sessions for medical students or in healthcare settings, we emphasise the trust that parents place on doctors and paramedical staff, and therefore the value that the information they provide carries. In addition to why father involvement is important, we have focused on encouraging the same in antenatal period, birth, postpartum and infant care, and the benefits it entails for women, children and fathers. We also present some of the case studies of such programmes that have reached out to parents through hospitals and their positive effects. These sessions also end with a summary on how fathers can be involved in reproductive child healthcare.

Local Events as an Opportunity to Reach Out

We have put up stalls in NGO fairs (locally called a *mela*), which is a platform to showcase social development work in the city. Similarly preschools also organise such fairs for parents and public. We put up poster exhibitions; have interactive slide shows; and create spaces where fathers can engage in joint activities with children. We have even arranged competitions for fathers on story-telling, dressing up a child, or engaging for a stipulated time without toys and the like. Fathers also take a quiz on their knowledge of children's needs and child rearing. The response has been positive as it generates enthusiasm and is fun. Post-activity time is used for a feedback to parents and discussion about the what, why and how of fathers' involvement. Another way is to have a focused discussion on handling difficult situations with children. It helps fathers share experiences and learn from each other in non-threatening ways.

Although we do not have any systematic evaluation of the impact of these programmes, formative evaluations through a variety of means such as feedback forms, follow up thank you letters, and individual phone calls indicate that such programmes are well received and have opened up a new way of looking at parenting—fathers. Some professionals also express a desire to engage in initiatives at their organisations and feel more responsible towards involving men and fathers. Another positive feature is the resource base that is built up. We have summaries from 90 children' stories, which portray a warm nurturing/humorous father or father figure; examples of fathers from epics, photographs of involved fathers, film clippings from father-centred Hindi films, clippings from films of Amitabh Bachchan as a father; 100 Hindi commercials shown on television that have a father or father figure; personal experiences and anecdotes—all of which help us build an image of an involved father. We have a collection of poems, essays, stories and anecdotes published in regional language as a book titled *Pitrutvana Panthe* (On the Path to Fatherhood), and a brochure titled "I am an involved father". Our powerpoint presentations and a set of 20 posters that showcase various aspects of involved fathering have been a useful tool to trigger a dialogue.

In Conclusion: The Way Forward

I have provided enough evidence from research and programme initiatives across the globe about the importance of acknowledging the benefits of involved fathering for children's well-being and gender equality. Indian studies on fathers in selected samples also break the image/stereotype of an uninvolved, psychologically distant father, and indicate that fathers in India are generative and involved in the lives of their children to different degrees. I believe there is scope to utilise this potential in positive ways. However, the nature of my profession (academics and university teaching) has provided only an opportunity to engage in action for promoting involved fathering, but not carry out long-term interventions aimed at transformation and evaluate them.

Despite this, I am convinced that engaging with men in their fathering role is a step in the right direction towards creating a gender equal and child-friendly society. Is there one place or a special programme for fathers? I say no! We need to build sensitivity to involved fathering across all programmes that focus on children and women, and all professionals and paraprofessionals who work with them. Involved fatherhood does not occur within a vacuum. Studies by White Ribbon Campaign (2014), Canada and Perry (2012) indicate that fathers were active members of their community, often accessed services from many different service providers and relied upon their communities for many aspects of the parenting process. Hence, I see the possibility of having programmes with all organisations and people who work with children and families. For example: currently, the fathering component can easily be built into ongoing reproductive health programmes, ICDS and other early childhood programmes. I see a lot of scope to provide opportunities for fathers to experience how it feels to be involved by arranging for them to be one-on-one with their children, inviting them to spend time with their children at preschool, Balwadi or a picnic, and engage in routine activities of caregiving for a stipulated period of time. Approaches like fathering day, and competitions that provide a platform to showcase fathers' abilities may also be welcome events in the community.

We have to rethink many issues such as—why link childcare service to women's employment? Why have diaper change stations in women's toilets? Why no paternity leave or flexible time for men? Can we make it a mandate for schools to play an active role to inspire involved fathering by demanding their participation in projects, everyday homework, reading, writing essays by discussion with fathers and the like? Can we provide a positive twist to social and print media images already put out on events like the Fathers' Day? It is a long journey along a winding path where we might have to make a stop, come back to reflect and take corrective action and move forward with new vigour. But I believe we can and should do it to create a better and more equitable world for the coming generations.

References

Ahluwalia, T. (2009). *Father Involvement in Daughters' Life and Career Choices—Daughters' perspective*, Unpublished Master's Dissertation. Baroda: Department of Human Development and Family Studies, M.S University of Baroda.

Allan, S. and K. Daly (2007). *The Effects of Father Involvement: An Updated Summary of Research Evidence*. Guelph: The Father Involvement Research Alliance, (FIRA) Centre for Families, Work & Well-Being, University of Guelph.

Beardshaw, T. (2004). *Involved Responsible Fatherhood and its Potential Impact on Men, Women, Children and Society*. Supporting Fathers: Contributions from the International Fatherhood Summit, "Early Childhood Development: Practices and Reflections", No. 20: 17-43 (Bernard van Leer Foundation).

Bronte-Tinkew, J., J. Carrano, T. Allen, L. Bowie, K. Mbawa and G. Matthews (2007). *Elements of Promising Practice for Fatherhood Programmes: Evidence based Research Findings on Programmes for Fathers*. Gaithersberg, MD: National Responsible Fatherhood Clearing House.

Burgess, A. and K. Jones for Bernard Van Leer Foundation (2012). *Advocating for Involved Fatherhood in the UK, (1999-2012)*. UK: The Fatherhood Institute Retrieved from *http://www.fatherhoodinstitute.org/wp-content/uploads/2012/09/Advocating-for-involved-fatherhood-in-the-UKAug2012.pdf*

Datta, D. (2007). "Overstretched Dads", *India Today* XXXII (23): 68-72.

Dollahite, D.C. and A.J. Hawkins (1997). "Beyond the Role-inadequacy Perspective of Fathering", in A.J. Hawkins and D.C. Dollahite (eds.), *Generative Fathering: Beyond Deficit Perspectives*. New Delhi: SAGE. pp.3-16.

Doucet, A. (2006). *Do Men Mother? Fathering, Care and Domestic Responsibility*. Toronto: University of Toronto Press. Retrieved from *https://books.google.co.in/books?id=G1p3v2soHToC&printsec=frontcover#v=onepage&q&f=false*

Fatherly Institute (FI) Research Summary (2014). *Fathers, Care-taking and Hormones*. January. Retrieved from *http://www.fatherhoodinstitute.org/2014/fi-research-summary-fathers-care-taking-and-hormones/*

Fletcher, R. (2013). *The Dad Factor*. Sydney: Finch Publishing.

ICRW (International Centre for Research on Women) and Instituto Pramundo (2007). *Engaging Men and Boys: How Can We Build on What We Have Learned?* Report of the International Seminar. Retrieved from *http://www.icrw.org/files/publications/Engaging-Men-and-Boys-to-Achieve-Gender-Equality-How-Can-We-Build-on-What-We-Have-Learned.pdf*

Kakar, S. (2010). "Father and Son: The Equation is Changing", *The Hindu*. 13 February. Retrieved from *http://timesofindia.indiatimes.com/home/opinion/edit-page/Father-Son-The-Equation-Is-Changing/articleshow/5565453.cms*

———. (1996). *The Indian Psyche: Intimate Relations, the Analyst and the Mystic*. New Delhi: Penguin.

Kaur, A. and R. Sriram (2011). *Fathering as a Process of Transformation in Men: Reflections of Involved Fathers*.Unpublished Masters Dissertation. Baroda: Department of Human Development and Family Studies, M.S. University of Baroda.

Kumari, A. (2008). *Father Involvement: As Children View It*. Unpublished Masters Dissertation. Baroda: Department of Human Development and Family Studies, M.S. University of Baroda.

Lamb, M.E. (2010). "How Do Fathers Influence Children's Development? Let Me Count the Ways", in M. Lamb (eds.), *The Role of Father in Child Development*. 5th ed. Hoboken, NJ: Wiley. pp.1-26. Retrieved from *https://netfiles.uiuc.edu/rferrer/VisitationSchedule/Various%20Topics%20Articles/LambRoleFather2010.pdf*

Lamb, M.E., J.H. Pleck, E.L. Charnov and J.A. Levine (1987). "A Biosocial Perspective on Paternal Behaviour and Involvement", in J.B. Lancaster, J. Altman, A. Rossi and L.R. Sherrod (eds.), *Parenting Across the Lifespan: Biosocial Perspectives*. New York: Academic. pp.11-42

Mathur, M. and M. Mathur (2006). *Between Fathers and Children: Experiences and Expectation of Indian Adolescent*. Unpublished Masters Dissertation. Jaipur: Department of Human Development, Maharani College of Home Science, Jaipur University.

McAlister, F. and A. Burgess (2012). *Fatherhood: Parenting Programmes and Policy: A Critical Review of Best Practice*. UK: Fatherhood Institute.

National Centre for Fathering (2009). *Fathering Court: Getting to the Heart of Child Support*. Retrieved from *http://www.fathers.com/documents/fatheringcourt/Fathering_Court_Booklet_Final.pdf*

Navalkar, P.G. (2010). "Fathering a Child with a Disability in India: A Perspective from Mumbai", *Childhood Education, International Focus Issue* 86(6): 389.

Palkovitz, R. (1997). "Reconstructing 'Involvement': Expanding Conceptualisations of Men's Caring in Contemporary Families", in A.J. Hawkins and D.C. Dollahite (eds.), *Generative Fathering: Beyond Deficit Perspectives*. New Delhi: Sage. pp.200-16.

Palkovitz, R., L.D. Marks, D.W. Appleby and E.K. Holmes (2003). "Parenting and Adult Development: Contexts: Processes and Products of Intergenerational Relationships", in L. Kucynski (ed.), *The Handbook of Dynamics in Parent-child Relationships*. Thousand Oaks, CA: Sage. pp.307-23.

Perry, A.R. (2012). *Man Up: Integrating Fatherhood and Community Engagement*. Posted in JCES Vol. 4(1). Retrieved from *http://jces.ua.edu/man-up-integrating-fatherhood-and-community-engagement/*

Pruett, K.D. (2000). *Father Need: Why Father Care is as Essential as Mother Care for Your Child*. Retrieved from *http://www.amazon.com/exec/obidos/isbn%3D076790737X/menwebA/103-4361537-2179045 K* (accessed on 5 April 2003).

Raju, S. (2001). "Addressing Men in Reproductive and Child Health", *Economic and Political Weekly* 36(49): 4589-92.

Roopnarine, J., and P. Suppal (2003). "Kakar's Psychoanalytic Interpretation of Childhood: The Need to Emphasise the Father and Multiple Caregivers in the Socialisation Equation", in D. Sharma (ed.), *Childhood, Family and Socio-cultural Change in India: Reinterpreting the Inner World*. New Delhi: Oxford. pp.115-37.

Roopnarine, J.L., E. Talukder, D. Jain, P. Joshi and P. Srivastav (1990). "Characteristics of Holding, Patterns of Play and Social Behaviours between Parents and Infants in New Delhi, India", *Developmental Psychology* 26(4): 667-73.

Russell, C.C. (2005). "Fathers Role in Social and Emotional Development of Young Children", *The Newsletter of Infant Mental Health Promotion* 42, Spring.

Sandhu, G. and R. Sriram (2008). *Father Involvement in Supporting Children's Achievement: A Context of Multiple Parenting*. Unpublished Masters Dissertation. Baroda: Department of Human Development and Family Studies, M.S. University of Baroda.

Saraff, A. and H.C. Srivastava (2010). "Pattern and Determinants of Paternal Involvement in Childcare: An Empirical Investigation in a Metropolis of India", *Population Research and Policy Review* 29: 249-73.

Sarkar, R. and R. Sriram (2014). *Children's View of Father Involvement in Military Families*. Unpublished Masters Dissertation. Baroda: Department of Human Development and Family Studies, M.S. University of Baroda.

Shah, M., and S. Kapadia (2007). *Parent-Child Perceptions About Parenting and its Relation with Children's Self-esteem*. Paper presented at the National Seminar on Human Development: Commitment to Processes of Change, Nirmila Niketan College of Home Science, Mumbai, India.

Shukla, A. and R. Sriram (1998). *Father's Role in Child Care: Knowledge, Beliefs and Practices*. Unpublished Master's Thesis. Baroda: Department of Human Development and Family Studies, M.S. University of Baroda.

Singh, R. and R. Sriram (2014). *Do Fathers Nurture Gender Equality in their Beliefs and Practices? Daughters' Experiences*. Unpublished Master's Dissertation. Baroda: Department of Human Development and Family Studies, M.S. University of Baroda.

Sinha, M. (2013). "Managing Constructive and Destructive Emotions: Indian Psycho Spiritual Perspective", in D.M. Pestonjee, S. Pandey (eds.), *Stress and Work: Perspectives on Understanding and Managing Stress*. New Delhi: Sage. pp-278-302.

Snarey, J. (1993). *How Fathers Care for the Next Generation: A Four Decade Study*. Cambridge, MA: Harvard University Press.

Sriram, R. (2003). *Subjective Experiences of Fatherhood and Motherhood: Realities and Reflections*. Unpublished PhD Dissertation. Baroda: Department of Human Development and Family Studies, M.S. University of Baroda.

———. (2011). "The Role of Fathers in Children's Lives: A View from Urban India", *Childhood Education* 87: 3: 185-190, DOI: 10.1080/00094056.2011.10521719.

———. (2011a). "Evidence of Change and Continuity in Fathering: The Case of Western India", *Marriage & Family Review* 47: 625-647.

Sriram, R and G. Sandhu (2013). "Fathering to Ensure Child's Success: What Urban Indian Fathers Do?" *Journal of Family Issues* 34(2): 159-81.

Sriram, R. and P. Navalkar (2012). "Fathering in India: Understanding Challenges and Opportunities", in J. Pattnaik (ed.), *Father/Male Involvement in Young Children's Lives: An International Analysis*. USA: Springer.

Sriram, R., K. Dutta and K. Bhojak (1998). *Mothers' Perception of Postpartum Health Care Needs and Problems: A Case Study from Baroda*. Unpublished Paper. Baroda: M.S. University of Baroda and Population Council.

Sriram, R., R. Karnik and R. Ali (2002). *Social Construction of Fatherhood and Motherhood: A View from within Families*. [Mimeo]. Baroda: Women's Studies Research Centre, M.S. University of Baroda.

Takwani, D and R. Sriram (2014). *Paa, Papa, Daddy: Representation of Father's and Fathering in Hindi Films*. Unpublished Masters Dissertation. Baroda: Department of Human Development and Family Studies, M.S. University of Baroda.

United Nations (2011). *Men in Families, and Family Policy in a Changing World* (sales no E.11.IV.1). New York: Department of Economic and Social Affairs, Division for Social and Policy Development.

Verma, R.K., J. Pulerwitz, V. Mahendra, S. Khandekar, G. Barker, P. Fulpagare and S.K. Singh (2006). "Challenging and Changing Gender Attitudes Among Young Men in Mumbai, India", *Reproductive Health Matters* 14(28): 135-43.

White Ribbon Campaign (2014). *Give Love, Get Love: The Involved Fatherhood and Gender Equity Project*. Toronto: White Ribbon Campaign. Retrieved from *http://www.whiteribbon.ca/pdfs/fatherhood_report.pdf*.

Section II

Gender, Socialisation and Theatre

6

HANNE M. de BRUIN

Gender @ Crossroads

Introduction

As I have argued in my introductory essay to *Between Fame and Shame: Performing Women—Women Performers in India*, professional female practitioners of rural, marginalised 'folk' theatres suffer from a double stigma: firstly, on account of being a woman performer defying the accepted rules of female propriety, and, secondly, on account of the low status attributed by society to the folk performances in which she acts (de Bruin, 2011: 20).[1]

There are no figures available about rural women performers involved in professional theatre performances in Tamil Nadu (TN), but it seems fair to assume that their number is not very large. In my fieldwork area in north Tamil Nadu, as well as in other parts of the state,[2] professional actresses were held in low esteem. Most of them performed in what was locally known as drama or *natakam*, while some of them were or had been involved in small travelling circuses and "Record Dance" performances. They belonged to the lower end of the social continuum and often had mixed caste backgrounds. They performed on makeshift stages as part of unregulated travelling

1. The term 'folk' (as well as its counterpart 'classical') needs to be problematised as it is often used in a pedantic and derogative manner whilst the perceived differences between 'folk' and 'classical' are not at all clear, (see, for instance, Krishna [2013: 20-23]) for a discussion on folk music). Ananda Lal writes in his introduction to *The Oxford Companion on Indian Theatre*, that in contemporary discourse among conservative, city-based Indian theatre workers, "folk and traditional forms do not even qualify as 'theatre'" (Lal 2004: ix). For me, 'folk' when applied to the Kattaikkuttu theatre embodies the organic wholeness and power of the form which, unlike other, more 'classical' theatre forms, has not (yet) separated out the medium of voice from the principal performer who requires complex skills of combining singing/speaking, acting and movement to produce and embody the text in performance.

2. See for instance Seizer (2005) on the Special Drama actresses in the Madurai region.

troupes mostly "owned" and dominated by men. The contributions to the informal rural arts scene of these women drama performers, and of their local predecessors, rural Devadasi actresses,[3] have largely remained hidden, because dominant scholarship has failed to recognise and value their personae and performances sufficiently to record them. Public visibility, mobility, interaction with men other than their close relatives and, most importantly, the display of their bodies to the male gaze, are prerequisites for women performers to carry out their profession. Yet each of these factors impacts negatively on a woman's respectability, in particular when she enjoys no high status patronage that can neutralise these "deficits".

The fact that rural professional women performers do not fit the accepted norms of female behaviour has required them to remain invisible to the world at large. Would the acknowledgement of their presence contaminate the idea of what India, as a modern nation, has come to consider collectively as the ideal "new" woman, defined as the safe keeper of the home and upholder of the nation's spiritual values?[4] Similarly, would the recognition that many of these folk forms possess a richness, complexity, rawness as well as subtlety of their own, negatively affect the status of their classical, urban counterparts? The goals of folk theatre performances taking place outdoors as part of sacral village temple festivals differ from the goals of a classical music, dance or theatre performance on a secular, urban, indoor stage. The different outcomes expected form these performances are reflected in their different modes of production and aesthetics. The appeal and meaningfulness of folk forms are apparent from the volume of rural audiences they attract. Yet, no statistics and economic figures are available as to how many rural women and men make a living through performing—and the number of spectators they entertain. Based on my own observations with regard to rural Drama and Kattaikkuttu theatre performances, I feel

3. On the rural Devadasi tradition, see de Bruin (2007).

4. For a discussion of the ideal of the "new" women that emerged as a part of the nationalist project, see for instance Chatterjee (1993) and the discussion in de Bruin (2011: 14-15). For examples that project Tamil Nadu's late 19th century (rural/folk) stage in a negative light terming it "crude" and "primitive" see de Bruin (1999: 94-96) and de Bruin (2011: 12-13).

confident to say that the number of spectators watching theatre in rural areas throughout the year is much larger than that watching live, "elite" or modern theatre, music and dance performances in Chennai. Where then does the myth that Tamil Nadu's folk theatre is dying stem from? From the urban-intellectual's uneasiness with these alternative, expressive forms which they see as incompatible with the dominant paradigm of their "modernity"? Or from a disaffection with and dissociation from the practitioners of these forms who represent the uneducated and lower classes and castes of society?

Women's Absence from Kattaikkuttu

On quite a few occasions my husband, P. Rajagopal, was questioned by Chennai-based theatre specialists and the media about the absence of women from his profession, the Kattaikkuttu theatre. He usually would reply that women had not come forward so far to train as Kattaikkuttu actresses. More often than not his answer would be set aside. The hidden promise, coming from a traditional, rural, male performer, of being prepared to induce women into the secrets of his profession if only they would present themselves, did not seem to fit some of the pre-conceived urban notions about rural women—and about the willingness of a traditional male performer to initiate female students into an all-male theatre genre.[5]

Rajagopal's first effort to introduce women in Kattaikkuttu dates back to 1996. Over a period of four months, he trained a group of 13 women and produced together with them an all-night version of the traditional Mahabharata play, *Vilvalaippu* (Bending of the Bow) or Draupadi's Marriage.[6] His students were actresses involved in Drama, a genre which is as popular as Kattaikkuttu, but which uses a rather different style of performance. This is not the place to go into the differences between drama and Kattaikkuttu. Suffice to say that Kattaikkuttu represents a typical heroic style of performance, which is considered physically demanding, while the drama style of

5. In addition to P. Rajagopal, Kattaikkuttu Guru Purisai Kannappa Thambiran also has taught women students as can be seen in the documentary *A Profile of a Doyen* by K. Penneswaran (*https://www.youtube.com/watch?v=dzDMk44RG9A*).

6. See chapter 7 by A. Mangai in this book.

performance is a forerunner of the acting that can be witnessed in the early Tamil cinema.[7]

Rajagopal's adventure was looked upon with considerable cynicism, not only by his male performer colleagues and members of the rural audience, but also by urban representatives of the feminist theatre movement. Rural spectators questioned Rajagopal's professional association with these female drama performers. Many rural informants considered itinerant drama performers to have scant respect for accepted social and sexual norms and suspected them of theft and prostitution. Our interviews with representatives of the Drama confirm that some of them were indeed involved in activities of such a nature (de Bruin and Rajagopal, 2001). However, it seems unfair to question their different life style and values given the economic and social circumstances some of these (semi-) nomadic women and/or women from mixed caste descent faced.

The appearance of rural drama actresses in the roles of *kattai veshams*, Kattaikkuttu's typically male heroic characters, shattered the myth that women could not perform in the Kattaikkuttu genre. Until then, many people believed that the physicality of a kattai character as performed by a male actor could not possibly be matched by a woman (in spite of the fact that rural women are involved in physically demanding jobs in agriculture and the construction industry). Women would be unable to carry the heavy wooden crowns, shoulder and breast ornaments and display the appropriate stage behaviour that goes with this ornamentation. This stage behaviour emphasises a heroic character's masculinity and proudness. It requires the elaborately costumed performer to make a vigorous entry into the performance area using a prescribed song and dance routine behind a hand-held curtain. Performing a *kattai vesham* demands the execution of exacting dance steps and high-speed pirouettes that mark the heroic and often angry stage presence of such a male character.

7. For further information on Kattaikkuttu, see de Bruin (1999), passim; for a discussion of Drama in north Tamil Nadu and related hybrid forms of theatre, see de Bruin (2001), passim.

Others were of the opinion that women were forbidden from participating in a ritual/sacral theatre, such as Kattaikkuttu, because of their monthly periods (de Bruin 1999: 127; footnote 34). I am not sure whether this assumption derives its validity from academic discussions foregrounding the Brahmanical idea of the importance of ritual purity. Within the context of village performances taking place on the occasion of religious festivals, the distinction between ritual purity and impurity seems less relevant. The festivals follow distinctively non-Brahmanical practices, such as offering live animal sacrifices, and employ low caste ritual specialists, including Kattaikkuttu performers, whose principal task is to handle impurity (Brubaker, 1979: 133). The assumption that a woman performer's temporary impurity would prevent her from performing was emasculated by contemporary Drama actress M. Shanmugavalli. Even though Drama performances have a more secular character, they often take place, like Kattaikkuttu performances, on the occasion of religious village festivals. Shanmugavalli told me that she could not financially afford to miss a single performance and would perform, irrespective of the fact that she would be having her periods. And with a smile she added: "I don't know what all the fuss is about when the Goddess herself gets them too!"[8]

The production of *Bending of the Bow* initiated a thought process of how best to introduce girls and young women into professional Kattaikkuttu training and onstage performances. Not only in India, but also elsewhere in the world, there is an unstated tendency to judge women performers on the basis of their onstage and offstage relationships first and only thereafter on the quality of their performances. While the concept of quality is a complex one comprising acoustic, visual and emotive aspects (Krishna, 2013: 4), the quality of a woman's performance is normally compared to that of men performing in the same genre—and found to be "different" or lacking in quality. The criteria used to judge her performance are derived from the male paradigm, leaving her with a "substandard" performance—whether perceived or real—that can be blamed easily

8. Personal communication with M. Shanmugavalli, 18 November 1998.

on the fact that she is a woman, in particular when she has the guts to perform in a theatre genre that traditionally features male performers only. Therefore, among the many things that are needed to break the social stigma on rural women performers, their ability to deliver high quality performances is pivotal. This requires women to have access to professional theatre training and to (male) teachers like P. Rajagopal, who are willing to transfer their artistic skills and practices to female pupils aspiring to become professional performers (and potential competitors in the same field). The preparedness of male teachers to teach female students in the oral transmission mode from *guru* to *śisya* becomes all the more important when the aspirant performer has had no or little access to the tools of reading and writing. The following quote of drama actress, M. Shanmugavalli in conversation with Kattaikkuttu actor, P. Rajagopal illustrates this:

> I cannot read, sir. Therefore, I depend on the willingness of others to teach me. I will listen, even when they get impatient. It will bring me greatness.[9]

Rajagopal dropped out of the formal educational system at the age of 10 when he joined his father's company as a childactor. Based on his own experience, he recognised the importance of education for all—not only to round out the overall development of young performers, but also to sustain the institutionalised transmission of a theatre tradition. Ever since he had seen that other states had established centres for the transmission of their local language theatres,[10] it has been his dream to offer rural children and young people in Tamil Nadu access to professional training in Kattaikkuttu and comprehensive education under the same roof.

Kattaikkuttu Gurukulam

In 2002, Rajagopal founded the Kattaikkuttu Gurukulam. The Kattaikkuttu Gurukulam is administered by the Kattaikkuttu Sangam, an association of professional Kattaikkuttu performers

9. Video interview with M. Shanmugavalli, de Bruin and Rajagopal (2001).
10. For instance Kalamandalam in Cheruthuruthy, Kerala (established in 1930) and Yakshagana Kendra in Udupi, Karnataka (established in 1971).

(see also *www.kattaikkuttu.org*). The Gurukulam is the first-ever co-educational residential school where rural boys and girls (6-18 years) can learn Kattaikkuttu without having to give up their formal education. Its students hail from several different districts in the north of Tamil Nadu and, although this is not a condition for admission, come from disadvantaged backgrounds. Most of them spend between four and eight years at the school.

The Kattaikkuttu Gurukulam is at the cutting edge of tackling gender inequality, social disadvantage and the barriers that prevent rural girls and boys from making theatre their profession. It offers quality artistic training and academic inclusion, equips and empowers its students with important life skills and creates sustainable employment in the field of the performing arts. Being at the Gurukulam allows girls and boys to experience a period of adolescence—and its accompanying, often confusing, feelings of emerging sexuality and attraction between the genders. For rural girls in particular, this extension of their childhood is a bonus that allows them to explore their own identities and feelings. In the long run, we hope that it will help them to become clearer on their own value position and their fundamental right to take decisions. In contrast to rural boys, many rural girls still do not have the opportunity to experience a gradual transition into adulthood, because early marriage and motherhood cut short their teenage years.

Having opened up professional Kattaikkuttu training to girls, the Gurukulam deliberately challenges the dominance of men in Kattaikkuttu, not only in the field of professional performances, but also in the areas of direction and theatre management. As part of its artistic curriculum, workshops in theatre, physical movement, voice and other (performing) art forms take place conducted by (international) female and male guest teachers. These workshops have the aim to widen the artistic horizon of the students, introduce them to different ways of making theatre and stimulate them to value different aesthetics. In combination with new productions in which gender, gender roles and barriers to attain greater gender equality are explored, these workshops and the day-to-day operations of the Gurukulam have opened up ongoing and many-layered discussions—

intimate, face-to-face and more formal—about what it means for a rural girl to be on the stage as well as the (perceived) reasons why girls/women should/could or should/could not perform. These discussions involve pupils, teachers and support staff of the school, as well as parents, guardians, siblings and other family members of the children. They extend also to professional (male) Kattaikkuttu performers who are members of the Kattaikkuttu Sangam and rural male and female spectators watching the performances of the Young Professional Company. The Kattaikkuttu Young Professionals Company (KYPC) consists of senior students and graduates of the Kattaikkuttu Gurukulam. Set up in 2010 to provide hands-on performance experience to young performers of the Gurukulam, the KYPC is the first professional Kattaikkuttu theatre company with a mixed-gender cast.

What the Gurukulam tries to achieve through its empowerment of girls on and off the stage links up to a much wider debate that covers the position of girls and women in (rural) society. Central to this debate is a woman's freedom of choice—whether for a partner, a lifestyle, a (gendered) identity or a career in the performing arts. The involvement of girls and women in public performances continues to be seen as extremely problematic, not only in India, but in many other cultures, too. In Europe, acting began to be considered as a "respectable profession" only towards end of the 19th century (de Gay, 2003: 25-28). In rural Tamil Nadu, women's (sexual) autonomy and sexuality are perceived as the subjects of strict (patriarchal) control. As theatrical performances involve the display of the female body—and by extension the display of a performer's sexuality—on the public stage, acting by a woman continues to be identified as highly undesirable, if not disrespectful. The social stigma on female performers is reinforced by the context and conditions in which they are presented on the stage, the kind of roles they get to perform and the circumstances of their work (de Bruin, 2011: 16). In my fieldwork area, makeshift stages, open-air performances, the (un)availability of dressing rooms, seating arrangements close to the performers, performers' modes of transport, ways of costuming and conventional gesture and body language used on the stage, all had the potential of marking a performance as "low culture" and its practitioners as "dishonourable". As brought to the fore by Susan Seizer in her groundbreaking work on Special Drama actresses in Tamil Nadu,[11] transgressive double entendres by male performers and male spectators emphasise how dominant male performers disempower actresses on the stage.[12] These *asingam* (dirty/scandalous) remarks perpetuate the stigma on rural women performers. This ground reality undermines the status and rich potential of the Drama genre when it is kept alive by its own performers and their audiences. While the financial insecurity of male and female Drama and Kattaikkuttu performers might explain why they feel forced to play into the perceived need of male spectators for cheap (sexual) vulgarity, they do not seem to realise that they herewith confirm the label of "low culture" that the urban elite has attached to their profession and its artistic expressions.[13] It makes us realise how long the way to go still is, before Rajagopal's dream of ensuring that Kattaikkuttu and rural theatre in general, will become a dignified profession—for both men and women.

In 2008, the Gurukulam organised a "Family Day". The aim of the Day was to take yet another step in sensitising the parents/guardians of the students towards gender issues and inform them about future career options open to the pupils at the school. Through activities, brief (comic) performances about gender stereotypes and gender inequality and a public discussion with women who had settled as performers, the Kattaikkuttu Gurukulam hoped to contribute to a more informed idea among parents of the realities their daughters and sons would face once they left the school. The discussion also focused on the challenges and rewards that come with different work

11. Special Drama is found in the southern parts of Tamil Nadu; it is a genre akin to what is known as Drama or *Natakam* in north Tamil Nadu.

12. Seizer (2005), passim; interview with M. Shanmugavalli in de Bruin and Rajagopal (2001).

13. Many performers said that the need for implicit and explicit sexual jokes and for the show of physical violence, including the beating up of women characters on stage, was also an imitation of what the contemporary Tamil cinema has on offer. As concerns the students of the Kattaikkuttu Gurukulam, it is clear that the popular films provide an important example of positively-valued angry, masculine behaviour in the absence of other attractive role models (and often also in the absence of own fathers).

possibilities, including a career as a (Kattaikkuttu) performer. There is an ever-growing divide between the reality and expectations of and opportunities open to the rural poor and the urban and/or "educated" middle classes.[14] The Gurukulam felt it was important to make some of the differences in expectation and reality, in particular with regard to gender equality, education, job opportunities, clear to the families of its pupils. The latter find themselves caught between what they learn at the Gurukulam and what is demanded from them at home, with their parents often having the ultimate say over their future. The Family Day was vital in showing what the Gurukulam offers and encouraging a more long-term vision concerning the students' futures. It also was an attempt to convince the parents that the Kattaikkuttu Gurukulam is on their side and wants to work together with, and not against, them to build a more optimistic future for this young generation.

Kattaikkuttu Girls: Pioneers and New Role Models

As compared to their rural predecessors, the rural Devadasis and drama actresses, the Kattaikkuttu Girls are pioneers of a new kind.[15] Their access to institutionalised, co-educational artistic training and education appears to have boosted self-image and confidence of the girls, whilst successful performances have made them proud of being female Kattaikkuttu actors.

Somewhat ironically, the safe environment offered by the Kattaikkuttu Gurukulam seems to play a dual role: It allows for

14. This became apparent also during a performance by the Kattaikkuttu Gurukulam's All Girls Company at Rangashankara Theatre in Bangalore in 2010. The performance was preceded by a power point presentation which stated the challenges rural girls face, if they decide to train as a Kattaikkuttu actress. Many people in the urban middle-class audience appeared not to be aware of, and at times unable to relate to, these difficulties and the negative evaluation that the profession of actress receives.

15. From my fieldwork I came to know about the widespread tradition where young girls were dedicated through marriage to rural Goddesses. From the scant data I have been able to collect, it appears that the rural Devadasis custom was quite different from the custom where girls were dedicated to the male deities of *agamic* temples. The rural Devadasis were involved in song and dance performances for the deity. After their participation in these traditional, ritual performances became impossible as the result of the changing social and political system, some rural Devadasis became full-time actresses in companies comprising a large number or women performers (de Bruin, 2007, passim).

the sensitisation of girls and boys with regard to gender and gender equality within its own walls. It also provides a safe context for experimentation, for instance with a novel interpretation of traditional female roles and the casting of girls in male roles. However, many of the girl students do not seem to fully realise that the same might not be possible in the world outside, including their own homes. Only a few of the senior girls and young women graduates have begun to realise that they, as actresses on the public stage, challenge accepted gender roles and defy the socio-cultural image of women. This ideal image confines women to the domestic sphere—modest, chaste and dependent on and subservient to the males in their families, be it fathers, brothers or husbands. The young women's realisation of the complexity of their choice, if they were to become Kattaikkuttu actresses often came as a shock to them. It was triggered by negative judgements the girls had received at home and/or their exposure to negative comments outside the Gurukulam.[16]

In spite of the Gurukulam's efforts, the agency of adolescent rural girls/young women—and for that matter also of adolescent boys/young men—remains restricted and cannot grow without the approval and support of parents, grandparents, older siblings and fellow male students. Fearing social repercussions and difficulties in finding suitable marriage candidates, parents and siblings may not be supportive of their daughter's or sister's choice for a career in the performing arts. The desire to get access to higher paid, white collar jobs often results in students opting for further education, overriding an obvious talent and passion of the young person in question. Cultural convention makes it difficult for both girls/young women and boys/young men, to act against the wishes of their (older) family

---

16. In order to prove her own agency and acting skills, one of our graduate female students who is a highly talented actress employed as a junior teacher at the Gurukulam, decided to participate in the performances of a professional (all-male) theatre company over the 2014 summer holidays. Apparently, she did so with the approval of her mother, but without the approval of her father. The latter approached the Gurukulam asking it how she could have been allowed to perform in public in a company other than the Young Professionals Company. He did not realise that with the completion of her studies and artistic training, she, as a 20-year old, was no longer in the care of the Gurukulam. She was recalled home three days into her performances and was allowed to continue her job at the Gurukulam only on the condition that she would no longer "perform outside".

members. Violation of this convention is perceived as disobedience (*peccu ketka mattal/mattan*) and a blotch on the family's honour.

The senior-most Kattaikkuttu Girls started their training in the period 2002-2004 and, if not removed prematurely at the moment of attaining puberty or out of their own choice, graduated in 2010-2012.[17] The Kattaikkuttu Girls have a number of firsts to their name: they are the first educated young women to perform on stage together with male colleagues; they count among themselves the first ever female player of the *mukavinai* (a small oboe-like instrument that used to be the prerogative of males of the barber caste only), and they are the first Kattaikkuttu actresses to have travelled abroad to participate in an international youth-led theatre event in Liverpool, UK, in 2008.

The first female graduate of the Kattaikkuttu Gurukulam, P. Thilagavathi, is from a family of marginalised professional performers. Thilagavathi has successfully negotiated her performance career—shifting the boundaries of the possible back home from wanting to become a Kattaikkuttu musician to becoming a leading actress in the Kattaikkuttu Young Professionals Company. This is a significant move when one realises that the occupation of musician at that time appeared more acceptable to Thilagavathi's family than that of female performer. While a musician's position is static being seated on the musicians' bench centre backstage, an actress has to move on the stage. In doing so, she displays her body to the audience and, possibly, to the roving gaze of unknown male spectators.

The full embodiment that a live theatre performance requires remains one of its most stigmatising aspects, in particular when women are involved. The removal of the female body from view or substituting it through material objects are means by which performances of women performers have been "purified" and elevated to a higher status. Rai (2011: 123-33) has described how a

17. The term Kattaikkuttu Girls was introduced at a time when the Gurukulam had the possibility to run an All Girls Programme and an All Girls Theatre Company funded by Mama Cash. This enabled us to organise additional events focusing on girls and their specific problems, such as the Family Day, and productions featuring only girls. Ever since this funding has been aborted, the Gurukulam tries to achieve greater gender equality within its general educational and artistic activities.

skilled female folk singer of the Paddana genre in Tulunadu suddenly found recognition when her performances were broadcast. Limiting her performance to the recorded soundscape, which eliminated the physical presence of her (low caste, female) body, conferred greater prestige on to the performance and the performer. Lea Griebl and Sina Sommer (2011: 135-52) have illustrated how amateur women performers of the Siri Cult in Karnataka, often under pressure of male relatives, have opted out of performances in which they become possessed. Modern Kannada society has come to see the "uncontrolled" display of female bodies in public as an expression of "undesirable" and "abnormal" female behaviour. As a result, the number of female devotees participating in what is in essence a devotional practice has declined. Many of the women have substituted possession as a way of service to the Goddess with the disembodied, individualist service of gift giving or *kanike*.

Kattaikkuttu Girl, P. Thilagavathi featured in a contemporary dance performance, Mayakkam-Oxymore, which was part of the Bonjour India Festival 2010 and travelled with this performance to France. Mayakkam-Oxymore was a collaboration of Indian and French artists fusing different dance styles, movements and digital arts. Thilaga's contribution as a female dancer was inspired by the powerful movements and body language of Kattaikkuttu's heroic male characters. Together with storyteller Craig Jenkins, she devised a workshop focusing on Surpanakha, the character she performed in P. Rajagopal's *RamaRavana*, a critical re-interpretation of the Ramayana epic, commissioned by the Adishakti Ramayana Festival 2011. RamaRavana blended the Kattaikkuttu style of performance with elements taken from the Drama and rural Devadasi traditions. The production saw five of Rajagopal's talented girl-students in the leading roles of Sita, Lakshmana, Ravana, Hanuman and Rama. Recently, Thilagavathi has found employment as an after-school drama teacher with a Chennai-based NGO (non-governmental organisation), after completing a three-year long apprenticeship at the Kattaikkuttu Gurukulam.

Thilagavathi and her immediate successors, S. Tamilarasi and R. Mahalakshmi, have been/are leading actresses in the KYPC.

Tamilarasi has been invited for a residency at the Scuola Teatro Dimitri, a school for physical theatre in Switzerland. She hopes to acquire new theatre and teaching skills which she intends to use on returning to her artistic teaching job at the Kattaikkuttu Gurukulam. She also hopes to introduce the art of Kattaikkuttu, of which she feels she is a proud representative, to the world. The importance of the first Kattaikkuttu Girls as role models for the younger generation of girls in the Gurukulam cannot be sufficiently underscored. These young women have helped lowering the cultural and social barriers of women's access to the male domain of Kattaikkuttu. They have revealed that women can perform in a physically demanding style of theatre. They have helped to extend the period of time that girls are now allowed to continue their artistic training and public performances. Finally, we hope that the example they have set will make the choice of becoming/being a woman performer easier for the girls that follow them.

So far the Kattaikkuttu Gurukulam has addressed and overcome three major barriers: firstly, by attracting an increasing number of rural girls to the Kattaikkuttu theatre; secondly, by keeping them involved in artistic and academic training and performance after they have attained puberty; and thirdly, incorporating them into a professional mixed-gender Kattaikkuttu company en route to a professional career in the performing arts. The Kattaikkuttu Gurukulam started in 2002 with three girls (14%) out of a total of 21 students. The number of girl students escalated faster than we thought possible: since 2010, girls represent between 35 per cent and 45 per cent of the total student population of about 45-50 children. After initial traumatic experiences with girls being removed by their parents from the Gurukulam against their wishes upon reaching puberty, this has not happened recently. Girls come of age at the school and are allowed to continue their artistic training and education. Most of them are not even called home to undergo a series of rituals that mark their transition from girl to young woman.

When the first group of girls passed their 10th or 12th standard exams and completed eight years of artistic training, a fourth barrier to this ongoing experiment surfaced: to some parents, this educational achievement signalled that their daughters were able to do well educationally—education being the preferred explanation/excuse to justify to the outside world why these girls are at the Kattaikkuttu Gurukulam. It marked also the moment when pressure on the girls increased to give up performance in favour of further studies as a prerequisite for a 'decent' job and/or marriage. For the young women who did go on to perform, and who joined the Apprentice Programme of the Gurukulam, the questions arising soon, will be when, and for some perhaps, they want to get married and whether they will be able to continue their professional careers as actresses post-marriage.

We expected the setting up of a mixed gender Kattaikkuttu company to be much harder than it turned out to be. We believed that an All Girls Kattaikkuttu Company would be required as an intermediate step in the direction of a mixed gender ensemble. However, the mixed gender company took shape quite naturally and within a short time of the Gurukulam producing its first graduates in 2010. The huge success of the KYPC can be attributed to the powerful performances of its young performers, their high energy, acting qualities and professionalism and the attraction of new repertory written and directed by their mentor and guru, P. Rajagopal. However, it is in particular the presence of the Kattaikkuttu Girls, which makes the KYPC particularly sought after.

The reception by rural audiences of all-night performances by the KYPC has been quite remarkable. As compared to the performances by regular (all-male) Kattaikkuttu and Drama companies, those of the KYPC attract many more (women) spectators and children. On several occasions, individual women and a women's self-help group (SHG) have commissioned a performance. Women spectators said they had stopped attending regular Kattaikkuttu and Drama performances because of the increasingly lewd dialogues and sex jokes and the undisciplined behaviour of male spectators who were often under the influence of alcohol. Young men would whistle, walk across the stage and, on some occasions, refuse to heed to the warnings of older people and organisers of the performance not to disturb the play. Women said they preferred to stay indoors and watch TV serials to cope with their feelings of "bored-ness". Some of them considered this in-house entertainment more respectable than attending outdoor public performances. However, others were drawn to see the performances of KYPC—and the novelty of women performers in its cast—and some of them talked about their passion for the theatre and their desire to watch many more Kattaikkuttu performances. They said that the presence of girl performers provided them with an argument to convince their male relatives that they should be allowed to sit in a mixed gender audience and watch an all-night Kattaikkuttu performance.

Both male and female spectators appeared eager to see real women, instead of cross-dressed male performers, act Kattaikkuttu's principal female roles, including the characters of Draupadi, Draupadi disguised as Kuratti, Karna's wife Ponnuruvi, Subhadra, Gandhari and the other Kaurava queens. It was not entirely clear whether they found these roles now more "realistic" or—for the male spectators in particular—whether they were secretly drawn to the novelty of seeing female bodies in performance. However, the appearance of women in the physically demanding roles of *kattai veshams* had a special appeal for rural spectators. These roles demanded the acting out of typical heroic masculinity which, ironically, now had fallen into the hands of female performers. Many rural spectators found it hard to believe that women could do this and wanted to see a performance with their own eyes.

The audience volume and the demand for KYPC performances underline the ambiguous fascination of rural audiences with the new phenomenon of female Kattaikkuttu performers. It shows the readiness of rural spectators to accept women on the Kattaikkuttu stage—that is, as long as these women are not their own sisters, wives or mothers.

Reworking a Traditional Texts: Disrobing of Draupadi

The initiation of women performers in Kattaikkuttu has opened up multiple possibilities for new interpretations of female and male Kattaikkuttu characters and of dramatic themes looking at them from a woman's perspective. It has also enhanced the scope for the expression of emotions and viewpoints of the female dramatis personae and for working on the mise-en-scène and body language of female characters. Interpretation and direction are powerful instruments to subvert the stereotyping of female roles which so far have been performed by men, in addition to counteracting dominant norms and values regarding the culturally accepted performance of gender. Professional theatre training lends girls and young women access to the power that theatre represents. It allows them to hold the stage in front of a critical audience and to make their voices heard. This empowerment is another important reason why patriarchal societies have denied women access to acting and have attempted to make women performers invisible by, for instance, writing them out of the history of the legitimate stage.

Rajagopal's work with talented young women performers has stimulated him to rethink and reformulate parts of the traditional Kattaikkuttu repertory so as to bring out more clearly the voices of its female characters, in addition to creating new work (see also Rajagopal, 2014). He feels that some of the Kattaikkuttu Girls are his best students, and that, ironically, his tradition and his style of performance will continue through the female line.

In 2010, the KYPC produced a condensed version of the all-night play *Dice and Disrobing* (*Pakatai Tukil*). The Young Professionals performed a first version of this production at the Rangashankara Theatre in Bangalore. Later versions of the same play involving different actors were staged in March 2013 and again in March 2014.[18]

Dice and Disrobing is the *pièce de résistance* of the Kattaikkuttu repertoire. The multiple textual and dramatic layers offered by the traditional Kattaikkuttu text ensure that our engagement with it will remain work-in-progress for ever. The scene that I will elaborate upon below is the one where Duhsasana challenges Draupadi to come to the court. Upon her strong refusal to comply, he drags her by the

18. These later versions elaborated on Draupadi's troubling question (*Sanskrit Praśna* and *Tamil Valakku*) to the assembly of kings: Was she staked and lost before or after he (Dharma) lost himself? No body of the assembled kings speaks up, except for Vikarna, the youngest of the Kaurava brothers. This part of the play also served as a starting point for a corporate workshop focusing on the theme of speaking your mind freely and the consequences of speaking up.

hair from within the women's quarters into the assembly of kings. The verbal and physical exchange of the two protagonists prior to and during this hair-pulling scene takes the form of *tarkkams*—question-answer or debate songs. During the 2013 rehearsals for this scene, it became more and more clear that the text/meaning of Draupadi's songs and her movements—which were dictated by the traditional musical framework and mise-en-scène—were incongruent.

Draupadi's language in this play is quite explicit and she certainly does not willingly subjugate herself to Duhsasana's violence. Duhsasana, too, is not an indifferent recipient of Draupadi's insults in this heated scene. He purposefully challenges her when he addresses her sarcastically in a *viruttam* as "Respected Draupadi" (*matittu turaupadaiye*). Showing some of his own desire for her, he proceeds to ask her why she would shy away from the "love" of all the hundred-and-one when she already enjoys sexual relationships with five other men (her husbands). Draupadi retorts by calling him a "Foolish Brother-in-law", who addresses her without a grain of respect "as if he's been drinking." Duhsasana taunts her by describing how Draupadi's husband, "the famous son of Dharma", got engrossed in a game of dice in which he lost everything, including his four brothers, himself and his wife Draupadi. "He's shrunk to nothing. Come and see for yourself!", he challenges her. He tells Draupadi that she cannot change what is bound to happen. He will haul her in front of his older Brother, tame her, break her arrogance and put her to shame in front of the assembly.

Moving towards Duhsasana, still behind a hand-held curtain that separates her from him, Draupadi throws her hands across the curtain in a threatening and insulting gesture:

Draupadi's Song (ādi talam)

"Get going", you bray, "to the noble assembly (*vãrãy vãrãy enru*)
That hosted this shameful game of dice."
Would that be right for a woman like me?
Get out of my sight! (*pōtā*)

Draupadi's use of the impolite form *pōtā* to address her male opponent provides, as pointed out by the Kattiyãkkaran, an example of strong language that is underlined by insulting him through gestural language. Yet slowness of the melody and rhythm to which Draupadi's song is set, make it sound rather like a lament than a protest. In contrast, the traditional repertory offers Duhsasana here a fast-paced rhythm with which he, enraged, breaks through the curtain and grabs Draupadi by her long hair. In performance, Draupadi's hair is symbolised by an extended black rope attached on one side to the actor's own hair and on the other side to a stick which she clutches in her hand as convention forbids Duhsasana from touching his female protagonist physically. The cord limits Draupadi's movements and freedom on the stage—she is "caught" and cannot run away; it forces the actress to bend over deeply while bending her head sideways. Keeping one hand on the rope she has little other option than to subject to the movements of Duhsasana who drags her across the stage and makes her pirouette around him.

The body language of the performers creates a strong visual impression of Duhsasana's power and masculinity and Draupadi's subjugated position. Her song as well as Duhsasana's sung response, are in *tirupatai talam,* and the *adavus* (dance steps) used by the two performers are quite complex. This sequence uses a choreography that confines and restricts Draupadi's movements and, therefore, her agency. If not totally pre-empting, it does dampen her protest against Duhsasana's violent and humiliating treatment of her. In contrast to Draupadi's body language—bent over with her head to a side—her sung text remains as forceful as before when she calls Duhsasana a "bastard" (*pāvi*) and threatens him that he will pay for his misbehaviour with his life:

Draupadi's Song

Let go of my hair, bastard!
If my husbands come to know
Of your misbehaviour
You will pay for it with your life!

In Rajagopal's reworked version, Draupadi, performed by S. Tamilarasi, reacts strongly to the violence meted out to her by Duhsasana played by M. Greenkumar. Tamilarasi is a powerful and very physical actress. She graduated from the Kattaikkuttu Gurukulam in 2012 and now works as an apprentice and junior theatre teacher at the school. Tamilarasi has also performed the role of Duhsasana. She is, therefore, aware of its content and standard interpretation. Different workshops at the Gurukulam, and Rajagopal's direction, have helped her look at the role of Draupadi from a gendered perspective. Already during the curtain entry she, as Draupadi, visually acts on and reacts to Duhsasana's show of virility and his improper demand to escort her to the assembly of kings. Her facial expression and her strong body language clearly tell him to keep his distance. At this moment in the performance, she is still separated from Duhsasana by a curtain (*tirai*). The curtain symbolises the invisible border between the inner apartments of Gandhari, Draupadi and the other royal women and the unnamed outside where Duhsasana finds himself. In contrast to all-male theatre companies, the curtain is held here by two women performers. This ensures a greater female presence on stage and offers a degree of protection to Draupadi as long as she manages to remain within the imagined women's quarters.

Forcing his entry into this domain—which he probably is allowed to do as Gandhari's son—Duhsasana chases Draupadi around and underneath the curtain. The two girl students holding the curtain move in sync with Draupadi while turning the curtain 360 degrees (in both directions) keeping her on the inside while Duhsasana tries to catch her. Ensuring a moment of comic relief in the building tension that characterises this scene, the Kattiyãkkaran counteracts Duhsasana's wild chase by getting in between him and Draupadi. Blinded by a combination of anger and desire, Duhsasana mistakes the Kattiyãkkaran for Draupadi and embraces the clown. Duhsasana's embrace is a blend of fury and lust. Thus the clown's action seems to comment indirectly on the fact that Duhsasana's reactions cannot be reduced to unmediated anger only, but also involve his (sexual) desire for Draupadi. While the performers seem to be aware of the erotic aspect of Duhsasana's relationship to Draupadi, cultural inhibitions and age make it difficult, if not impossible, for the young female and male actors of the Kattaikkuttu Gurukulam to bring their own sexuality and desires into play.

When Duhsasana slits away the curtain with his sword, Draupadi attempts to escape creating a distance between herself and her opponent that visually strengthens their opposition. It takes Duhsasana sometime before he can get hold of Draupadi's "hair", symbolised by the black cord. Once he has done so, he restrains Draupadi holding her in a tight grip and bending her head and body sideways while forcing her, at the end of the song, to kneel in front of him. In a conventional performance, the actor impersonating Draupadi usually surrenders to Duhsasana immediately and without protest. However, in the following sequence, Tamilarasi moving backward opts to follow Duhsasana's lead, but then surprises him by suddenly moving forward. Duhsasana is taken aback and Draupadi uses his momentary alarm to regain her liberty. The two performers now slowly move around each other on stage, creating a much more loaded and threatening atmosphere than the traditional "close-hold" scene does. And Duhsasana has to go to a much greater extent to try and catch his unwilling victim again.

The length of the cord by which Duhsasana holds Draupadi by her "hair" leaves little distance between the performers. It forces them to collaborate closely whilst they need to create for the spectators the opposite image of struggle and resistance. When Duhsasana "swings" Draupadi by her hair, this entails mirroring sets of *adavus* (steps) from both performers—one moving backward and the other moving forward. Duhsasana is instrumental in letting Draupadi pirouette around him by holding the cord high and swinging her underneath it. This requires considerable agility on the part of the performer playing Draupadi as well as care on the part of the actor playing Duhsasana as to not unbalance his opposite number. Rajagopal is persistent that his actors should not strain the rope that binds them: the subtlety of this scene lies in conveying the powerful emotions experienced by both these epic characters through a stylised acting out of violence—that is without allowing these emotions to erupt into real anger and physically violence. While the powerful text of Draupadi's songs does not match the traditional body and movement language, it is possible that the rather slow, atypical rhythm and the choice of *ragas* used in this scene help to contain the emotions unleashed here from having "real" and violent consequences.

Conclusion

The Kattaikkuttu Gurukulam brings under the same roof education, gender and theatre—not as three separate fields but as parts of a holistic whole. The full achievement of the Gurukulam's aims is a long- term process with a closer collaboration between the arts and formal educational along with gender-equality practiced as an integral part of the curriculum. At this moment in time, it also requires a more whole-hearted support from the government, which needs to ensure that quality education and professional artistic training in a theatre that rural people consider their own cultural heritage, will be accessible to rural, disadvantaged children and young people. Training in the performing arts can act as a powerful tool to bring about greater gender equality, bodily awareness, the confidence to speak and act in public, collaboration with others, and to stimulate girls to think critically and independently about one's self and one's right to choose and take important decisions. Instead, the rigidity of the legal system appears to provide barriers rather than support to the work of the Gurukulam. Recent guidelines with regard to the care and protection to girl students, for instance, carry the risk of accomplishing an artificial separation between the genders and placing even normal contact between girls and boys in a suspicious light.[19]

The Kattaikkuttu Gurukulam experiment is about stretching the boudaries of social norms, attitudes and (artistic) imagination in order to break the stigma on female performers, make the rural performing arts more inclusive by providing talented rural women performers with the opportunity to express themselves artistically and act on a par with men. The groundbreaking work of the Kattaikkuttu Gurukulam at the frontier of social and cultural experimentation has created ambitious (and at times ambiguous)

19. These well-intentioned guidelines were issued in June 2014, following the rape of two young girls living in a private hostel, catering to the needs of the disadvantaged.

expectations for social change among its students and teachers. Even though some of the Kattaikkuttu Girls strive to gain unconventional freedoms and economic independence, their position within their own families and within rural society at large is not an easy one. Their choice to become women performers is not accepted without problems. In order to realise a successful career in the performing arts and wrest themselves from situations of perpetuating and debilitating poverty and dependence, they need to be exceptionally motivated, focused, critical, independent, courageous, and (socially) smart. Above all, they require, like P. Thilagavathi and S. Tamilarasi, initiative and negotiation skills to mediate their own choices *versus* the aspirations that their families have for them.

The Kattaikkuttu Gurukulam is also about facilitating rural girls and women in this complex mediation process so as to augment their freedom of choice and (artistic) expression and make their voices heard on as well as off the stage. This process involves the long-term process of shifting the artistic boundaries of a traditional theatre in order to make its performances representative of/for the different genders, aesthetically pleasing, powerful, meaningful, dignified and economically viable for women and men.

Gender in Performance

With the entry on stage of young women trained in Kattaikkuttu, the need to have a closer look at the depiction of female and male characters in the traditional repertory became immediate. Song texts and prose passages (*vacanam*) of female characters, traditionally spoken by men, often take on a different meaning when sung or said by a woman performer, even if she does not change a single word in the text.

In the second part of this essay, I have tried to capture some of the experimental changes that have taken place under the direction of P. Rajagopal in the performance of the "hair-pulling scene" in the traditional Kattaikkuttu play *Pakatai Tukil*. The challenge Rajagopal and his actors had set themselves was to create a greater scope for Draupadi to express her feelings and register her resistance; to make her onstage presence more "truthful" to the persona that the powerful traditional Kattaikkuttu song-text implies she is or should be; and to provide her with agency and not diminish her at the hands of Duhsasana.

Keeping the song-text intact (as it is difficult for a traditional performer to touch upon this part of the tradition that has been transmitted by previous *vattiyars*), they worked on creating a greater balance in the stand-off between Draupadi and Duhsasana. Through direct eye contact with her opponent (instead of evading the male gaze) and providing a greater focus to the direction of gestures and body language, the actress performing Draupadi (re-)appropriated space for her character. Her reacting on Duhsasana's violent conduct (rather than putting up with it) created opportunities where both performers would be temporarily released from the tight grip in which the hair-pulling scene engages them. The distance thus created offered a visual image quite different from that of a subjugated woman at the hands of a furious man, in addition to conveying a greater menace through the gaze and the movement of both performers when they faced and encircled each other. It also allowed the actor performing Duhsasana to bring into his acting other emotions than anger alone.

Information about historical performances of the hair-pulling scene in *Pakatai Tukil* is scarce. It seems reasonable to assume that the powerful songs and *viruttams* used by Draupadi in *Pakatai Tukil* in her response to Duhsasana are more or less the same as those used three or four generations ago. As seen above, the song-text depicts Draupadi as a forceful woman who refuses to be cowed down, a lady who dares to ask questions. It is, therefore, difficult to ascertain how "traditional" the subdued visual image is of Draupadi that is presented in current performances by all-male Kattaikkuttu companies. The depiction of epic characters, in particuar when these aqcuire a divine status, is subject to changing social and religious norms. Draupadi's outspoken character, her violent warrior identity as well as the demonic character traits she is said to possess have increasingly become to be seen as undesirable for the canonised and Brahmanised goddess Draupadi Amman in the present modern rural society (de Bruin 1999: 321). The contradiction between the ferocious warrior Goddess and her subdued Parvati-like avatar, which is arguably closer to the stereotyped ideal of the "good woman", is reflected in the discrepancy between the traditional performance text and the ways in which today's male Kattaikkuttu performers tend to interpret this text taking into account the expectations of contemporary village audiences. Let's hope that Draupadi's next incarnation will have her emerge from the fire of Kattaikkuttu Gurukulam with her warrior identity intact.

References

Brubaker, Richard L. (1979). "Barbers, Washermen, and Other Priests: Servants of the South Indian Village and its Goddesses", in *History of Religions* 19(2): 128-52.

Heidrun Brückner, Hanne M. de Bruin and Heike Moser (eds.) (2011). *Between Fame and Shame: Performing Women: Women Performers in India.* Wiesbaden (Germany): Otto Harrassowitz Verlag.

de Bruin, Hanne M. (1999). *Kattaikkuttu: The Flexibility of a South Indian Theatre Tradition.* Gonda Indological Studies Volume VII. Groningen (The Netherlands): Egbert Forsten.

———. (2001). Seagull Theatre Quarterly 31 (September 2001) on "Hybrid Theatres in India". Ed. and introduced by Hanne M. de Bruin. Calcutta (India): The Seagull Foundation for the Arts.

———. (2007). "Devadasis and Village Goddesses of North Tamil Nadu", in Heidrun Brückner, Elisabeth Schömbucher and Philip B. Zarrilli (eds.), *The Power of Performance: Actors, Audiences and Observers of Cultural Performances in India.* New Delhi: Manohar. pp.53-83.

———. (2011). "Contextualising Women and Performance in India: An Introductory Essay", in Heidrun Brückner, Hanne M. de Bruin & Heike Moser (eds.), *Between Fame and Shame: Performing Women—Women Performers in India.* Wiesbaden (Germany): Otto Harrassowitz Verlag. pp.11-35.

Bruin, Hanne M. de and P. Rajagopal (2001). *In Their Own Words: The Unheard History of the Rural Tamil Stage as Told by Four of its Professional Exponents.* Interviews on video. Leiden: International Institute for Asian Studies.

Chatterjee, Partha (1993). *The Nation and its Fragments: Colonial and Postcolonial Histories.* Princeton, New Jersey: Princeton University Press.

de Gay, Jane (2003). "Naming Names: An Overview of Women in the Theatre, 1500-1900", in Lizbeth Goodman with Jane de Gay. (eds.), *The Routledge Reader in Gender and Performance.* London, New York: Routledge. pp.25-28.

Grieble, Lea and Sina Sommer (2011). "Siri Revisited: A Female 'Mass Possession Cult' without Women Performers?", in Heidrun Brückner, Hanne M. de Bruin & Heike Moser (eds.), *Between Fame and Shame: Performing Women—Women Performers in India.* Wiesbaden (Germany): Otto Harrassowitz Verlag. pp.135-52.

Krishna, T.M. (2013). *A Southern Music: The Karnatic Story.* Noida (India): Harper Collins Publishers.

Lal, Ananda (ed.) (2004). *The Oxford Companion to Indian Theatre.* New Delhi: Oxford University Press.

Rai, Viveka B.A. (2011). "Gender in Folk Narratives with Special Reference to Tuluva Society, in the West Coast Region of Karanataka, India", in Heidrun Brückner, Hanne M. de Bruin & Heike Moser (eds.), *Between Fame and Shame: Performing Women—Women Performers in India.* Wiesbaden (Germany): Otto Harrassowitz Verlag. pp.11-35.

Rajagopal, P. (2014). *Paarkdatal, Vituttal, Raamaravanaa. Three Kuttu Texts.* Chennai: Kalachuvadu Publishers.

Seizer, Susan (2005). *Stigmas of the Tamil Stage: Ethnography of Special Drama Artists in South India.* Durham, London: Duke University Press.

7

A. MANGAI

Staging Feminist Consciousness

Voicing Silence

Theatre is one of the crucial contexts in and through which feminist political ideas are played out. Apart from public protests against violence and the mobilisation of women on the streets, this period, from the late 1970s, saw consciousness-raising efforts organised in different parts of the country. The idea was to rethink politics as pedagogy, and for newly emergent women's groups this meant both unlearning and relearning ways of thinking about the self, family, community and the world. Much of this learning and relearning evolved in and through practical work sessions, which were guided by teaching modules developed by peer educators across the world, especially where anti-race and anti-class ideas were in circulation. Training programmes used games and activities, in short, performative skills, to elicit information. As far as women's groups and feminist activism were concerned, 'performing' in public to raise public consciousness of particular issues has remained a staple since that time. In the world of theatre, the times pushed many of us to re-examine our work, and, while some of us connected with women's groups and worked with them in their campaigns using our theatre skills and putting our feminist concerns on board, others came to do theatre with an explicit focus on women's experience from a feminist perspective.

Voicing Silence, a unique effort at gendered theatre that acted as a catalyst in the process of women's awareness and empowerment, began as a project of M.S. Swaminathan Research Foundation (MSSRF) in 1992. It was initiated with the objective of giving "voice to the voiceless" and theatre was the primary medium of its interventions. It aimed to address women's empowerment through women's theatre. Gender, culture and social activism are the three major concerns of Voicing Silence. It has combined three main strands of work such as: (a) Developing plays on women issues or from a feminist perspective, (b) Organising collective sharing of experiences or women's theatre festivals, bringing together cultural workers, theatre persons, social activists and NGOs (non-governmental organisations, and (c) Working with different communities of women, supporting them to use theatre as a tool for self-expression and empowerment.

In *We Were Making History*, the editorial team (Lalitha and Tharu, 1989) says, "Women's history, then, is an intervention: its intent more political than archival. It is an assertion that women have a history, although that history has been distorted, even erased by the biases that pervade our culture and our scholarship." They were referring to Telengana struggle within a specific region, during a particular moment in the history of the new nation called India. The same can be applied with varying degrees to almost all aspects of participation of women in public sphere. In the case of theatre, the problem is much more complex, since it is ephemeral even for those who participate; its production process is as varied as there are groups; it is regional and therefore local; and rarely can the experience of theatre be repeated with the same momentum, cast and audience response. While this is true of all theatrical experience, the question of gender most often does not figure as a criterion at all, unless one zeroes in on it consciously or is led by a consciousness that considers gender as central to any aspect of life, including theatre.

Attempts have been made to bring gender and theatre in focus by many academicians and a few practitioners [Subramanyam (2002), Mukherjee (2005), Singh and Mukherjee (2013), some earlier volumes *STQ* and *Theatre India*). Very rarely have they made the connection between the efforts of women playwrights, artists and directors to the women's movement. And this trend is mutual. Rarely do we find women's movements of various shades acknowledging the contribution of performance. Uma Chakravarti (2012) records how the issues of dowry and rape were major preoccupations of the 1980s and how "the process of addressing the politics of social change itself created a new imperative both in thinking critically about culture and in finding ways of intervening in the practice of culture and in democratising it (Chakravarti, 2012)." She also brings out the struggle Anuradha Kapur and Maya Rao had faced in Miranda House as students to perform "relevant plays, moreover in Hindi". There was uproar when Anuradha translated Gorky's *Mother* and Maya Rao did the lead role.

With such democratic impulses and the enthusiastic improvisations of the women in Stree Sanghatana, Om Swaha a play performed by women as street theatre in Delhi to tackle the dowry issue was poignant, analytical, and after repeated re-workings of the end, even hopeful of bringing about change in society."[1]

It is this nexus between the women's movement and the role of women in cultural production that I would like to focus on with Voicing Silence as a case in point.

My discussion is classified into three major aspects in terms of content: creating alternate images of women, also corresponding to three stages of the work of Voicing Silence foregrounding sexuality as a crucial aspect of understanding gender and mobilising the feminist consciousness at work in the realm of theatre. These three aspects seem to have geared the course of Voicing Silence and also fashioned our formal aspects. The narrative I put forth is however not chronological, neither does it claim to be complete.[2]

Creating Alternate Images

Alternate images of women from one's own history were seen as the need of the hour. Countering the arguments of feminism as a Western import and retracing the steps of our fore-mothers were the two major concerns that pushed us into this journey. Staging the life story of Manalur Maniamma was the initial effort that brought Mina and I together. She was fresh in Chennai, having moved from

---

1. Eugene Van Irwen has documented the beginnings of feminist activist theatre. But there are factual controversies in his narrative.
2. I would like to place on record the conversations between Mina Swaminathan and I while working on this paper; the intense emotions of the re-lived moments and her painstaking effort to make this paper come to its present shape.

Delhi. I was an All India Democratic Women's Association (AIDWA) cadre trying to do a play for the State Conference at Nagappattinam with and for the attending delegates. The rehearsals were in the Party office at Perambur. Hours of waiting for the group to assemble, being exhausted after a campaign to mobilise funds or people, as well as completing their household work often unaided by men, most of them in their late thirties and forties from backgrounds that did not ensure stable health conditions, did not deter her from helping us put the first version of the play together.

Therefore, when Voicing Silence took off, we wanted to redo that play with another group. *Chuvadugal* was born thus in 1994. We kept the structure of the play as we did in AIDWA. The scenes were re-worked to bring out the energy of the protagonist. Maniamma, a Brahmin girl from Thanjavur, widowed at the age of nine, moved on to join Congress and later, the Communist Movement in the 1940s. Disillusioned with the Party, she assimilated the Periyarist ideals of caste annihilation and self-respect, and died mysteriously hit by a pet deer brought up in a landlord's farm. She died at a time when the party had not elected her as a delegate for the district conference at Tiruvarur. Her funeral became a procession of the party conference delegates in homage to Amma, as she was referred to by people in the area. She had cut her hair short, wore a *dhoti* and *banyan* with a red towel thrown around her shoulders, rode a bicycle, mastered the martial art of *Silampam*[3] and avidly read party literature and Periyar's writings. Rajam Krishnan, one of the major progressive writers in Tamil, has written a novel based on her life entitled *Paathaiyil Patintha Adigal*. We also did fieldwork to collect the stories of people in and around the area in Thanjavur. Rukmani Ammal, her young friend, was a member of the Communist Party and lived in Chennai at that time.[4] Of course, there is no portrait/photo of Maniamma in the Party office in Thanjavur, and rarely do the leaders mention her.

---

3. *Silampam* is a martial art of Tamil Nadu performed with bamboo sticks. It is a self-defence form.

4. NSR or Rukmani Ammal, as she was referred to, was a mentor to me. Her life story is yet to be written. Part of her early life and decisions about her intimacy with Com. Natarajan has been dealt with in Kamala Visweswaran's *Feminist Ethnography*.

Yet she lives on in the narratives of oral lore. And remains till date an inimitable woman yet to be explored. This play is one of the most favourite ones for both of us.

The issue of representation posed a challenge to us. Theatrically, we did not want to visualise Maniamma as a heroine of sorts. We wanted to emphasise that her spirit is latent in all of us. The story unfolded as a ballad with as many as six people taking on the role of Maniamma in different scenes, signified by her red towel and dhoti on stage. While we did the AIDWA conference production, this technique was considered to be too confusing in an otherwise inspiring narrative. But we were determined to have her role played by many actors. We used the songs sung by the agricultural workers of the region, which document Maniamma's death. We also used contemporary songs on Dalit resistance composed by Makkal Kalai Ilakkiya Kazhagam.[5] The most significant one was the song on cycling that became popular in Pudukkottai district, a neighbouring district of Thanjavur that was an offshoot of Arivoli Iyakkam (Literacy Movement). So, the play was representing Maniamma, yet with a contemporary resonance written over her life.

Other alternative images of women were gleaned from Tamil classical literature. I have written elsewhere about how the Babri Masjid demolition and the communal clashes that followed shook the sensibility of those who believed in democracy. For me, now, it was a questioning of the use of Hindu myths that provided scope to question patriarchy in theatre. I was searching for an alternate resource to build a critique of patriarchal notions of womanhood.

Classical Tamil texts proved to be a major reservoir of such resources. Inquilab, a major progressive poet of Tamil Nadu and a Tamil Professor, initiated the whole journey. *Avvai*, the first play, was a find in many ways. It retold the story of Avvai, popularly depicted as an old, wise woman, almost saintly, who developed a moral code in poetry, and is still taught to school children in Tamil Nadu. Exploring her history, we focused instead on the Sangam period when she was

5. Makkal Kalai Ilakkiya Kazhagam is the cultural front of one of the Marxist-Leninist groups in Tamil Nadu. They were very active in composing and disseminating songs of protest and resistance on contemporary political issues in the 1990s.

a sensuous young woman, yet led a community of bards as a skilful composer and singer of ballads. I have documented in detail our process of working on *Avvai* (2000) and the impact of our questioning of the popular image.

So I would like to focus on Manimekalai, a courtesan-turned-Buddhist-nun in the Tamil epic by the same name, written by the poet Sathanar, exploring the intricate relationship between caste and gender. The twin epics in *Tamil Silappadhikaram* and *Manimekalai* represent Jain and Buddhist thoughts, respectively. In the former, we have a merchant prince Kovalan, marrying Kannagi; leaving her enamoured by the courtesan Madhavi. Kovalan and Madhavi have a daughter named Manimekalai. When Kovalan returns to his wife and the couple move to Madurai for establishing their life, Kovalan is wrongly murdered; Kannagi seeks vengeance on the Pandya king and the city of Madurai. Kannagi is therefore the icon of chastity and is invoked often in Tamil Nadu political contexts as a symbol of Tamil Woman. Madhavi, on the other hand, has her daughter to bring up; also she detests her courtesan life. She joins a Buddhist convent along with her daughter.

Manimekalai is sought after by the Prince Udhayakumaran. She oscillates between sexual desire and the norms of a Buddhist nun. She is protected by numerous goddesses at different points in the epic. Finally she acquires the never-empty *Akshaya Pathra*—or *Amudha Surabhi*—out of which she feeds the poor and hungry.

What is most interesting is that the play was performed by professional female stage artists from in and around Kanchipuram area. The group consisted of 12 women, most of them bound by kinship ties and ranging from 17-70 years of age. Only four of them could read and write. Since childhood, they had worked with a form of popular musical performance tradition known as *Isai Natakam* (or Special Drama). While they remain familiar with older plays, they perform them very rarely. Over the years their form has mutated into something called 'novels', a form specific to northern Tamil Nadu. These are stories as well as tales of kings and queens interspersed with song and dance sequences. Music, both songs and musical delivery (of dialogue), is common to both forms.

I wanted to experiment with a story that was not part of the traditional *Isai Natakam* repertoire, but which, like other stories, possessed an epic context. Further, *Isai Natakam* exponents are familiar with the *Kovalan Kathai* based on the story of Kannagi—and written and performed by the legendary Sankaradas Swamigal in the early 20th century—and therefore I did not consider my drawing on the sister epic, *Manimekalai* as anomalous. The crucial difference though was the status of the central character that refuses love as well as courtesanship and instead chooses to become a *bhikkuni*. This was completely unexpected and new in the context of *Isai Natakam*, as were a few other elements, such as the reinterpretation of Buddhism as a liberatory faith in the modern sense and as interpreted by B.R. Ambedkar and Periyar.

This team of women had been trained in Koothu by Rajagopal in 1997.[6] The 1997 *Kulavai* workshop (discussed later in this paper) created a space and context for them to speak of their lives as performers, especially its everyday material aspects and examined women's contribution to theatre. In the course of and following the workshop, the women artists who had learned koothu from Perungattur Rajagopal, worked with Gunasekaran on *Isai Natakam* form. They also worked on their music, with a Madurai-based senior musician.

Voicing Silence started working with them during off-season, 1998 onwards. Two plays were directed respectively by Gunasekaran and Vengadesan[7] with this group in 2000 and next, we did *Manimekalai* with the group. The group consisted of women who performed for a living. They were trained in a specific form called *Isai Natakam* that uses music as the primary mode of rendering. Although they had

---

6. P. Rajagopal has founded the Kattai Koothu School in Punjarasanthangal, which is a history in the making. Please refer chapter 5 of this volume by Hanne M. de Bruin.

7. Prof K.A.Gunasekaran works in the Sankaradas Swamigal School of Performing Arts, Central University, Pondicherry. He began as a folk singer and Dalit activist in the Communist Party of India (CPI) and Communist Party of India (Marxist) (CPM) circles. Vengadesan is a member of the group called 'Aazhi'. He was student of the Drama school in Pondicherry and continues to be active in theatre till date.

begun with Sankaradas Swamigal's[8] repertoire of plays, when they settled in the northern parts of Tamil Nadu, they began to be part of a form called 'Novels'. Their range of skills was amazing, and could perform male roles with ease and power. Their acrobatic skills enable them to play comic roles in abandon—something which they rarely had opportunity to do.

Among the several memorable plays that we did with this group was a comedy called *Pavalakodi Alladhu Kudumba Vazhakku* based on Arjuna as a lover with a roving eye, and his multiple wives, and Krishna being an accomplice in all these adventures. Mina Swaminathan recalls in her personal communication how,

> this emerged from a workshop of improvisations with the women, using material drawn from their regular performances, and was their own creation, with some involvement from us. It was then scripted and directed by K.A. Gunasekharan. This hilarious comedy was a roaring success, showing that traditional arts could be a success in an elite urban milieu. Unfortunately, it later became an ugly controversy when our collaborator claimed copyright! We had to extricate ourselves from this unexpected complication.

After about four years, this experiment with the traditional women artists could not continue.[9]

---

8. Sankaradas Swamigal (1867-1922) is a pioneer of Early Modern Theatre, which was a combination of mythological plays, back curtains and accompanying musical instruments. He also formed Boys' Companies, a unique feature of Tamil theatre history.

9. Realising that they did not have enough scope for their skills in their own milieu, although they could scrape together enough to support their families as chief breadwinners, and also recognising that they could not survive on occasional urban performances organised by us, we tried to arrange a compromise by suggesting to their regular company manager/ agent to start a women's company in which these women played all roles (as is normally done in all-male companies without anyone turning a hair). He accepted our suggestion, thinking perhaps that it might be a new way to attract audiences. Alas, the women's company had to fold up in about a year, as the regular rural audiences were still unprepared to accept women playing all parts. Similarly, Rajagopal, who had trained them in *koothu* tried to absorb them in regular performances. In his famous one-night *Mahabharata*, in which more than 50 actors from several companies took part, he included several of these women. Interestingly, in all the scenes where male-female partners were involved, he cast all these women in the male roles, and the men as their female partners. All of them being consummate actors, they brought this off brilliantly, but it was never to be repeated. Hence this turned out to be one of our many experiments that could not take off; but we tried nevertheless.

In 2001, when these women heard the story of Manimekalai, they totally identified with her urge to escape from the courtesan tradition and also her spiritual quest to appease the hunger of those who suffer from the same. So, Inquilab's text was re-written with songs in the traditional style by A.K. Selvadurai. The epic, replete with branch stories, magical creatures and Buddhist philosophical tenets on rebirth came alive in the popular theatre form, transforming us to the turn of the 20th century. Considering that only four women in the group could read and write, the musical mode helped them learn their lines through means that were familiar to them: listening and rote learning. It was heartwarming to get an invitation from Tirutthani Murugan temple for a performance of this play during their annual festival. The Hindu temple hosted a show on this Buddhist epic and the audience received it with warmth.

Scholars of early Buddhism and Tamil literature have pointed out how *Manimekalai*, the epic, portrays the aspects of gender and spirituality: (a) it recognised the right of women to join the *sangha*; (b) Forced the *sangha* to recognise women's right to be leaders; (c) Advocated that a woman can develop her own personality and individuality independent of any male support; (d) Broke the myth of family and male children; and (e) Privileged women's education. The best part was that Manimekalai did all these within the literary conventions of Tamil tradition. Paulo Richman explains how the protagonist, a Buddhist nun, gives rice, not receive it; and in so doing, she combines celibacy of the renouncer while upholding the practice of a devoted laywoman. Unlike the epic proportions of characters in Greek, Tamil epics deal with the *Vanigar/Ganika*, and the rulers as titular. It is not accidental that the twin epics have female protagonists. The number of female characters in *Manimekalai* should throw light on the universe peopled by women from different walks of life: Chithrapathi, Madhavi, Vasanthamalai—Ganika; Sudhamathi, a Brahmin woman given asylum in the Buddhist convent after her endless travails; Kayasandikai, a Gandharva cursed with unending hunger until Manimekalai feeds her; Athirai, whose chastity entitles her to give the first morsel of rice to Manimekalai; and the queen. There are also many female deities: mother-goddesses who provide the directions to Manimekalai—Sambapathi tells her that her teachings are different from what the Vedic Brahmins preach; Sindha Devi tells her the story of the magic vessel—*amudha surabhi*; Deeva Thilagai teaches her to eradicate hunger, and Manimekala goddess leads her to many journeys.

Manimekalai also does not initially project the heroine as a nun who is tonsured. In fact, it appears only after she establishes her argument contending with other schools of thought, guided by Aravana Adigal. In many ways, *Manimekalai* tries to present a sexuality that is sublimated to mothering thousands of people. The peak of Manimekalai is the way she combines appeasing physical hunger with changing the consciousness of people condemned as criminals. She experiences imprisonment and torture, and yet stands up for justice against the State.

Manimekalai questions caste stratification by leaving her traditional *ganika* conventions of dance, which also make women sexually available to the powers-that-be. Aputhiran in the epic openly questions the caste practices of exclusion, notions of purity and pollution and the hierocracies of the Brahminical forces. Apart from working on her own self-realisation, she extends both charity—feeding the hungry—and *gnana*—changing the consciousness of prisoners through goodwill and trust. Above all, she defends herself against torture and fights for justice.

Interpreting and drawing contemporary connections of *Manimekalai* by social movements is not new in the Tamil context. In the 1930s, Tamizh Pathugappu Kazagam (Tamil Protection Society), a lesser known social movement, published the Aputhiran story of the epic as a separate booklet. And it is commonly quoted when discussions on prison reforms are held. What became a new aspect in this production was the focus on Manimekalai's renunciation and her yearnings for Udayakumaran, the prince—her husband in her previous birth—as an existential dilemma. It also poetically shows how she sublimates her sexual desire by feeding the hungry: "She walks as a river-/converting thousand breasts into *amudha surabhis*/ she walks;/with the warmth of blood, and coolness of the spring waters/she walks as a river." *Manimekalai* provided a trope to explore spirituality and sexuality; address caste and gender variables; and also embodied the ethics of care.

Foregrounding Sexuality

Desire as a significant component of feminist politics has always been a contested terrain, while violence as a rallying point has been easy to articulate in public in a way desire was not. The turn of the millennium in India saw the rise of sexuality as a major rallying point. Women's movements had initial hesitations (some of them still do). LGBTQ (lesbian, gay, bisexual, transgender, queer) movements with or without feminist politics began to mobilise their own communities for basic rights. Voicing Silence had begun the debate with its play *Pani Thee* (Frozen Fire) based on the Amba-Shikandin myth about masculinity and femininity as constructs. The original play and its production with Usha Rani performing the main role used two modes of performance—*Koothu*, a martial and male-dominated form, and *Isai Natakam*. The queer consciousness fell into place when we started working with a group of transgenders who wished to form their own cultural group.

There were other important differences between these and earlier activist theatre groups; the composition of the groups, for one, and therefore their sense of what they were doing. Since the actors were themselves 'stigmatised' people, they did not seek to convert or mobilise the ones 'out there' so much as speak about themselves, and call attention to what they were and what they endured. The tone of their presentations was also quite unlike that of consciousness-raising activist theatre, almost as if they were bearing witness to a marginality no one wished to acknowledge; and finally, the themes were different too, since many were overtly concerned with 'taboo' subjects centreing on the body and bodily practices. Perhaps the most startling feature of this theatre had to do with the way 'representation' came to mean 'embodiment' in a novel sense, for the bodies on stage were not 'playing' non-normative bodies, but themselves! And so, these very bodies now presented to public gaze, in themselves, and irrespective of which character they played, served as fit counters to the stereotyping that had gone into the 'imagining' of these people.

It started with a legal case filed by some transgender groups to obtain electoral identity cards in 2003. Sudar Foundation headed by Priya Babu and Vasanthi wanted to do a play as part of their campaign and to advocate their cause in the context of the court case. The play was to focus on a single message: *aravanis* had to be treated as citizens of this country. As with our other plays addressing compelling social issues, we relied on the workshop process and on improvisations. The play was called *Manasin Azhaippu* (Call of the Heart, 2003). We listed their realities as we went along: their lives had been tragic right from childhood: driven out of home, they begged in the streets and/or danced to earn a living and in the process were sexually abused by members of the audience; and also had to hunt for a rented house. These experiences informed the episodes that we eventually featured in the play. Since the play was about citizenship, we needed to have a figure, an icon that could mediate the *aravanis*' (common Tamil name for transgenders) claims to equal citizenship. We chose to have a Queen as the arbiter of citizenship (J. Jayalalithaa was the Chief Minister!). The play concluded with the choric narration of a poem by the poet, Inquilab that challenges social hierarchies built around caste and class. "If the society can identify them only on the basis of an organ or the lack of it, they would rather stamp on it and walk ahead with their hair tied up".

The primary visual image in the play was the row of long wigs (false hair) hung as a back drop. At different points, the hair was used to refer to their desire to be women. In the last scene, they had plaited the hair in a variety of ways. Hair, as is well known, is a major cultural symbol in India. Letting one's hair loose signifies wantonness, allure or bereavement and tragedy. It is not for nothing that we have Draupadi vowing not to tie her hair up until she could anoint it with the blood of Dushasana, who disrobed her in public.

This play, invited and promoted by some NGOs, had over 100 performances across Tamil Nadu, giving public visibility to their cause. Audiences wept, ashamed of their own earlier behaviour; collections were huge, and media showered attention on them.

Sadly, the women's movement and leading women's groups would have nothing to do with it. In about two years however, the women's groups invited the articulate leaders of transgender groups to participate in their events.

Eventually, Sudar Foundation won its court case and identity cards were issued to the community granting them the right to announce themselves as male or female. In a more fundamental sense, they, and *aravanis* in general, became 'visible' in the government's eyes, and many concessions were provided, including a Transgender Welfare Board, making Tamil Nadu the best state for aravanis. The play, we could safely surmise, played its own modest role in making this possible.

The group, calling itself *Kannadi Kalai Kuzhu,* then began work on its second play in mid-2005. It was hard to arrive at a decision about the theme of the play. By then many other transgender groups had emerged in Tamil Nadu, and there was a proliferation of AIDS awareness content in the cultural work they did. After many discussions and arguments, the group zeroed in on the theme of family acceptance. Unlike the earlier occasion when the improvisation sessions proved cathartic, this time around they turned out to be disturbing for all concerned. Many of them relived their horrible experiences of being rejected by their loved ones, and some even carried scars on their bodies, caused by wilful hurt and violence. Personally, I was skeptical about the idea that family support could serve as an antidote or solution to their problems. But I could relate to their craving for it.

As we prepared for the play, we realised that the moment of change, for better or for worse, happened during the crucial adolescent phase of their lives, and if at this point families were more accepting, there could have been the possibility of their lives turning out to be very different from how it actually happened. We learned too that acceptance or rejection was never total. Some of them had mothers who supported them, while the men in the family threw them out, sometimes after the mothers died. There were other factors that also shaped family responses: property, lost loves, betrayals and sheer physical torture.

Eventually, we chose to work on six stories. We juggled the stories around so that no one played their own life. But we were stuck when it came to the story of Selvam, the only 'female to male' (F to M) in the group. He had to tell his story himself. He was the most brittle person emotionally, yet he was convinced that his story should be told, since most people do not know of the existence of people like him.

The play titled *Uraiyatha Ninaivugal* (Unsettled Memories) unravels these stories through photographs that are discussed by the group as possible material for a competition on the best family. That becomes the context and link to express both nostalgia and critique of the idea of family. After the stories are told, the players pose as themselves for a group photograph and ask the audience to judge if theirs doesn't make a good family photo. At one level, the play communicates a simple but powerful message about acceptance, but actually it does more. The *aravanis* actually interrogate the idea of a given or birth-based family. In fact, the play may be seen to "interrogate the notion of family while talking about their experiences with their natal families as well as their adopted family of *aravanis*. They conclude that a family can be of different kinds and it is a space of acceptance, warmth, care and mutual support" (Ponni Arasu, "...And the flame shines on" 3.2.2007, WFS).

Community theatre in the exact sense of the term was attempted by Voicing Silence in the work with the transgender communities. Workshops with communities were not new for Voicing Silence in terms of understanding the nuances of the issues and self-articulations of the same. We have done it on many occasions, with quarry workers in Pudukkottai or Dalit women in Tirunelveli district. But with the transgender community, they provided the content and had to enact the same. We remember many humbling and startling moments of how accountable we have to be, for many of them to share their lives with us. That experience stays fresh even today.

Mobilising Feminist Consciousness in Theatre

Activism and artistic efforts do not always seem to go hand in hand. They are difficult companions. The endless arguments about individual creativity of the artist and the prerequisite of activism lead us nowhere. Especially in theatre, which is primarily collective in nature, the understanding of 'coming together' should not be that difficult. But in reality, as we know, the two are at loggerheads. Voicing Silence always felt the need to have a conversation between the two aspects—art and activism.

From 1996, we realised the need to have discussions within the community of theatre practitioners, men and women, about the whole phenomenon of gender in terms of participation, working process and aesthetics. We began to organise *Kulavai* festivals and workshops, *Kulavai* being a Tamil term for women's ululation on ritual occasions). In the first *Kulavai* held in 1996, we had a scroll on which the respective words for ululation in all the languages represented in the meet were recorded. It was like the quilt made by women and men, acknowledging the abstract call of celebration made by women in many countries, including India.

Mina Swaminathan recalled in her communication how in *Kulavai* 1996,

> Women activists using theatre as part of their work from seven States, including many Northern ones, and speaking seven different languages, participated. Consisting of discussions, workshops led by theatre persons and performances, the occasion was an eye-opener for all participants as well as organisers! To begin with, there was no formal arrangement for translation. Instead, each of the seven groups was provided with one or two multi-lingual persons who functioned as informal two-way translators, from the group to the whole and the whole to the group. This arrangement, made out of desperation, turned out to be the main factor in the success of this *Kulavai*. It depended, of course, on the availability of people who were both multi-lingual and interested in theatre, but led to a sense of full participation and hence satisfaction by all.[10]

While the 1996 Kulavai was a National Workshop-cum-Seminar on Women and Theatre, 1997 Kulavai was a state-level workshop of Professional Women Artists from various genres and districts

10. Kulavai (1996) has been documented in detail in STQ Issue 9, April 1996. Thanks to Anjum Katyal who was present throughout the workshop.

of Tamil Nadu. This turned out to be more of a documentation of women-based forms and perfomers. Each spoke not only about her own form, but also about their difficulties and how they had overcome them.[11] What was unique about this effort was to actually trace the lineage of women in performance. Apart from the *Isai Natakam*/special Drama artists, female artists working in urban *sabha* drama and contemporary modern theatre were together on the same platform discussing what it was to be a woman and in theatre. Personally it was an eye-opener, that women need not feel lonely in this field, since they have waded through the trials and tribulations for many decades in this form.

The 1999 Kulavai was a Regional Workshop on Community Theatre at the South India level. It followed the same patterns as the previous one, combining performance, documentation and interaction, with formal translation, and including folk forms as well as activist theatre. But we were unable to monitor its impact or engage in follow-ups in the other three states.

2002 Kulavai was a National Seminar-cum-Festival of Women Directors titled 'Towards Feminist Theatre', where presentations, demonstrations and discussions during the mornings were combined with performances led by the invited directors in regular theatre venues and open to the public—for the first time bringing women's theatre into the larger public view as something different from other theatre. This was a new experiment combining public performance forms along with workshop atmosphere and in-depth discussion with fellow-workers, and was at a different level.[12] More than arriving at specific answers, this Kulavai posed complex questions such as, what makes a theatre work feminist, or does it become feminist just because a woman has directed the piece, or are there certain unique aesthetic processes that make for a feminist experience and so on.

11. Performances and brief introductions were recorded on video, and it remains a rich source of archival material, particularly as some of these forms and their practitioners, are disappearing, or being absorbed in other forms. A handbook entitled *Pen Medai Kalanjargal* based on the fieldwork was edited by J. Amaithi Arasu and published by International Institute of Tamil Studies and Voicing Silence in 1997.

12. There is video documentation of Kulavai 2002, produced by Voicing Silence.

The reflective nature of the questions raised, allowing for various views on the matter without pushing for an agenda, was indeed a memorable experience to cherish.

The last Kulavai in 2003 was a national festival of solo performances by women. The nine artists, ranging from folk to classical to musical to modern, and coming from several different states, performed for about 45-50 minutes. The performances ran continuously from 10 in the morning to 9 at night on a Sunday, with short breaks for the changes of scene. For the organisers and volunteers, who also had to ferry the artists from the place of stay to the venue and back, it was a Herculean effort. Mina Swaminathan shares how,

> We had expected that people would drift in and out, during the day, and that there would be a varying audience profile at every moment of the day. In fact, however, most of the seats were filled up when the show started. People went out for a snack or a chat whenever they felt like; invariably coming back to their seats after a short break. So it became ever more crowded towards evening; as the early birds firmly retained their seats. It was the first time that we had seen audiences glued to their seats for nine hours during the day, though still a common spectacle in India at night, for traditional performances (even in urban areas).

In several ways, Voicing Silence was a new experiment in its time. Only *Expressions*, organised by Madhushree Dutta and Flavia in Mumbai, had earlier brought together women from various fields of art in 1989, and Purva—an Asian Women's theatre festival was organised by Kirti Jain at the National School of Drama in 2003. The first decade of the 21st century, however, saw many women's theatre festivals, state-sponsored and otherwise.

These workshops and seminars opened up new areas of discussion. Apart from drawing attention to themes that engaged the playwrights and directors, they brought out the differences in the processes at work. The discussions proved that there was a phenomenon of women's/feminist/gendered theatre that has been in practice for over two and a half decades in India. This notion of gender has not taken the easy recourse to male-masculine/female-feminine binary. It has worked on the intersections, however painful it is, of gender with class, caste, religion, language and sexuality. It is a healthy trend to have many shades of feminism or gender activity prevailing in theatre. It might not fit into neat boundaries that are expected in academia, but the best part of Indian performing arts is the cacophony of many voices and there is a need to maintain that in all its glory.

Even though Voicing Silence was evolved and supported as a project of MSSRF, it functioned unlike other projects. There were enough stumbling blocks and re-workings of the project as the journey progressed. The nature of the work, participants and reception did not fall neatly into any project report pattern. Nor were we trying to fit ourselves to size. We wanted the space to remain painfully exploratory and very often introspective. What Voicing Silence attempted was to make the activist movements, especially women's movements, recognise the role of culture and to remind the cultural workers of their legacy of feminist politics.

To me personally, what began as an accidental coming together of interests with Mina Swaminathan, turned out to be a journey of bringing together various aspects of my own life. As individuals seeking reviews and reassurances ever so often, we had wonderful moments of heartbreaking criticisms and the most moving mutual compliments and love for each other. To achieve that with over 25 years of difference in age in the Indian context is no joke. But as always, I think it is our feminist politics that made possible the co-existence of happy, fearless irreverence and unswerving mutual support.

References

Chakravarti, Uma (2012). "Cultures of Resistance: Women's Movement as Performance", in Panjabi, Kavita and Paromita Chakravarti (eds.), *Women Contesting Cultures*. Kolkata: School of Women's Studies and Stree. pp 58 -71.

Dalmia, Vasudha (2006). *Poetics, Plays and Performances: The Politics of Modern Indian Theatre*. New Delhi: Oxford University Press.

Dharwadker, Aparna (2008). *Theatres of Independence: Drama, Theory and Urban Performances in India since 1947*. New Delhi: Oxford University Press.

Erven, Eugene Van (1992). *The Playful Revolution: Theatre and Liberation in Asia*. Indiana University Press.

Lalitha, K. and Susie Tharu (1989). *We were Making History*. New Delhi: Kali.

Mangai, A. (2000). "Theatre of Protest and Resistance: Avvai", *Indian Journal of Gender Studies* 7(2): 217–230. July-December.

———. (2006). "Presenting the Past: Classical Tamil Texts on the Contemporary Stage", in M. Kannan and Carlos Mena (eds.), *Negotiations with the Past: Classical Tamil in Contemporary Tamil*. Pondicherry: Institut Francais De Pondichery and Berkeley: Tamil Chair, Department of South and Southeast Asian Studies, University of California. pp.307-20.

Mukherjee, Tutun (2005). *Staging Resistance: Plays by Women*. New Delhi: Oxford University Press.

Richman, Paula (1998). *Women, Branch Stories and Religious Rhetoric in a Tamil Buddhist Text*. Foreign and Comparative Studies, South Asian Series.

Singh, Anita and T.T. Mukherjee (2013). *Gender Space and Resistance: Women and Theatre in India*. New Delhi: D.K. Printworld.

Subramanyam, Lakshmi (ed.) (2002). *Muffled Voices: Women in Modern Indian Theatre*. New Delhi: Shakthi Books.

Swaminathan, Mina, (1998). *IIAS Newsletter* No. 17. *http://www.iias.nl/iiasn/17/regions/17CBCD01.html*

8

JOLLY ROHATAGI and MINA SWAMINATHAN

Lok Doot: The People's Messenger

Gender Awareness Through Theatre

This piece is presented as part of the section on communication in this collection, and hence I must explain what a visual book is doing here, trying to communicate both content and form through a medium of communication other than the academic essay.

Between 1975 and 1983, the two authors, Jolly Rohatagi, an artist and student of folk art, and I (Mina Swaminathan), a teacher specialising in early childhood and drama, worked together with a unique theatre group, called Lok Doot, or People's Messenger, to develop theatre for communication. Set up by Mobile Creches, with a few talented members of its staff, this group had grown out of the literacy programme on the construction sites, from a felt need for greater communication with the construction labour for whom it was intended. Efforts began with a series of humorous sketches to motivate the audience to join the literacy classes. From these simple beginnings, we were gradually able to develop a series of shows, transforming the repertoire into an ongoing dialogue between the actors and the audience, using a variety of forms and techniques. Over a period of time, the messenger transformed itself, and became, not only a messenger to the people, but of the people.

Now, nearly 40 years later, during which we have each gone our separate ways, although always in friendly touch, we have come together once more to work on communications through another popular medium—this time, not theatre on a stage, but the pages of a visual book. Combining words with pictures, the medium is intended for the many whose visual literacy goes far beyond their formal literacy. Ideally, to reach such a public, the book should be in an Indian language, as we hope our next one might be. For now, it demonstrates our approach, transferring our learning(s) from one medium to another, and learning afresh as the medium suggests.

Both then and now, gender issues are introduced at two levels—both by mirroring the life and difficulties of a woman from the same community as the one being addressed, and by the use of language and action that offers the woman both voice and space. We knew that issues affecting the life of the people can be dealt with, on the one hand, through traditional stories, tales and myths as content; and on the other, by using the people's own idiom—its sayings, language, songs, music and dances to narrate the tale, including the traditional device of the *Sutradhar* or narrator. Form and content, both were drawn from the people to convey the message.

At that time, folk visual aids to storytelling, from some parts of the country, such as puppets, *phada* or scrolls, *Pata Chitra* or pictures, and *Kavad* and *Katha Peti* or story-boxes, were used to attract close attention to the content, as the forms were already familiar to the audience; here, we have based ourselves on a modern example, the comic book. Again, we assume that the audience would always include both adults and children, the usual Indian practice, and structure the story to engage both sections. Other strategies used to promote reflection in the case of theatre were alternative endings, audience participation and choice, and parallel stories. We have tried to introduce some of these elements in ways appropriate to a visual book.

Focusing on today's gender issues, we present a village woman who not only had the possibility, but also the courage, to make a non-traditional choice, lucidly explaining her reasons for doing so, and still be accepted by the community, although breaking the barriers of class, caste, religion, gender and sexual orientation. This may not have been a realistic possibility in another time and place; but that is precisely the point of storytelling—it can alter both past and future to suit the tale.

From the first few pages, which show the man idling, while the women (and girls) work all the time, every page shows a familiar situation which suggests questions and challenges thinking. The possible questions and answers of the readers/audience are anticipated and resolved through the two *Sutradhars* on each page—one a foreign woman upholding gender equality, but unfamiliar with the fabric of Indian community life; the other an Indian boy who, we learn much later, was raised by aware and informed village women. Their conversation carries the tale, with a message on every page.

Importantly, those who participated in the making of the book also took part in the emotional and intellectual journey. The woman artist who drew the pictures was moved to tears on several pages, which reminded her of her own trials and tribulations in life; while the one who did the lettering of the text, himself a rural youth with limited education, thought deeply over each page and reviewed his own responses. Thus again, as in the earlier case, did messenger become both the people's medium, and the people's message.

Hmm.. looks like a sleepy little village!
The Lemon Tree
Wait and see...
Vivek,a journalist,comes to village Sultanpur, at the edge of the forest, where a great lemon tree is king. Only these lemons are offered to the deity here, where thousands come. He and his wife, Marianne,from Paris, are travelling in India
1

God,let them say yes! Four more to marry off!
My son's fair,she's dark..
Looks simple, obedient- she'll do
He thinks she's plain
Soti Lal of Sultanpur went with his parents to find a bride. He was ambitious, wanted to own a business. When Pushpa was sixteen, they came to her house. The marriage was fixed.
But he's fat,too...
2

Tea cold!Roti too hot! Your girls are worthless.Teach them house work! I cycle miles daily just to feed you.
They're your children too! Why are you angry ?...
He says Pushpa brought bad luck, so his parents died!
Also he blames her for two daughters!
Soti lal 's parents died in an accident during pilgrimage soon after the wedding. He is a shop assistant in a nearby town.
3

Going to school secretly ?
To hide it from him!
Kela,Santara, go quietly behind the houses.. let no one see you !
Yes Amma
Once Soti lal had left for work, Pushpa would quickly get the girls ready for school. and send them off secretly
4

Dear tree,he drinks,then beats me every night ....please help...
Where did the money go?
..in a hole under the hearth - for the girls' education!
After housework, Pushpa went to collect wood. Hugging the lemon tree,she cried, and fruit rained down. She sold them in the temple market.
5

Oh....I'm alone!
Lemon tree,
you are all I have!!
Omi looked after his sick mother till she died.
Now an orphan, alone in his hut!
The tree shook down fruits which he too sold to meet his daily needs, and continued his studies. Nature is bountiful.
6

My sons are nasty!
-God, call me soon!
Amin's three sons complained that he did nothing...
......and their wives often locked him out at night !
The third visitor was old and lame Amin. He plucked Champa flowers to make garlands for sale at the temple.
7

They've got together ...
Who are you, what's wrong!
I am Pushpa!..let's all work together!
Now there is hope!
No-we are here --- your sisters Kela and Santara
I have no one in this world ...
I never see anyone here! Who are you?
Once,Soti Lal drank late,was late to work-so the girls missed school. They all went to the lemon tree and met Omi and Amin
8

....and Omi run from forest to temple to sell with me.
Then we will sell more !
We'll do this --,Amin dada sit and sell,I make garlands, gather fruits,girls help after school..
So the business grew,and they began to save ....
...........they got organized,and grew closer!
Daily,they collected fruits and flowers and sold them. Then,Pushpa made another plan.They built a shed,got a shop in the market,and became partners.
9

Friends-- we sell flowers and fruit in the market. And you?
See-- our sisterhood. Rejected by society and family...
Who are you? Why are you here?
...and makes a family.This is our family
...we help each other and live together.
An aunt adopts a few youngsters....
Soon the hijras served a hot meal, and the friends offered each a lemon and some flowers.
One evening, hearing songs and laughter close by...
.......they went to look...
10

What a happy,united,family-- they love each other, live and work together--
How do you earn?
We are artists, we sing and dance, going from place to place.
We perform in people's homes and public spaces.
We want to study and work, like others, but are not allowed to!
Next day the camp was silent, the hijras had gone. But sometimes they could hear the sound of music.
.... and none related by blood!
....but each is different
11

Omi is the son I never had,and Amin Dada is my father now. Yes-I too will come home here...
Amin,turned out of his house,brought his things to sleep in the shed,and Omi began staying there.Pushpa too, badly beaten by Soti Lal,decided to join her "new" family
A village woman with the courage to leave her husband and ..
.......move in with strangers ! Wonderful!
12

Girls,make tea for everyone
Omi,you're our brother and Amin dada our grandfather.
Bless you all!
I told you to wait and see...
Next morning,Pushpa prepared food for her husband,sent him off,then ran with the girls to the lemon tree. The new family worked happily all day.
It's a new kind of family!
13

Pushpa! Santra! Kela!
Have you seen my wife and children?
They must be in their shop in the market as usual.
What sh ..sh.. shop?
No light in the house, no smoke, no sounds of laughter! No tea, no food, no slaves!
She is a businesswoman, he is a shop assistant! He's jealous!
Finding the house deserted, Soti Lal ran in search of Pushpa, shouting furiously. Everyone said she must be in the market, then about to close.
14

Pushpa! Are you mad? Humph ! It is night - come home right now!
Go away
I am not going home. They may not be blood relatives,but they are my family now -
hhshh .. for the last time ... are you coming with me ?
No! and the girls stay with me !
Finding his way to the market,and seeing Pushpa working with others,Soti Lal began to shout,but had to leave with head down.
He cannot respect her.Will men ever learn?
Lets see what he does now
15

Outsiders have taken your land and built a hut there-my wife is with them too..
Is that so? Let us go to father at once!
From the time of Mahabarata, people have fought bitterly and killed for a piece of land.....
Soti Lal ran to the owners of the land, where Pushpa's new family lived, to complain. The landlord's sons were angry and rushed to tell their father.
Its just the same today .....
16

Father,those people have taken our land! Why are you silent ?
But when you die it will be ours-- you must keep it safe for us
Be patient ! it is still my land - I am making the decisions
I am not dead yet. Hmmm......
Hmmm......
Soti Lal appealed to the two sons to save their property, but their father refused to listen to then.
.... but the ending may be different!
Now its Mahabharata in Sultanpur......
17

My wife has run away with strange men, and is living outside the village
Let us go and see-this may ruin the village prestige.
Did I tell you she was my grandmother? And most village women were on her side....
I am glad a woman of that time was ready to defy customs!
Soti Lal and the two sons complained to the village headman and asked for his support. The Headman agreed to go with them to investigate.
18

This land is ours...
She is my daughter. The land is ours. We have paid for it, and have all the papers.
And to this young lout
How are you related to this woman?
I'm a mother of three and can decide where and how to live. You gave me only misery. I will live with my new family-.
Now lets go see what else there is in this country!
Pushpa won! just imagine!
The Headman could find no fault with them, so everyone left,and the family slept.The sound of music and the scent of lemon wafted through the night.
19

Concept and Design - Jolly Rohatagi
Story - Jolly Rohatagi and Mina Swaminathan
Text - Mina Swaminathan
Art Work - Hira Devi Kant
(Madhubani)
Text lettering - Dhiraj Jaiswal
20

9

AMIT MITRA

Patriarchs and *Dhakans*

Exploring Gendered Socialisation in Dungarpur

Introduction

Stereotypes of greater gender equality among India's tribals, rooted in the romanticism of colonial anthropologist missionaries and administrators persist in developmental thinking. Strong evidence of inequality, such as gender discrimination in birth, healthcare, educational attainments notwithstanding, the ideologies and cultures of misogyny underlying and reinforcing patriarchy are ignored. In this paper, using the example of Dungarpur district in Rajasthan, with a population of 70.8 per cent STs (scheduled tribes) (2011 census) belonging to the Bhil family, I interrogate some of these assumptions. Ninety-four per cent of Dungarpur's population is rural. The district is poor and underdeveloped. In 2007, its Human Development Index (HDI) was 0.409, ranking it 32 out of Rajasthan's 33 districts (IDS, 2008).

Departing from the popular usage of the term meaning hatred, I conceptualise misogyny as an ideology that propagates that: a) women deserve to be denigrated as they are inferior to men; and b) being superior, men can and do dominate women in all spheres of life, ritually and violently (Sirnate, 2015). Patriarchy as a system of power thrives on misogyny, including appropriating women's consent in everything and defining and setting limits to dissent. For the women, the ideologies of misogyny are a day-to-day lived experience (Sirnate, 2015). I argue that in a patriarchal system, women also practice misogyny both against other women and themselves. "Misogyny functions as an ideology or belief system that has accompanied patriarchal or male-dominated societies for thousands of years and continues to place women in subordinate positions with limited access to power and decision making" (Flood, 2007). Patriarchy thrives on misogyny wherein men also are victims. For reasons of space, I do not discuss the impacts of patriarchy and misogyny on men.

I analyse how cultural beliefs about women set and perpetuate the ideologies of misogyny in their lives, ranging from ownership of their bodies, to property and decision-making, as well as physical violence (Section 2). The diverse impacts of these ideologies on women, especially girl children, from survival and health issues to education are analysed in Section 3. I argue that assumptions of tribal egalitarianism do not lead to gender equality. Tribal areas, including Dungarpur, are severely development deprived and discriminated against. Women face multiple discriminations and deprivations due to their location, ethnicity and gender.

Methodology

This paper draws on a scoping study on gender relations in Dungarpur district (Mitra, 2010). The data was collected primarily by listening to individuals: women, men and children, mostly tribals from impoverished households. Some teachers and health delivery personnel were interviewed.

Intensive fieldwork was conducted in Banra and Junagraha villages[1] of Bicchiwara and Dungarpur tehsils between March and June 2010. Ten households were selected randomly from each village for the primary interviews. Mothers apart, I listened to the children of school-going age in the household. Generally the 'husbands' in these households were not contacted because of: a) their unavailability b) their refusal to be candid in front of women and c) my apprehension about the possible violent repercussions. Where possible, the older sons were interviewed. Men's views were collected from discussions with them in eateries of Dungarpur, with men standing around at the bus stand or waiting to find work along the town's main road. Observations and getting the children to enact

1. All names, including of villages, have been changed to protect anonymity of the respondents.

role plays were other methods of data collection. Discussions with women were facilitated by local women associates.

Many interviewees were visited multiple times. Their narratives were discussed with the local facilitators and other respondents. Census documents, ASER Reports, DISE data and the District Human Development Report (IDS, 2008) have been used extensively.

Gender Ideologies and Relations in Dungarpur

All Women are Witches

Kansli matar dhakan (*every bodice, implying a woman, is a witch*) goes an old Bhili saying (Koppers and Jungblut, 1976: 250). Every tribal woman in Dungarpur is considered a potential witch with varying powers to harm, including 'eating' their own children. It is believed that "girls born on Saturdays are generally *dhakans* (witches), especially those who are born on new moon days that happen to be Saturdays. Girls born on a Saturday coinciding with the new moon day before Diwali will invariably grow into a witch," said Sachin Damor (35), a male driver of a car rental agency, articulating a popular perception. These views, held by both men and women, prevail widely in Dungarpur.

Witchcraft is strongly attributed to Indian tribal women. Women are frequently tortured and killed for witchcraft. The Rajasthan government in 2015 passed a bill against declaring a woman as a witch.[2]

Men do not become witches. Such beliefs, often dismissed as 'superstitions,' reveal the role of misogynous ideologies in 'controlling' women. It is as if society were telling women, "Cross the line and you will be branded a witch." The 'declaration', often covert, socially kills the woman, but such covert declarations and the social killings are outside the purview of the law. Effectively, it is the conversion of non-conformist women to non-beings for "sucking the life of their nearest, including husbands and children" (Rao, 2008: 4).

2. The Rajasthan Prevention of Witch Hunting Bill, 2015 (*http://rajassembly.nic.in/BillsPdf/Bill20-2015.pdf*)

Symbolically, blood/life can represent the social norms and structures of control in patriarchy when the woman seeks to assert her identity. This is not restricted to rural/tribal women only, but even highly educated urban women are attributed the same qualities if they question patriarchy by being labelled "bad mothers" (Rao, 2008: 4).

Ideologically, such attribution sets the environment which denigrates the very existence of women, undervalues their reproductive and productive work, controls their labour and fertility and renders them second rate citizens. This form of 'control' is more of a punishment, but socialisation and inculcation into the culture is achieved by several other means. These include marrying girls off early, ensuring that they produce children at a young age and denying them any material property.

A Girl's Home is Not Her Home

"I will marry off my daughter when she is capable of fetching water," says Radha (14) of Banra. Her daughter is just two. Radha was married at menarche at 10. No one in her or her husband's family has ever been to school. But she and her husband, Raju (29), took a major decision to defer another child until her daughter, Bimla, grew up a couple of years. This annoyed her in-laws.

Usually, the girls are married around menarche (10-13 years) expressed as *kapda chad gaya*.[3] The groom is usually 3-5 years older.[4] Interestingly, the Annual Health Survey (AHS) 2012-13 found only 5.9 per cent girls married before 18 years, pointing to reportage issues.

The usual explanations/justifications given for child marriages, common to the country, are that girls belong to their in-laws (husband's) home and are guests in their mother's; puberty renders them vulnerable and marriage ensures their safety. A married woman can be violated, but then the responsibility lies with the

3. She has started using the cloth.

4. In the absence of systematic registration of births, the ages are at best approximations, even in the schools. A school teacher explained, "We assume that children getting admitted for the first time are six. It is we who give them a date of birth, taking care not to repeat birthdays in a batch of students. This birthday is theirs permanently and will be in all future records."

husband. Males equate pubescent girls with cows. "Their body heats up. Nature's laws are violated if girls are not married off and start bearing children early."[5] Sachin Damor said:

> A paddy seedling flourishes only when it is transplanted from the nursery to another field. It has to be transplanted at an early age or it dies. Girls have to be sent to their homes early so that they can develop and blossom. If she goes off at an early age she will be rooted better in her new environment. You cannot transplant an old tree.

Child brides are expected to procreate within a year of marriage. She is 'allowed' at the most a couple of years to produce a child or else there is a threat that the husband will remarry. Alka (38) of Banra was married at 13. Her first pregnancy at 16 ended in a stillborn girl. A son born nine years later died in infancy, as did the third, a son. Her husband, Ramesh, brought Ramila in a *nata* relationship (*nata pratha*) from Sabarkantha in Gujarat six years ago. Alka has a son and a daughter now. She recounted the daily taunts and physical abuse for being 'barren'. Sarala of Junaghara, with four daughters, is under pressure to produce a son. Sarala miscarried male foetuses twice, leading to the suspicion of her being a *dhakan* who "ate up her two sons." Her eldest daughter (13) is to be married soon. Sarala says, "*Ladki ab pani lane layak ho gayi hai*" (the girl is now old enough to fetch water) and asks "Girls destiny is to get married, so why delay the inevitable?"

Generally, childhood ends with the onset of puberty. For the girls and boys, childhood means learning to obey the parents. The girls are socialised into becoming women and learning their role in life. The latter includes doing the household chores, tending to the cattle, poultry, and younger siblings and 'sacrificing' to the needs of males, including brothers, both older and younger. Most girls denied overt discrimination in intra-household food distribution, but admitted eating after the men and compared to their brothers "they felt less hungry as after all they were girls and their bodies needed less food."[6]

5. Discussion with Hajabhai, a labour contractor, in Dungarpur, 24th March 2010.
6. Interviews with Paro and Moti in Thamka and Radha in Banra. Suchitra (Auxillary Nurse Midwife, or ANM) opined that female bodies "are made in such a way that they need less food."

A Strong Son Preference

A strong son preference prevails in Dungarpur (like in the rest of South Asia). Often by the time a woman is 18-20 years, she has 4-5 children. While the desire for sons often leads to having daughters until a boy is born, having a son as the first born does not stop more children. "At least two sons are needed," said Sushma, 17, of Junaghara. Sushma, married three years ago, is in trouble with just a daughter.[7] Presently, having 4-5 children is the norm, *vis-à-vis* 7-8 in the previous generation. Many women want 'operations' after 2-3 children, but as Urmila of Banra said, "The decision about the operation doesn't really depend on us [women] but the man."

The average inter-birth spacing is 1-1.5 years. Male perceptions of women being responsible for the sex of the foetus, along with the threat that with failure to produce sons another partner would be got, puts tremendous mental pressure on the women. Both Sarala of Junaghara and Urmila of Banra recounted the ignominies they have had to suffer because of not bearing sons.

Bearing many children, in a state of hunger and malnourishment, and hard toil, takes its toll. By their 40s, many women are in a very poor state of health, the ill-health accentuated by the poor healthcare infrastructure and attitudes towards disease (cf Section on Healthcare). Many just die. This is reflected in the age-specific sex ratios: sex ratios between 40-49 years drop drastically compared to the previous cohort (cf Table 9.2). Only after 60 does it pick up again.

Nothing to Call their Own

"Having many daughters impoverishes due to the wedding expenses," said Gauri of Junaghara, mother to five daughters. The bride's family has to give a wedding feast, utensils, clothes and if they can afford it, a bedstead and bedding. "But she brings back nothing, while a boy, despite the expenses on the wedding, brings back a woman who can work," many articulated.[8]

---

7. It is tempting to conjecture that the view that at least two sons are necessary is the cultural influence of the Rajputs. Amongst the elite Rajputs, this view prevails even today, and also finds mention in fiction (Cf Archer, 2010).

8. Interviews of Sarala, Puja and Kalpana, Junaghara.

Bride price is a misnomer for *dapa*. Customarily the bride has to be given at least five silver ornaments, weighing about a kilogram. About ₹1 lakh is spent on *dapa* by even the poorest of families perforce borrowing from local moneylenders at high rates of interest.[9]

Dapa is not given to the bride's family but to the bride, who brings it back to her marital home. She has no control over the jewellery, except wearing it for social gatherings. She cannot pawn or sell the ornaments for her own expenses or spend on her natal family members' medical treatment, unless permitted by her husband. Usually the women pawn/sell the jewellery to construct a house (hutment) soon after marriage.[10] The other frequent use of *dapa* ornaments is to pay for the treatment of her husband or sons when needed. In case of a divorce or separation, the woman has to return the jewellery without any deductions for her labour.

Women apart from their clothes do not have any possessions or assets of their own. They do not inherit land even after widowhood. It passes on to sons or grandsons or nephews when there are no sons.

The World of Work of Women

Reproductive work is the responsibility of women. Environmental constraints of a drought prone area additionally burden women. On an average, a woman in Junaghara walks 8-12 kilometres daily (in 4-5 rounds) to fetch water, balancing 20 kilograms on her head. The problem is compounded with four of the village hand-pumps malfunctioning. Some men deliberately damaged a hand-pump to punish a defiant widow. Women walk several kilometres to get scarce fuel-wood.

Elder girl children help mothers to cook and tend younger siblings. Slightly older girls graze cattle, scavenge for fuel and pick *mahua* (*Madhuca longfolia*), missing school if enrolled.

Women tend the family fields and perform most tasks related to cultivation, except ploughing the land. They prepare the fields, sow,

9. Testimonies of Sarala, Kalpana, Gauri in Junaghara, FGD (focus group discussions) with women in Chatri.

10. The source for this is the same as above and Asha, field facilitator.

weed, harvest and thresh. Older girls help in this; and it is included in the responsibilities of a new bride. Bhulabhai of Tijor, explained, "My wife has been ill for long. She cannot go to the fields. I do what I can, but I have a shop to mind. There is so much work to be done at home and outside. So I want to get my eldest son married." Women accept they have to work both inside the home and outside. In Junaghara, Kalpana's daughter (9) had skipped school to help her mother harvest the wheat. Kalpana said, "I cannot manage alone. If the wheat is not harvested, what will we eat? My husband is a labourer in Dungarpur. How does it matter if Neeta misses school? This learning is more important. She will have to do this work all her life. She will attend school after the wheat is brought home." Kalpana asks, "I studied till class 7 but how has it helped me? I wanted to study further. I was married off against my will despite resisting for two years. My brothers overruled my objections. My mother had no say."

Many women work as casual labour. Many work in NREGS[11] for cash incomes, but it is gender unfriendly, resulting in women getting less than stipulated for a day's full work (₹100). The work is divided into light and heavy, with the men being allocated the task of cutting/digging the earth and women removing the boulders/carrying the stones away on their heads in iron containers (*tapelas*). Labour-saving devices like handcarts are not used to reduce women's drudgery. A few rounds of cutting later, the 'tired' men retire to the shade with their *biris* and the women take over the task of digging/cutting the earth with heavy pickaxes under a scorching sun, ensuring all along that their veils don't slip off. At the end of the day, the allocated task is not completed and the women get less than what they should have, despite working the full day.

On an average, despite the leakages, the women make about ₹7000 for 100 days of work annually.[12] This money eases somewhat

11. The Mahatma Gandhi National Rural Employment Guarantee Scheme (MNREGS) is expected to provide 100 days of guaranteed work to any adult who demands such work, at the minimum wage.

12. Computed from the passbooks of several women for 2009. Pankaj and Tankha (2010), based on a sample of 103 women from Dungarpur, calculate the average amount earned by the women to be ₹ 7855 for 2008-09. The average number of days worked by these women was 77.

the family's financial burden. Some Banra women had been to Ahmedabad to work with their husbands as casual labour, but said that it was their husbands who received the money and not them. And even when they got cash directly, they had to hand it over to their husbands.[13]

Contemporary discourses often assume that enhanced earning opportunities for women translate into their greater control over such incomes and lead to positive impacts on the children. Thus, Pankaj and Tankha (2010: 46) argue:

> The NREGS aims to meet the practical needs of women workers in the short run and their strategic needs in the long run. Women are able to buy food, clothes and medicines from their NREGS earnings that addresses their short-term needs. Their reduced dependence for these basic needs on male family members also addresses the issue of subordination and subjugation in the long-term.

Such generalisations need careful consideration. Firstly, women are not an undifferentiated lot. Apart from class and caste/ethnic variations, the status of the woman in terms of demography, household size, social position and the overall social and economic position and composition of the households makes a big difference. Secondly, even if some practical needs are met, it doesn't necessarily imply that their strategic interests will be met unless some basic institutional structures are questioned.

Sujata, of Chatri, was widowed five years ago. She has four children (three daughters, one of whom is hearing and speech impaired). As long as Shiva (her husband) was alive, they stayed with his parents. When Shiva died, his youngest brother threw Sujata and the children out of the house. She started staying in a hut owned by another brother-in-law, who has now become abusive and asks her to vacate the hut. She is beaten regularly by her brothers-in-law. Yet, Sujata gets a widow pension and earns sometimes from NREGS. Part of the money is appropriated by her brothers-in-law. She has applied for a house unsuccessfully under the Indira Awas Yojana (IAY). As she says, "With my husband not there, who will pursue my case? Even if I

---

13. Cf Interview of Alka in Banra.

get the house, will I be able to stay in it?" She cannot afford to feed all the children, so the eldest stays with her brother and studies in Class 8 now.

In households where both husband and wife are alive, the overall economic situation and the number of children is an impacting factor. Thus Sheetal and Jitesh (of Banra), spend most of their earnings on debt-servicing. The remainder is spent on buying minimal amounts of food for bare survival. As Urmila (of Banra) says, "If I don't work, we will starve. I have so many children. My husband is a drunkard."

The amount earned is important. Putlibai and others in Junaghara spoke of the high rates of inflation and the rising costs of food, clothes, and medicines, and asked "What is ₹7000 a year these days, especially if there are 5-7 mouths to feed?" Indeed, to what extent then are even the practical needs met, even if it be assumed that the women have control over their incomes?[14] Clearly, a lot more attention has to be paid to the household structures and household cycles in specific contexts, before making generalisations around factors contributing to gender equality.

Male perspectives on work follow the usual patterns elsewhere, including non-tribal society. Men's work is considered more important, heavier and more arduous. Women's work is not considered work. Even in NREGS, men label women's work as mere helping and sacrificing for the family. Men's work necessitates consuming alcohol to relieve the "tiredness." Women do not drink even ceremoniously. A 25-year-old Ghanshyam's (of Junaghara) mother was widowed when the children were young. Ghanshyam, BA, BEd, is unemployed. He says he finds it difficult to till the land or work in NREGS. He owns a bicycle. His mother had gone to fetch on foot the monthly quota of wheat (28 kg) from the Public Distribution System (PDS) shop 4 km away. Asked if he helps his mother fetch the

14. In Pankaj and Tankha's (2010) study, 50 per cent of the women in Dungarpur said they could retain upto 25 per cent of the NREGS earnings. The average income per woman is ₹7,855, so this is ₹1,963. Apart from 'keeping' being different from 'controlling', ₹1,963, even if spent on food and clothes does not amount to much in terms of actual commodity consumption. Assuming these women had four children, it is less than ₹500 per annum per child.

wheat, he replied, "She goes with her friends enjoying each other's company. What shall I do there? Anyway, she might not let me do it and I will not enjoy it. It gives her something to do and keeps her occupied. Why should I not let her have her enjoyment? She worked so hard to bring us up." Ghanshyam pontificated on the qualities of good men and good women. To him bad men don't exist. Even alcohol consumption (though he says he doesn't drink) is an act of necessity (other men equated it with manliness). There are only educated men and uneducated men, but again lack of education is not in the hands of men but of fate. But women are potentially bad and need proper guidance and control or they go astray. Good women work hard and sacrifice for others. He vehemently opposes love marriages as such women are spoilt and turn their husbands against their families.

Chronic alcohol abuse by men combined with poor nourishment often leads to health complications. Many men die young (cf. Table 9.2). Diabetes, tuberculosis and sickle cell anaemia[15] are rampant.

The Myth of Greater Freedom

Tribal women are believed to have greater 'freedom'. Often this is a slanted reference to an assumed greater libido of tribal women (and men). There are instances of women leaving their husbands and children and going off with another man. So are examples of men getting another spouse or just a woman (*nata jodna*).

Young, articulate and having studied till the tenth standard, Suchitra is a temporary ANM living in a big modern house. Her husband is a school teacher. Suchitra is the second wife. Her co-wife is much older as is her husband, her former teacher. She articulates:

> I know my marriage is illegal. I do not have any legal rights to his property. I will never be confirmed in my job. But his kin will give my sons (she has two male twins) some land. But forget the law. Even otherwise, if I were the sole wife of somebody, would I have any claims on the property?

15. cf Choubisa (1990).

Asked about widow remarriage, she said that no one really wants to marry a widow. Many of course don't mind having an affair with her.[16] And why don't women walk out on abusive men since apparently tribal society allows it? She replied:

> What is the guarantee that the next person wouldn't be abusive? In non-tribal societies, divorces and re-marriages are legally accepted. But how many women can exercise that choice? It's not so easy, even with economic independence. It's not a question of tribal vs. non-tribal society but more of men and women in this system.

An old widow in the same village, with a much younger co-wife now dead, said, "He brought her to satisfy his lust as I was growing older. But when I was younger, I wouldn't dare look at another man for the fear of being thrashed."

There is not much difference between tribal and non-tribal society in this aspect. Interviews with families/children of the mothers who seemingly abandoned their husbands and children to elope with someone revealed such abandonment followed years of mental and physical torture and agony. The husband didn't allow the woman in question to leave with the kids, nor did the new man want them.[17]

Bhim of Banra met Babli when she was 13 and he 28, already married with a son. He brought her home in a *nata* relationship after two years, ignoring her parents' objections. Bhim had driven out his first wife. He thrashed her whenever she visited the son who is now a casual labourer in Gujarat. Now Babli is in her mid-30s, and has

---

16. Allegations of widows having affairs are common. There is a Vaghdi saying, "*Randi bairi nu desh ghani*" meaning that a widow has many homes and no one questions her. In Junaghara, Gauri is alleged to have a "setting" (the local term for an affair) and "even her son doesn't stay with her" (a neighbour). Single women are targeted both by men and society. Dressing up is looked down upon and taken as an indicator of being involved with other men. A field facilitator was shocked to see a widow Jayanti, in Samota village, wearing ornaments, a clean sari, eyes kohled, and "even nail polish." She was certain that Jayanti was having an affair because, "a widow is not supposed to dress up so much." Many widows are labelled *dhakans*.

17. Abandonment is not by choice and the *nata* relationship has many exploitative elements. Young widows are driven off by in-laws after taking the *dapa* back. In one instance, a widow had been driven away and the father in-law was trying desperately for the last few years to get the ₹10,000 that the widow had been given by the government. He has kept the passbook. She can't withdraw it and the father-in-law was cold shouldered by the bank manager, despite the offer of a cut if the withdrawal was allowed. The *dapa* was kept by the in-laws.

four sons and three daughters. Bhim has become an alcoholic. He was jailed for two months for setting a neighbour's house on fire and last year set fire to his own house. He frequently thrashes Babli. One day he just threw her out. She went to her parent's in Charwada with her youngest daughter. The education of the other younger children has been stopped and they roam about Banra dirty and hungry. Sometimes Babli sends some maize but the economic condition of her parents' home is not very good. Babli says that she can't elope with someone with so many children.

Not all parents are as supportive as Babli's. Reema, 20, was driven away from home by her parents in Rama fala, when she was seduced by someone at 13. She went off to Dodio and got involved with someone from Surta village. Her parents brought her back, pregnant. The parents of the boy and the girl came to an agreement, and Reema went to live in Surta. But there would be fights daily and Reema would be beaten. She came home, gave birth to Priya, stayed for a year: a year of daily humiliations. Finally she went off to Gujarat and has not returned. Her parents refuse to talk about her. They are somehow bringing Priya up: the five-year-old kid looks emaciated and often goes hungry. She has burn marks on her right shoulder and a part of her head. Her grandparents say she fell into the fire while playing. But from the burn marks, it doesn't seem that it was an accident.

The greater freedom myth is shattered by the high levels of physical and mental domestic violence. Both child marriage and child-motherhood are extremely violent acts physically and emotionally. Just plain beating is a part of life for the women. "Husbands have the right to beat us for mistakes. But the beating should not be so severe that we cannot work," refrained many. Sheetal (23) of Banra says, "Jitesh, my husband, is really a very good man. He has never given me even a *dhap* (hard slap) when I make a mistake." The 'mistakes' usually relate to serving food on time, ensuring that the *rotis* don't become hard or get burnt. The discourse on violence, amongst the women, then gets relegated to whether it was 'due' or 'justified.' Getting beaten for not looking after children (evidenced by their crying too much) or hobnobbing with other men is justified. Thrashing for not producing sons is unjustified (since the gods decide the gender) as is complaining if the husband drinks or talks about (and sometimes does) re-marrying.

Although women can abandon/divorce their spouses, they have to leave behind the children. This is an important constraint for women to opt out of broken marriages. Moreover, "younger women are the most attractive marriage partners in the eyes of the men, being divorced and older and with children makes it hard for a woman to get married again" (Nielsen, 2010: 83).

Decision-making

Men decide major matters like family size, marriage of children, their education, buying clothes and seeking healthcare. Women have some say about food, but they cannot prioritise purchasing of milk over alcohol or *bidis* and *gutka*, irrespective of whether they earn or not. Hooji of Gamdi says that despite earning from NREGS, she cannot take her sick daughter to the city doctor. She can take her to the village quack if permitted by her husband, Sachin. "How can I spend without asking him? We are deeply in debt because of the loans to build the house?" she asks. The men decide the crops to be cultivated and borrowing money, but may order their spouse to borrow from a neighbour or her maternal relatives. If there be acute shortage of food, a woman might go and borrow some maize from a neighbour.

Local customs, traditions and the advice of kinsfolk influence male decisions. Personal idiosyncrasies, beliefs and notions of honour are important, alongside exposure to the outside world in decisions about children. Thus Bela, 23, of Rakhodia village, who studied in Gujarat says, "My father, as a driver in Gujarat, used to see girls attending college. My mother did not want me to study beyond class 8. Initially my father sided with her. But when I explained to him with examples why I wanted to study, he permitted me despite mother's objections." Bela says that if her father disagreed, she would not have been able to study.

Impacts on Children

The previous section analysed how misogynous ideologies shape the lives of Dungarpur's tribal women. Such ideologies impact and influence every aspect of their being. This section discusses three major areas: child survival, health and education.

Child Survival

Dungarpur has high child mortality rates compared to the rest of the state due to low birth weight, anaemia, pneumonia, dehydration and diarrhoea. Each of these originates either in early marriage and poor postnatal care (poverty, illiteracy, lack of extension services), or low quality drinking water supply (IDS, 2008: 64) (see Table 9.1).

Table 9.1

Mortality Rates in Dungarpur versus Rajasthan

Unit	*Rate*	*Persons (Total)*	*Male*	*Female*
Rajasthan	IMR	55	51	60
Dungarpur	IMR	63	61	65
Rajasthan	U5MR	74	68	81
Dungarpur	U5MR	81	79	85
Rajasthan	NMR	37		
Dungarpur	NMR	41		
Rajasthan	Post NMR	18		
Dungarpur	Post NMR	23		

Note: IMR - Input mortality rate; U5MR - Under five mortality rate; NMR - Net mortality rate.

Source: Annual Health Survey (AHS) 2012-13.

The health infrastructure is weak and malnutrition rampant. According to the AHS 2012-13, 42 per cent children had birth weights below 2.5 kg. Immunisation of children is poor: 18 per cent children did not get the polio vaccine and 5 per cent did not get any vaccine. Some instances were found where the mothers refused to immunise their sons, especially if he was born after several girls, on the apprehension that it might lead to a fever or other illnesses.

The weak health infrastructure should affect all children equally. But as seen from Table 9.1, all the mortality rates for girls are higher. Discrimination against girls is most visible in the sex ratios.

Sex Ratios

The overall sex ratio in Dungarpur fell from 1022 in 2001 to 994 in 2011. The child sex ratio (0-6 years) dropped from 955 in 2001 to 922. Yet, when compared to the rest of the state (928) or the country as a whole (940), it might appear that women are better off in the district than elsewhere or that the status of women is relatively better in a tribal society. However, the *Human Development Report* (IDS, 2008: 62) had pointed out for the 2001 census that if age-specific distribution is considered, then in the lower age groups (below 14 years), boys outnumber girls. The sex ratio is balanced only because surviving women outlive men in older age groups. The 2011 data shows a similar trend (Table 9.2), indicating that a high sex ratio of the whole population does not indicate gender equity.

Table 9.2

Sex Ratios in Dungarpur

Age group (Years)	*Sex Ratio (Total)*	*Sex Ratio (ST)*	*Sex Ratio (non-ST)*
0	884	907	805
0-4	925	948	844
5 to 9	928	954	843
10 to 14	931	952	867
15 to 17	957	998	854
All children (0-18)	932	957	852
15-19	1001	1049	886
20-29	1029	1032	1023
30-39	1059	1043	1092
40-49	999	976	1046
50-59	959	948	978
60+	1170	1175	1161

Source: Census 2011.

Sex ratios are better among tribals than the non-tribals. But among the tribals, the sex-ratio in the first year of birth and in the 0-4 age group reflects the possibility of sex selective abortions, female infanticide as well as a lower social priority for the survival of the girl child. This was corroborated in the field. "Do you understand the plight of the parents when they have one daughter after another? After a few deliveries, if a son is not born, some parents get desperate. Those who can afford go to Modassa and other small towns in Gujarat to get an ultrasound done. The foetus is aborted if it is a girl. It usually costs about ₹2,000-2,500," says Sachin. This was ratified by two ANMs.

Many rely on indigenous methods of female foeticide and infanticide. "If the foetus is a male, the woman pales (*sookh jati hai*) and the abdomen protrudes in front. If it is a female, she glows, puts on weight and the abdomen spreads laterally," says Putlibai, a midwife of Junagraha. This view was ratified by several others including Shanti, a midwife of Banra who claims to know herbal abortifacients.[18]

Several women reported having miscarriages. While miscarriages can be due to a host of reasons, especially the poor state of nourishment and the age of the mother, it seemed too much of a coincidence when in successive miscarriages of the same mother the foetus was a female. On the other hand, in some cases the foetus was a male. If abortifacients were used, it shows the unreliability of indigenous methods of sex determination of the foetus.

Female infanticide is shrouded in a veil of silence. The most common methods are suffocating, throttling or administering the latex of the *jangli thoor* (*Euphorbia caducifolia*) or *akdo* (*Calotropis procera*). Both plants grow abundantly in the region, the former being used for green fencing. Vandana (7) of Banra is the sixth of eight siblings. Soon after her birth, Ranjit tried to throttle Vandana but broke her collarbone. He administered her the latex of jungle *thoor*. Urmila left home for Gujarat after he brutally beat her. Their neighbours, Shanti and Bharat, who didn't have a daughter rescued Vandana. Timely treatment (and perhaps an underdose of the latex)

18. Some of the common abortifacients in this area are: (a) *Sainjna* (also known as *Sajjan*, Latin: *Moringa oliefera*) bark and root; (b) *Ringni* (*Solanum virginianum*) root decoction is administered and can be used for aborting foetuses upto five months old. Sometimes this is mixed with the tuber extract of *Kalihari* (*Gloriosa superba*). It can be fatal in high doses.

saved her. Shanti and Bharat have now adopted Vandana through an affidavit signed at the local police station.

The mother and the child are cloistered after delivery for 5-6 weeks for boys and 4 weeks for girls. Even close relatives are not allowed. This makes medical treatment, when needed, difficult, if not impossible. In emergencies, the taboo is broken for boys but not girls. In Banra, a girl child died during the ritual cloistering due to lack of medical attention in Ratanlal's house. The child would not have died if it were a boy. The argument given was that Ratanlal's father died during this period so the child got neglected.

Healthcare

Dungarpur has a very poor healthcare infrastructure (cf. IDS, 2008: Chapter 6). There is a shortage of doctors, of nurses and so on and the existing personnel often play truant. Travelling to the urban centres is expensive. There is a proliferation of quacks, locally known as Bengali or Gujarati doctors dispensing spurious medicines. The water and sanitation situation is pathetic, leading to diarrhoea, worms, amoebiasis, and giardiasis. While government schemes stipulate the construction of sanitary toilets, nowhere are these to be found. Children and adults defecate in the open and the former rarely wash their hands. Some women said, "How can we monitor where the children go and defecate during the whole day? We tell them to wash their hands but do they listen to us? Sometimes the younger ones don't even wash their bottoms."[19] Vector borne diseases like malaria (including *P. falciparum*) are prevalent.

Poor sanitation impacts women and girls' health, especially in the neglect of menstrual hygiene. When girls start menstruating, they do not discuss what to do with their mothers. Instead they handle the situation themselves, sometimes discussing with their peers. Using cloth is the norm and the menstrual cloth is washed with water and sometimes with soap powder. Other aspects, like swelling, white discharges or excessive bleeding are just not discussed and the girls learn to live with the problem.

19. FGD with adult women, Chatri, 11th June 2010.

While generally disadvantaged, deep probing brings out the gender discrimination in child healthcare. Dungarpur's *Adivasis* believe diseases are caused by *dhakans* (witches) and *matas* (female deities). *Matas* cause paralysis and have to be appeased, as did Kanu of Samota. She claims that after the appeasement, she can now walk with two sticks. If children have a persistent cough, *Dhekli Mata* has to be appeased by putting the child's old clothes on a babool tree (Mitra, 2010).

Dhakans dominate even when contemporary allopathic treatment is sought. Sujata of Chatri said that her husband and three of her brothers-in-law died in a short span of time with similar symptoms: wasting, coughing blood and fever. They consulted the best of doctors. She is convinced that her eldest sister-in-law is a *dhakan* who 'ate up' all her brothers-in-law.

The *bhopa* (indigenous faith healer) determines whether a *mata* or a *dhakan* has caused the illness. His cures involve sacrificial offerings and sometimes some herbs of limited (or at best psychosomatic) efficacy. If the disease be self-limiting, the psychological effects are tremendous. But when the disease recurs or continues, the services of a Bengali doctor is sought. Only after that (and if the patient survives till then), the child is taken to a proper qualified doctor.

The following discriminatory trends were seen. (a) For sick girls, the waiting period before the treatment (irrespective of form) is longer than for boys. (b) The interval between going to a bhopa and a Bengali doctor is shorter for boys. (c) Lesser numbers of girls than boys are taken to a regular doctor. (d) Even when a girl child is taken to a proper doctor, the full course of medicines/or sometimes the full prescription is not administered. Sometimes the more expensive medicines are dropped from the list, those often being the actual therapy.[20] The final decision of what kind of healthcare to seek is taken by males of the household. This holds irrespective of the nature of an illness and extends to disabled children.

Apart from diseases, a further source of health disadvantage emerges from gendered roles and socialisation. Cooking is done

20. FGD with women in Chatri; discussions with some ANMs, Accredited Social Health Activists (ASHAs), a quack, and a qualified medical practitioner and my own observations.

using bio-fuels like wood, dung and crop residues. The mother and the girl children, helping their mothers or even themselves cooking, are most affected by the smoke from biofuels, which contains several hazardous pollutants, like particulate matter, carbon monoxide, nitrogen dioxide, formaldehyde, polycyclic organic matter including carcinogens like benzopyrene. Exposure to indoor air pollution (IAP) from combustion of unprocessed biomass fuels are an important cause of morbidity and mortality. IAP can cause acute respiratory infections (ARI), chronic obstructive pulmonary disease (COPD), lung cancer, asthma, tuberculosis, low birth weight, cataract and eye irritation with various degrees of evidence (Parikh *et al.*, 2003).

Overtly, there is no gender discrimination in food allocation. But the girls are inculcated into eating less. A typical response is "I eat one roti in the morning and another in the evening. I don't feel hungry", said Paro, 13, of Banra. Paro makes the rotis as she doesn't go to school and her mother goes to the NREGS site for work. She justifies her brothers and father eating more as they are "hungrier", and "men need more food as they work harder and do heavier work."

Education

Education supply in Dungarpur is dismal. With an overall literacy rate of 60.78 per cent according to the 2011 Census, Dungarpur remains the worst district in Rajasthan and India as a whole. The gender gap in literacy showed some improvement, from 34.2 per cent points in the 2001 Census to 26.7 in 2011.

The District Information System for Education (DISE) data for 2013-14 shows that the primary level Net Enrolment Ratio (NER) was 82.4 per cent and 61.4 per cent for the upper primary level. The retention level was 68.1 per cent for the primary level. Other supply-sided factors, including non-compliance with RTE[21] norms and learning acquisition remain weak (ASER, 2014: District Performance Tables). The ASER data shows that 51 per cent pupils in third to fifth

21. The Right to Education Act, 2005, ensures all children from 6-14 years, the right to free, quality education.

standard could not read a first standard text and 82 per cent could not subtract.

Against this background, what is of interest here is how the existing schools and the educational supply reinforce patriarchy and misogyny. Krishna Kumar (2012) argues that teachers perform certain "civilisational functions" which are intrinsic to the reproduction of society. The job of primary school teachers, in addition to teaching the three 'R's, is to enable children to become social beings.

Kumar is correct inasmuch as the teachers in Dungarpur and perhaps elsewhere, being part of the patriarchal system, reproduce it well. At the national level, articulation of the importance of gender equality goes back to the Kothari Commission (GoI, 1964-1966) and the National Policy on Education 1986 (GoI, 1986), and its Plan of Action in 1992 (GoI, 1992). The Sarva Shiksha Abhiyan (SSA) and the District Primary Education Programme (DPEP) have also stressed gender mainstreaming (Bandopadhyay and Subrahmanian, 2008: 3).

Ideologies shaping gender identities, mutually reinforce each other, across institutions such as the family, workplace, and community (Kabeer and Subrahmanian, 1999). The school is such a site. Jha and Jhingran's (2002) study of schooling in communities across 10 districts showed the continued belief in the importance of early marriage for girls, and of maintaining asymmetries between men and women in educational attainment as a marker of relatively greater male social status. As a report for the National Commission for Women (NCW) argues, stereotypes about responsibilities, roles and opportunities, to which children are initially exposed in family settings, are endorsed in educational institutions (Walikhanna, 2013: 14-15). So schools are places where the socialising process is reinforced and given legitimacy and authenticity (Bourdieu and Passeron, 1977). The social knowledge relating to gender is constructed, validated and perpetuated by schools through textbooks, pedagogy, assessment and the academic milieu, what Stromquist *et al.* (1998) have termed the "hidden curriculum". In the textbooks, women/girls are represented as weak, dependent and stereotypically shy, and confined to the home, whereas the male characters are shown as strong, independent, innovative, outgoing and responsible for the outer world (Walikhanna, 2013: 14-15).

Diverse views on education emerged in the field, but what stands out is the strong desire to study amongst the children. This extends to even those who never went to school, especially the girls. They wistfully view their friends attending school and want to study. Yet the role of the girl is seen as a homemaker by the adults around them. In an FGD with women, it was said: "*Surji bhanin hoon collector bani java ni hai?*" (Will girls become Collectors after studying?) Says Gita of Chatri village, "Girls start flying in the clouds after studying a bit and refuse to perform household chores. If you ask them to do something they just open a book and bury their face in it." Adds Ramila, "Even if they study, they should help in the domestic work." Both Gita and Ramila married off their daughters soon after menarche.

Going back to the case of Vandana, she doesn't go to school either. Her foster parents say they will admit her in the next term. While Shanti says that they adopted her out of sympathy and pity, especially since they didn't have a daughter, Vandana does serve a very important function in the household. Her main task, apart from helping Shanti in the domestic chores and grazing cattle, is looking after, carrying around Kailash, the youngest child of Shanti and Bharat. He is six but physically and mentally challenged. The other reason Shanti said they wanted a daughter was that amongst them (they are Khants-ST), the sister has to perform the first *tilak* ceremony of the son when he gets married, and only after that the *tilak* is given by other villagers. If there be no sister, outsiders (kinsfolk) can do it but they will have to be given ₹1500-2000. The sister gets only ₹11 and a sari. What was obvious is that the couple are planning to have more children, as their eldest son Brijesh got married and left, and they want a son to look after them. Kailash cannot perform that task.

In most schools I visited, the domestication of girls was evident, as they performed reproductive tasks like filling water pitchers, sometimes sweeping the classroom and helping the mid-day meal cook. The boys performed 'heavier' tasks like moving furniture and sometime tending to the flowering plants. The general norm is to withdraw the girls after they reach puberty, around the time they are in eighth standard. This is partly due to fear for their 'safety' (given the high premium on female chastity and the parental fear that they might elope). "It is difficult for a girl to study after class 8. Everyone wants you to get married as soon as possible. What is the use of a girl studying is the question that is generally asked if ultimately we have to get married, bear children and look after the household." says Bela, 23, of Rakhodia. Bela resisted tremendous pressure to finish her master's degree.

The ideologies of misogyny are also reproduced in schools by corporal punishment (including verbal abuse) and sexual molestation, especially of the girl child. My classroom observations across several schools showed a tremendous level of fear in the children. The role plays enacted by the students showed that learning is not a joyous experience for children, but rather a very frightful one, as perhaps elsewhere in the country. Physical beatings, contorting the body in painful positions (*murga* posture), shouting, and abusing are rampant. Girls are not spared. Some women teachers outdo their male counterparts in terrorising the children.

"My class 1 teacher beat me so much that I wet my pants. She laughed. It hurts me so much even now," said Rani, a 2nd year college student in Dungarpur. "We want to study for we like it. We know it is important to study so that we can become something. But they beat us like cattle. We call Jitendra Sir [the Physical Training Instructor—PTI] Pitai (hitter) Sir. He comes drunk to class. We get beaten one day and don't go to school for the next 3-4 days. I get beaten regularly. The maths teacher doesn't teach. The English teacher beats us a lot. But if they stop beating us and start teaching, we will go to school regularly and study," says Harish, 11, a class 7 student of Tijor.

In effect, violence in schools subdues children, especially the girls. The pedagogy promotes superiority, aggression and dominance of the powerful over the weak. It also inculcates the value of submission to the powerful and being meek. "I will never go to that school again," says Maya of Thamka in a hurt tone and moist eyes. She dropped out of class 4. She was molested.

Misogyny thrives on suppression of women and the socialisation begins in school. Sexual molestation, especially of the girl child, even though legally punishable, is common. In role plays, the girl children showed how they were pinched all over their body, especially the chest. I came across instances of severe sexual molestation which according to the Protection of Children from Sexual Offenses Act, 2012, would be tantamount to rape. Yet a conspiracy of silence shrouds these incidents as the "family's and girl's *izzat* (honour)" is involved. The girl is withdrawn from school. In the records, such cases go down as left because of 'illness' or 'domestic work'. Women teachers do not molest but uphold the values of patriarchy in blaming the victim. "There were times when I would receive the unwanted attention of male teachers, especially around the time of puberty. There was no one I could mention this to, for I felt ashamed. One day I spoke to a lady teacher. Instead of taking action she blamed me. I felt so miserable that I didn't go to school for several days. Fortunately, the teacher was transferred. I don't know where he went but I used to feel bad for the girls in the school he went to," concluded Rani.

Conclusion

Patriarchy and by implication misogyny sustains itself by appropriating if not outright denying the right of women to say 'no'. Socialisation processes, specific in their manifestations, occur in ways that most women do not think it proper to assert themselves. This is not a result of "false consciousness" (Sen, 1990), but often the only option available to women in their particular social contexts. Enduring hardships is also a way of 'bargaining with patriarchy' (Kandiyoti, 1988), for the limited gains it may bring them, in terms of safety and food security perhaps. More so, given the deep-rooted nature of the ideology of female dependence and subordination across all institutions.

Using the example of the tribals of Dungarpur, I argue that idealising tribal society as egalitarian is not only erroneous, but also demonstrate how the various social institutions converge in suppressing women and simultaneously get them to internalise the suppression. This begins by appropriating the power to denigrate their social being (accusing them of witchcraft), killing them (foeticide and infanticide), and denying them property, assets, and decision-making powers. Their 'work' and identity is not respected. The ultimate is violence: verbal and physical including child marriage and pressure to produce sons in childhood.

Education, potentially liberating, seen in global discourses as the magic bullet for women's emancipation, fails in this objective in the local context, as patriarchal values are reinforced by the curriculum, the pedagogy and the teachers. Sara Longwe (1998), in the context of Zambia, went to the extent of seeing schooling as a tool for subordination of women and girls, rather than their emancipation. Perhaps in various permutations and combinations, this holds true across the country, in both tribal and non-tribal society, with girls being directed towards particular 'feminine' subjects, tasks and activities.

Women do protest in all possible forms used by the oppressed in any situation such as narrating to the outsider, flight, feet-dragging, and sometimes through the contemporary legal system, yet are bounded by the limits set by patriarchy. Support structures are limited, within both natal and marital families, as well as institutions of the state. Ultimately, to survive, they relent, and at best, shift allegiances from one man to another.

In conclusion, it has to be reiterated that a holistic analysis of the gender situation, including the role of ideologies is crucial for interventions to bring gender equality. Tokenism based on numerical parity leads only to superficial solutions.

References

Annual Survey of Education Report (ASER) (2014). *District Performance Tables, Rajasthan (http://img.asercentre.org/docs/Publications/ASER%20Reports/ASER_2013/District%20estimates/rajasthan.pdf)*

Annual Health Survey (2012-13). *Fact Sheet: Rajasthan (http://www.censusindia.gov.in/vital_statistics/AHSBulletins/AHS_Factsheets_2012-13/FACTSHEET-Rajasthan.pdf)*

Archer, Jeffrey (2010). "Caste-Off", in *Thereby Hangs a Tale*. London: Pan Books.

Bandopadhyaya, M. and R. Subrahmanian (2008). *Gender Equity in Education: A Review of Trends and Factors*, CREATE Pathways to Access, Research Monograph No.18. New Delhi: National University of Educational Planning and Administration (NUEPA).

Bourdieu, P. and J. Passeron (1977). *Reproduction in Education, Society and Culture*, London/Beverly Hills: Sage.

Choubisa, S.L. (1990). "Sickle Cell Trait in Damor Tribe of Dungarpur District, Southern Rajasthan", *Man in India* 70(4): 454-58.

Flood, M. (2007). "International Encyclopedia of Men and Masculinities". Cited in *https://en.wikipedia.org/?title=Misogyny*

Government of India (GoI) (1964-66). *Report of the Education Commission: Education and National Development*. New Delhi: Ministry of Education.

———. (1986). *National Policy on Education 1986*. New Delhi: Ministry of Human Resource Development.

———. (1992). *National Policy on Education 1986: Programme of Action 1992*. New Delhi: Ministry of Human Resource Development.

IDS (2008). *Dungarpur District Human Development Report-2007*. Jaipur: Institute of Development Studies (IDS).

Jha, J. and D. Jhingran (2002). *Elementary Education for the Poorest and other Deprived Groups: The Real Challenge of Universalisation*. New Delhi: Centre for Policy.

Kabeer, N. and R. Subrahmanian (1999). *Institutions, Relations and Outcomes. A Framework and Case Studies for Gender-aware Planning.* New Delhi: Zubaan.

Kandiyoti, D. (1988). "Bargaining with Patriarchy", *Gender and Society* 2(3) 274-90.

Koppers, W and L. Jungblut (1976). *Bowmen of Mid-India* (Vol. 1). Acta Ethnologica et Linguistica. Wein.

Krishna Kumar (2012). "What Teachers Do", *Ten Talks*. Bangalore: The Teacher Foundation. November *(http://teachersofindia.org/en/article/gender-inequities-school-teaching)*

Longwe, S. (1998). "Education for Women's Empowerment or Schooling for Women's Subordination"?, *Gender and Development* 6(2): 19-26.

Mitra, A. (2010). *Scoping Study on Gender Inequality in Relation to the Child Sensitive Social Protection (CSSP) Project in Dungarpur*. Unpublished report for Save the Children Bal Raksha Bharat (SCBR).

Nielsen, Jonas Østergaard, (2010). "The Outburst—Climate Change, Gender Relations, and Situational Analysis", *Social Analysis* 54(3): 76–89.

Pankaj, A.and R. Tankha (2010). "Empowerment Effects of the NREGS on Women Workers: A Study in Four States", *Economic and Political Weekly* XLV(30): 45-55, July 24.

Parikh, J., H. Biswas and S. Karmakar (2003). "Cooking with Biofuels", *Economic and Political Weekly* 38(26). 26 June-04 July.

Rao, N. (2008). *Good Women do not Inherit Land*. New Delhi: Social Science Press.

Sen, A. (1990). "Gender and Cooperative Conflicts", in I. Tinker (ed.), *Persistent Inequalities: Women and World Development*. New York: Oxford University Press. pp.123-49.

Sirnate, V. (2015). "When Marriage is Less than Sacred", *The Hindu*, 15 June, p.9, New Delhi edition.

Stromquist, N., M. Lee and B. Brock-Utne (1998). "The Explicit and the Hidden School Curriculum", in N. Stromquist (ed.), *Women in the Third World*. New York: Garland Publishing.

Walikhanna, C. (2013). *Report of the Expert Committee on Gender and Education*. New Delhi: National Commission on Women.

Others:

Census 2011, Various Tables, *http://www.censusindia.gov.in/2011census/population_enumeration.html*

District Information System for Education (DISE). *District Report Cards*, various years. Available at *http://www.dise.in/drc.htm*

Acknowledgements: This paper is based on the primary data I collected in Dungarpur for a scoping study on gender relations for Save the Children Finland, South Asia Regional Office and Save the Children—Bal Raksha Bharat. My thanks to Disa Sjoblom, Neema Pant and Harish for the many discussions and help they provided. My thanks to Mina Swaminathan for commenting on an earlier draft. Without Nitya Rao's persistence, encouragement and critical discussions on previous drafts, this paper would not have materialised. I am grateful to all the women, men and children who spoke to me in Dungarpur.

10

NITYA RAO

Mothers, Daughters and Well-being

Contentment and Conflict Amongst the Santals

Research on 'well-being'[1] has progressed from an exclusive focus on individual, 'objective' outcomes (such as literacy/schooling, health/nutrition and the ability to work and earn an income, as conceptualised in the *Human Development Report*) to being "a process that comprises material, relational and subjective dimensions" (White, 2010: 170). Varying with history, geography, across time, space and life cycle, the concept of well-being captures the dynamics of the relationships between these different elements in people's lives (White, 2010: 170).

However, a focus on binaries of poverty-wealth, well-being-ill-being, happiness-unhappiness persists in development discourses. Efforts to move people out of poverty (Narayan, 2009) often stress the material dimensions of people's lives, ignoring the relational, emotional and non-material, which are equally important for a person's well-being.

Families are major sites of gendered socialisation during childhood. Children observe the actions of their parents and as they grow older are socialised into gender roles, learning and reproducing, but sometimes challenging particular roles and responsibilities. Relationships are crucial in this process—with parents, siblings, peers and others. One of the key concerns expressed by parents relates to the life chances and future well-being of their children. The normative expectation of 'maternal altruism', where mothers are primarily responsible for the care of children and maintenance

1. McGregor (2008) has defined it as a state of being, which arises when human needs are met, one can act meaningfully to pursue one's goals and can enjoy a satisfactory quality of life.

of the household, however, poses a dilemma for women. While the well-being of her children is indeed a very important priority for a mother, she has to make choices: how far can she really be herself, how important is it to socialise the child, especially the daughter, to lead a life without bearing some of her own trials and tribulations, or is it preferable to sacrifice her own identity and possibly emotional well-being for the sake of the material well-being of her children and gaining a life of peace (cf Ahmed, 2014)? Women have to negotiate functional boundaries, and work out the extent to which deviations are permissible, within the larger context of patriarchy. When my own daughter was born, a dear friend of the family, now no more, sent me a congratulatory card, in which she wrote: "Never stop being yourself for the sake of your daughter. She will appreciate you for who you are, not what you gave up for her sake" (personal communication with Rosalind Wilson, March 1988).

While there has been a lot of attention to the mother-son relationship, especially in the context of debates around son preference in India, less is known about the mother-daughter relationship, perhaps because of its plurality, ambivalence and continuities (Hirsch, 1981), and the fear of exposing our pain, longing, nostalgia and struggles to retain our own identity. What little exists, relates to urban, middle/upper class, educated women, able to reflect on and write about their lives and relationships.

In this paper, I seek to add to this literature, exploring the relationships between mothers and daughters, and how it contributes to the shaping of well-being for both. While conscious of my own positionality as an urban, educated woman, and informed by my own experiences and relationships with both my mother and daughter, this paper is based on long-term, ethnographic work amongst the Santals in Dumka district, Jharkhand. It focuses specifically on unpacking the gender norms in relation to notions of 'reciprocity' amongst the Santals. As I explore in this paper, patrilineal inheritance practices relating to property and identity intensify the dilemmas and contradictions mothers and daughters face (Rao, 2008). A social context of male dominance reflected in institutions, both formal and informal, and relationships, force women to choose between the material and emotional aspects of relationships, especially *vis-à-vis* their daughters, at particular moments in time.

Yet the relationship is an important one because while material resources are exchanged between fathers and sons, a lot of the business of social reproduction takes place between mothers (or indeed fathers) and daughters. At times of ill-health or crises, daughters are called upon to support their parents, not just as an obligation, but as the result of a relationship built on notions of reciprocity and care, on emotional rather than material foundations. At the collective level, we have examples from the anti-dowry movement in urban, middle-class India which encouraged parents to take their daughters' voices seriously (Sen, 1994), treat them as one of their own, rather than 'paraya dhan' (someone else's property). At a more individual level, my own research amongst Dalits in Tamil Nadu revealed daughters' willingness to support their mothers, often abused, both financially and emotionally (Rao, 2014).

After briefly explaining the methodology and setting the context in the next section, I explore a few key dimensions relating to mother-daughter relationships conceptually and their links to well-being, before offering some tentative conclusions.

Methodology and Context

This paper is informed by long-term associations built over 15 years, in two villages, in different agro-ecological settings of Dumka district—one in the plains and one in hilly, forested terrain (Rao, 2008). Dumka district, the headquarters of the Santal Parganas division, has a majority Santal population. Despite small improvements, Santal literacy rates remain far below that of other social groups (Census 2011). Poverty and food insecurity are high. Santal women participate equally with their men in agriculture and other productive activities involving engagement with both labour and product markets. Mainly small-scale farmers, poor quality land, inadequate water (except during the monsoons) and lack of inputs have led to agriculture remaining low in productivity. Malnutrition and indebtedness are near-universal, and growing Maoism (an ultra-left, violent resistance movement) in the district has further restricted employment opportunities locally. Seasonal migration is rampant for both men and women—men often for longer periods to more distant locations in North India (Rao and Mitra, 2013).

Inheritance is patrilineal and residence generally patrilocal. There are instances where the husband stays in his wife's village for a certain period of time or even a lifetime (Rao, 2005a). The Santal customs in fact describe seven forms of marriage, ranging from arranged marriage to simple remarriage (following widowhood or separation) to elopement. Separation is common, with almost a third of the women and men I encountered, in their second or third marital relationship. Separation could be initiated by either men or women, and the causes often seemed insignificant. Women even mentioned their sense of not being valued or loved by the husband as a cause for separation (Rao, 2005b).

The high levels of marital mobility reflect a situation where women stand up for their rights, their dignity and their spaces, demanding mutuality in marriage. But in a patriarchal society, this often leads to parting with the children, with a potential negative effect on their own sense of well-being. While sons are left with the father, daughters are moved to the maternal grandparents or maternal uncle. In one stroke, in such situations the daughter loses both parents. There is a loss of trust, a letting down, in a psycho-emotional sense, but this also has material implications—in terms of her education, the food she gets and the work she has to do in her new home. Motherhood then is perhaps the one element that could lead to compromise in an unhappy conjugal relationship.

In this paper, I also draw on a specific piece of research on well-being, conducted with households with three living generations of men and women, in 2006-07. Thirty-one households were identified in the two clusters of villages. While all Santal, the sample is skewed in favour of the educated, often Christian, and those with regular employment, usually as teachers in state schools. Life expectancy is lower amongst the poor, those dependent on agriculture or wage labour, making three generations hard to find in these households.

A hundred and thirty-eight (138) people (61 men and 77 women) were interviewed. The numbers reveal excess male mortality especially in the oldest generation. In fact, there were not more than a handful of men above the age of 45 in the more remote, hilly cluster of villages, pointing to the importance of location in mediating the relationship between the personal and the material. The interviews began with questions on the individual's view on happiness and life satisfaction, and were followed up with questions on various dimensions of well-being such as work, assets, education, health, marital relations, social standing, politics, identity and others that they raised. Each interview took close to two hours.

The responses were ambiguous, especially in relation to feelings of happiness/unhappiness. For instance, for men, their sense of happiness and satisfaction with life was linked to appreciation of the efforts they were making in fulfilling their 'provider' roles, namely, ensuring the food security of their family. In a context of rainfed agriculture, high rates of indebtedness and lack of inputs, this was not guaranteed, but conditional on nature, their efforts and relationships. The uncertain realities of people's lives points to the problems of averaging across indicators to arrive at indices such as the gross national happiness index. Mooted first by the Kingdom of Bhutan to emphasise the importance of the environment and people's psychological well-being and community relationships, and not just economic or material development, it nevertheless masks differences within communities and over time. Further, people's priorities shift in accordance with their positionality (economic and social) and stage in the course of life.

Women placed importance on reciprocity and status, which included both material and emotional support *vis-à-vis* their larger family. Reciprocity for them includes support to parents, grandparents, siblings, children and grandchildren both in financial/material terms, as well as love, care and affection. It also includes the absence of quarrels and conflicts within the family. Status includes the ability to work, to earn, to have a stable job, to accumulate assets, have children, and successfully overcome adversity/difficulties. While men too laid emphasis on their children's well-being, for men it was linked to educational attainments, performance in school and the ability to get a job, while women articulated a more general notion of their children doing well, including their education, their ability to get good marriage partners, their ability to get a job and have a happy family life.

In this paper, I focus particularly on the nature, meanings and construction of reciprocity and status in the mother-daughter relationship. I give voice to women, both mothers and daughters, telling their stories without imposing any value judgement on their actions or emotions.

Understanding the Mother-Daughter Relationship

A key role for a woman is that of a mother. The biology of childbearing is in many ways seen to be responsible for the gendering of roles and division of work in society. Women are typically seen to be more concerned with private lives and reproducing for the family, and men with public spaces of decision-making, politics and engaging with the markets. The central role of motherhood in women's lives has been held responsible for the subordination of women (Edholm *et al.*, 1977). While not devaluing motherhood *per se*, examples of women resisting social domination in myriad ways and in 'everyday' forms, often very subtle, point to the need to question some of these stereotypes. Through the case studies presented in this paper, I demonstrate how women manipulate patriarchy, accepting certain elements to resist others.

At a more collective level too, the women's movement has been struggling to gain recognition for women as 'persons', refuting the idea of a family as existing by 'nature' (cf Ortner, 1974). There is nothing innate about biology, traditions, necessity or norms that make women better placed to provide love and care compared to other members of the household (Nussbaum, 2000). While the family does have virtues, emotions, attachments and affiliations are central human capabilities (Nussbaum, 2000), and it is hard to imagine ourselves as separate, individuated selves, it is also a major site of oppression—of violence and abuse, of potential discrimination and gender inequality in nutrition, health and educational opportunities. Recognising this duality in the role of the family as a source of solidarity as well as neglect, the women's movement in India has raised their voices for reproductive choices and rights on the one hand, while demanding social support especially in terms of childcare services on the other.

Rich (1976), by pointing to the silence around the mother-daughter relationship in her controversial work, set off considerable feminist, interdisciplinary work on this theme. While the mother-child relationship is perhaps the essential human relationship, it is often blamed for the domestication, confinement and subordination of women across contexts. As a result, it has contributed to a burden of maternal guilt, a constant reviewing of whether they have failed their children, or could have done better.

What then is meant by the nurture of daughters? At one level, it is trust and tenderness, a love not of the 'sacrificial' kind, but rather one that shows courage. While there is no end to the limits that society imposes on women, the most important thing one woman can do for another is to expand her sense of possibilities, her understanding of choices that she can make and the implications of these. It is important for the mother "to refuse to be a victim" (Rich, 1976: 246). This in fact corresponds to the concept of well-being, which is seen to ultimately be about people's goals and aspirations, and about the choices they make in trying to achieve these goals (cf Gough *et al.*, 2007). The quality of the mother's life and her struggle to expand the surrounding spaces, demonstrates to her daughter that these possibilities exist. Yet in the struggle for physical survival, a reality for many poor women in India, and the Santals, demonstrating the fighting spirit to their daughters almost always means absence, even long-term separation. It may involve migration for work; it may also mean leaving the child with a maternal uncle or grandparents during their critical growing-up years.

There is likely to be the deepest love but also the most painful estrangement between mothers and their daughters, a shared knowledge, but also a desire to be free of each other (Hirsch, 1981). The collection of oral testimonies from working class or lower middle class (British) women reveals how many women hated their mothers for constantly being tired, overworked and oppressed, yet doing exactly the same *vis-à-vis* their daughters (McCrindle and

Rowbotham, 1977: 4). If mothers were strong and independent, resisted their domestication and subordination, this too appeared selfish and was construed as neglect by the daughter, especially in her early years. More so, if the daughters ended up in mothering roles *vis-à-vis* their younger siblings. In retrospect, many of them saw these same actions as worthy of respect.

The birth of a daughter is not celebrated in most communities across India. For the mother, it can have several consequences—from the extreme and painful act of infanticide, to, more commonly, a period of neglect, and in some circumstances of being devalued as a wife, having to accept another wife or even separation. Sona's mother[2] recounts how the most difficult time in her life was when she gave birth to her third daughter—the failure to produce a son almost put her future in jeopardy. Fortunately for her, the next child was a son. The relationship with daughters then is often conflictual, but also changes over a lifetime. While some see closeness developing in later years (Fischer, 1986), others see this period as more demanding and difficult (Barnett, 1988). In their study of a group of adult, employed daughters, between the ages of 25 and 55, Barnett *et al.* (1991) found that quality of the daughter-mother relationship significantly impacted the daughter's subjective well-being and levels of distress. The same probably holds true for the mother.

Gulati and Bagchi (2005), exploring the lives of educated Indian women, including many academics, isolate several key elements in mother-daughter relationships. First of all, given the engagement of women with a large number of kin, it often became difficult to disentangle the relationship of oneself with one's own parent. Secondly, while several of these women made hard choices in terms of their careers as well as family life, the sense of satisfaction or happiness they express emerges not just from 'externally recognised success', but rather from having 'established a sphere of autonomy where they could make decisions that nurture themselves as well as others' (Gulati and Bagchi, 2005: 10). What many of these women remember is the strength of their own mothers and grandmothers

2. All names of people and places have been changed to maintain anonymity.

in dealing both with family crisis such as the death of a husband and related internal dynamics, as well as external social change. This included risky ventures such as negotiating with the bureaucracy and police in refugee camps post-Partition, or providing shelter to Muslim strangers from across the border.

An important defining moment for women, especially in a patrilineal, patrilocal context, is marriage—preparing the daughter for marriage (which implies also a break in daily contact with people with whom she is closest), arranging the marriage and post-marriage support. Despite the rhetoric around the sanctity of marriage, numerous examples of failed marriages exist, influencing in turn the relationship between mother and daughter. It becomes a test of their support and understanding for each other. Children are their proudest accomplishment, yet relations with children are often distorted due to their own lack of personal space as well as voice in influencing marriage decisions (Gulati and Bagchi, 2005: 19).

When speaking to women in the field, what commonly emerged was the coexistence of love and resentment. In isolating the causes of resentment, one is confronted by the contradictions inherent in patriarchy—the gendered access to resources it entails—and the choices it then poses in fulfilling material expectations. As some of the stories reflect, when mothers resist patriarchy and are punished through material deprivations, the daughters instead of challenging the structures of patriarchy, challenge/resent their mother. The notions of 'maternal deprivation' are constituted not just of material deprivation, but the feeling of helplessness to support one's child, particularly one's daughter. It is this contradictory element in women's relationships within patriarchy, the ways in which female experiences (both of mothers and daughters) are shaped by male structures (Hirsch, 1981), which are explored in the rest of this paper. The purpose is to highlight how 'well-being happens in relationships' (White, 2010: 171), the implications of relational shifts for women's emotional well-being and in turn ensuring their basic human capabilities (to use Nussbaum's phrase).

Perceptions of Reciprocity: Insights from the Field

The tensions between marital fulfilment and motherhood in a Santal woman's life play out most significantly in the relationships they build with their daughters, in material terms at least, as sons are expected to be taken care of by their fathers. I start this section with a focus on the feelings and emotions of the daughter, which range from hatred to resentment, from understanding to intimacy, often changing over time, depending on how their own futures work out. In presenting these cases, I explore the interlinkages between material, personal and relational aspects of well-being that they highlight. I then turn to the perspective of the mother.

Hating Her Mother

Sheela, 65, is a retired primary schoolteacher. She is educated, soft-spoken, helpful and reflective, well-liked by most people in the village. In 2010, she was elected *sarpanch* (head/leader) of her village local government (*panchayat*). I lived with her family in the village, and she became one of my closest friends. Her narration of her relationship with her mother, whom she hated, was poignant. Sheela's father, a school teacher, earned a meagre salary of ₹60 per month. Yet, he had four wives. The eldest had a daughter, Sheela was born to the second. The third wife had three children, and the fourth did not stay long with her father, finding the situation oppressive. While the social system allows polygyny, clearly this is not straightforward for the women concerned. Some may accept and adjust, while others resent the apparent absence of love and reciprocity from their spouse.

They were poor, her father did not have much land, and this too was disputed by his brothers. Yet, he insisted on educating all his children. Sheela and her elder sister (by his first wife) studied for a year or two in the local village school and were then admitted to the Moharo Mission School. Her father paid the fees, even though they had often to cut down on the food they ate at home. She recalled how other children would bring snacks from home to the hostel, but she never brought any. Both sisters studied hard, and ultimately both got jobs as teachers.

When her father married a third time, her own mother got upset and started demanding a share of the property for her upkeep. Sheela begged her mother not to insist, as this would affect their household condition and potentially her education. Yet, her mother persisted in her claims creating a permanent rift between them. While deep down she resented the social system which allowed polygyny, her anger was directed at her mother, whose actions (challenging her husband) potentially affected her personal interests. When she came home from school, she had to listen to the bantering of her step-mother who resented the fees being paid for Sheela's education. She grew up hating her mother, yet admiring her father for his commitment to education and to treating all the children equally.

Sheela felt that even though she was the only child, her mother preferred to take advice from others, harming their family's well-being in the process. After Sheela got married, her mother came and stayed with them, cultivating her share of the marital land. Sheela was annoyed, but being the only child of her mother, could not throw her out of the house. She apologised to her father for the behaviour of her mother, as the relationship with her father was central to her well-being. After his retirement in 1980, with failing health, her father and his third wife came and lived with them for six years, and this gave her an opportunity to reciprocate her feelings for him. Just the fact that her step-mother looked after her father until his death, has enabled a shared intimacy between them. She still visits her step-mother, who lives on the outskirts of Dumka town (with her son). She also takes pride in maintaining a range of relationships and affiliations, especially with her siblings: her sister, with whom she studied, was also her closest confidante. Her brothers, all employed, maintain cordial relationships and visit her occasionally.

This narrative of a fragile, emotional relationship, is not due to marital mobility and abandonment, but reflects the tensions of being in a polygynous household. When her father married a third time, if her mother had left him and moved away, perhaps Sheela's future would have taken a different turn. She may not have been able to continue her education, she may have had to work in the home of her maternal grandparents (as Maki's daughter Surajmani, discussed in the next section, did). Her mother claiming a share of the property, of course, made life difficult for the rest of the family, but things could have been worse for Sheela herself had her mother left the village. At least now her father, committed to education, continued to support all his children, without discriminating against her because of her mother's claims. Perhaps it was also a man's guilt—and recognition of his responsibility as a provider.

While polygyny is an affront to the woman's identity and one can understand why Sheela's mother was determined to fight for her rights, for the children, it provided a strong support base. Sheela's step-sister, as long as she was alive, and step-brothers have been a source of great emotional support. When one looks at the case from a gender perspective, rather than from the woman's perspective alone (Rao, 2005a), the father's position becomes somewhat more complex and ambiguous. To compensate for his shifting sexual and emotional needs, he was willing to provide equally for all his wives and children, including daughters, helping develop a sense of sharing and camaraderie amongst them. This semblance of equity and justice creates a dilemma for the mother—resisting the system only served in this case to evoke the resentment of her daughter, as their material and personal interests were opposed to each other, at that moment in time.

Daughter's Sense of Desertion

Surajmani (11 in 2006), was an unhappy child. She never knew her father, as her mother Maki left her marital home just before Surajmani was born. Maki was 18 then, ill, and her husband had no money for medical treatment. She returned to her parents' home. Her daughter was born, but her husband never visited, instead he remarried. Maki was deserted. When Surajmani was seven, she decided to marry a man from a neighbouring village. She hoped to keep her daughter with her, but her failure to conceive again, led to quarrels with her husband and mother-in-law, who refused to allow Surajmani to stay with them. She too didn't want her daughter to see her being abused. Maki wanted to educate her daughter and give her all her love, but they barely managed to meet once a month.

Outwardly, Maki seemed reconciled to this separation, keen to build a new family and a new life. Her main concern when we spoke was not her daughter, but rather the difficulty in conception, as reproductive failure could probably result in another failed marriage.

Marriage for her appears to be the only way to build a home of her own. Maki is a strong woman, and while living in her parent's house, over the past several years, she engaged in hard work. She would migrate several times a year to Bengal in search of seasonal agricultural work. Even now, she works on the fields of her second husband and also makes and sells liquor in the bi-weekly local market to earn some extra cash income. Despite her economic independence, she cannot imagine life as a single woman, as this she feels will deny her a 'home' of her own. Her parents barely have any land, and she has three brothers with whom it would have to be shared. The choices of women such as Maki get shaped by patrilineal inheritance practices that deny the daughter a share of her parent's property—the contours of emotional/personal well-being thus set by material constraints.

But more important, Maki cannot face the psychological state of rejection, the feeling of not being wanted. She does not want to be like her mother. Her father brought a second wife 20 years ago, from one of his migrations to Bengal, yet her mother stayed on with her four children. Her father gave her mother a larger share of his less than one acre of land, so she could feed the children. He also helped her plough the land. He built himself and his new wife a separate house next to hers. Her mother chose to accept this option—it gave her some security, and she had the children, which gave her social respect. While motherhood helped her realise her identity, it also closed down the exit option. Instead, she internalised her well-being as the happiness of her children.

But for Maki, still young, having a man is important, and a reaffirmation of her femininity. A reciprocal relationship, with a man who cares for her, is crucial for her personal well-being. She would not be happy as a mere 'working body', fulfilling the role of a mother. Her marriage gives her material security, yet is also a source of dejection. She is worried that if the marriage doesn't work, she would not only be rejected as a woman and a wife yet again, but would also in the meanwhile have earned the resentment of her daughter, and hence failed as a mother too.

Surajmani lives with her grandparents. Her mother's remarriage was a moment of intense distress, sadness and loss. The only person in whom she could confide was her friend, another girl from the village. While her grandparents are kind, after her mother moved to her second husband's village, there was one set of hands less to work, so she was roped into helping with a range of household tasks. Her main job however was to take the cattle out to graze each day, so even though she wanted to go to school, she couldn't. While she loves her mother very much and meets her once a month, she feels lonely in her absence and resents the fact that her mother got remarried and left her behind.

The emotional abandonment of the daughter by the mother has material consequences as well, in a context of poverty. Her mother completed her primary education, but Surajmani was unable to pursue her own aspirations. She sees her friends in school and she knows that her lack of education will affect her life chances. While she has enough food to eat, she is not optimistic about her future—it can only be a hard life filled with manual work. During a visit in February 2015, although I could meet neither Maki nor Surajmani, I learnt that Maki had left her second marriage and was now remarried a third time, while Surajmani too was married in a neighbouring village. According to her grandfather, she was happy.

And such cases are not isolated ones. Baha is 28 years old. She was married when barely 12, and a few years later had a son. When her son was three, her husband died. She stayed with her in-laws to look after her son, but her father-in-law tried to rape her. This upset her father, it became a matter of pride, and he brought her home. The child was left behind; being a male he would inherit his father's property. Baha was miserable, but in the clash of male egos, that of her father and father-in-law, she could do nothing. Two years later, her son died of illness, she knew it was from neglect.

Her parents then started pressurising her to remarry, she was only 20. She was not keen, but a man from the same village had lost his wife, so she was married to him. While her parents are kind to her, she feels that they cannot understand her pain and feelings. She never got an opportunity to study, and was married early. She lost the child she had. Her husband is a nice man and helpful, but they have had no children. She worries about this, as once he went to Bengal for seasonal agricultural work and there had an affair with another woman. He was fined, and apologised for his behaviour, but like Maki, reproductive failure is clearly a concern in terms of her future security.

Baha understands the attitude of her mother, who was herself abandoned as a child. Baha's grandmother was not happy with her first marriage, so moved out. She was then deserted by her second husband, after she gave birth to a daughter. Her grandmother got remarried a third time when her mother was about 10 years old, but left her mother behind in her natal home. A few years later, however, she took her daughter to stay with her in her new marital home. She did not have any more children, her husband, much older, accepted Baha's mother as his daughter. Through hard work, her grandparents gradually built up assets in the form of food stocks, goat and cattle. As her grandparents grew old, they came to stay with Baha's parents, bringing their cattle with them. Her grandfather died four years ago, but her grandmother continues to live with her mother's family, they feed her and take care of her, and in return use her cattle for their cultivation. Baha feels that perhaps it is the childhood experiences of her mother, both of being abandoned for a while, but then finding a new father and moving to a new home, that made her insist that Baha get remarried and make a new life for herself.

These two examples bring to light a range of extremely complex themes. Both Maki's and Baha's mothers supported them in their separation/widowhood, giving them a place to stay, and encouraging them to find new partners. They were concerned about their daughters' futures, wanting them to get remarried and find love and happiness in their lives. For the younger women, this meant abandoning their children, failing in their role as mothers, in an attempt to find themselves as women and secure their futures as wives. While Maki's daughter is alive, and now married herself,

Baha's departure from her marital home led ultimately to the death of her child. As mothers, they cannot forgive themselves. At times, this gets expressed as anger against their own mothers, for what they see as improper advice, and a failure to protect their own children.

The stories are not straightforward. The older generation of women were seeking to help their daughters, projecting their "own ambivalence about being female in a patriarchal culture" (Hirsch, 1981: 206). They did not just bargain with patriarchy, but also tried to reformulate and redefine its rules. Baha's mother and grandmother were perhaps more successful in this than Maki's mother, although she too managed secure access to land for herself and her children, albeit a small plot. The daughters, however, end up blaming their mothers for not giving better counsel, for forcing a separation between mother and daughter (son in the case of Baha), rather than finding alternate pathways that could continue to nurture these bonds and relationships.

There appears to be a generational shift too on what constitutes well-being and the contours of reciprocity entailed. It is important to point out here that this is bounded by class position and geographical location. While both were poor, Maki's mother lived in the plains village, with a small plot of land to cultivate, and Baha's mother in the forested cluster of villages, dependent on both land and forests for survival. With diversified livelihood opportunities including seasonal migration prevalent in the former, social bonds had already started to weaken, in contrast to the latter village. The general levels of social reciprocity and its correlation to the ability to access material resources also contributes to the shifting terrain of relationships between mothers and daughters.

Mothering Options: Material *versus* Emotional Needs

Given the link to material resources and personal security discussed in the last section, it seems clear that mothering and the 'maternal' is a social and not a biological category. It is constituted of what mothers do, rather than what they are. "Maternal thinking" can then be separated from the "ideology of womanhood (which) has been invented by men" (Ruddick, 1980: 345), and in fact the term 'mother' can be extended to include shared parental care. This thought is rather more radical than the current emphasis on motherhood and fatherhood as complementary (see Sriram in this volume), which itself is an improvement on near exclusive parenting by the mother. In this section, I explore different elements of "maternal thinking", to use Ruddick's phrase, *vis-à-vis* their daughters.

Providing Material Support

Hopni, 65 in 2007 (died in 2012), had a daughter, Nachni, and a son. When the son was about eight, he died of illness, and soon after, so did her husband. She was close to her daughter, wanted to stay with her, and get her married to a *gharjawae* (resident son-in-law) when she came of age (cf Rao, 2008). However, her husband's male kin got wind of these plans and made it clear that they would not allow her daughter to inherit her father's land. Hopni was at a loss on how to proceed, and ended up marrying a man from a nearby village. He did not let her daughter stay with them, as he already had a son, so the girl was moved to her maternal uncle's home. The uncle got Hopni's daughter married when she was still very young, but this marriage did not last. A few years later she married again. Hopni's second husband died in the late 1990s, and since then, she has been helping her daughter in myriad ways. When Hopni's stepson started resenting her support to Nachni, she demanded a partition of the property. Her grandson stayed with her to help with the cultivation. She gives any surplus to Nachni's family, as the latter's alcoholic husband is unwell and unable to do much work.

Although there were a few years when she and her daughter were separated from each other, the villages being close, they continued to meet. Hopni felt that by entering the second marriage, she was able to access property, which she could now use to help her daughter. This could have been more difficult in her first marital home, where there were many more people interested in the property. While perhaps at that moment of remarriage she failed in her role as a mother emotionally, but she feels that this has been compensated for. Over the past two decades, both materially and emotionally, while not owning much herself, she has been the main source of support for her daughter. Hopni negotiated a host of power relations, with the marital kin of her first husband (somewhat unsuccessfully in terms of securing her share of property), and with her stepson (in securing a partition of her husband's property), to support her own daughter better negotiate her marriage and maintain her household.

Resisting Remarriage

Despite the acceptance of secondary unions, and its common occurrence, several women have resisted remarriage, for the dependence it entails on another man. Jhumri is a case in point. She was widowed at 30, 10 years previously, a mother of two young daughters—the elder 10, and the younger 4. There was a lot of pressure on her to get remarried—she was young, she had only daughters, who would ultimately get married, so she needed to build a new life for herself. She refused, precisely because of the fear that a new husband might refuse to support her daughters, and she could not bear the thought of leaving them behind. She therefore fought for her share of her husband's property to maintain herself and her children. This was not easy, as she had no sons.

The support of her parents was crucial in enabling her to fight for her share of her late husband's property, permissible in Santal customary law, as long as the widow does not get remarried (Rao, 2005b). She cultivates her land and engages in wage labour, but occasionally if she is in need, her parents give her food or cash. She is educated up to grade 9 and was determined to educate both her daughters. The elder one was in college, living with her maternal grandparents, from whose home travelling to college was easier. Jhumri's father retired from the army, and from his pension, he contributes partially for her elder granddaughter's education. She is very grateful to them for this support, as she knows that single-handedly it may have been difficult for her to meet their educational needs in addition to all the daily necessities. Jhumri has chosen a life of struggle, and of independence, mainly to give her daughters all she has and the best chances in their own lives. They recognise this and study hard.

A second instance is Sona, 40, who too was widowed about 10 years ago; although a mother of six children at that time, the eldest daughter married, but the youngest less than a year old. On her husband's death, Sona faced harassment from her relatives—she was called a witch, abused and isolated. Yet, she never thought about remarrying, having five children to bring up. She is very close to her eldest daughter, Lalita, 20, who along with her husband, helps her cultivate the land, especially ploughing it for her on time. This was not easy for Lalita, as she too had to manage all the household tasks in her marital home. Yet she realised that at this moment, her mother needed her support. Lalita clearly recognises her mother's role in educating her (up to grade 8) and in supporting her marriage to a man of her choice. Apart from cultivation, Sona engaged in wage labour and brewed and sold liquor, in order to feed her children. In return for the support from Lalita and her husband, Sona gave them a field to cultivate for their own use. Mother and daughter meet every week in the local market and exchange news and confidences. They remain as close as they have ever been, both with their independent families to nurture.

What Do These Life Stories Tell us About Well-being?

The lifestories discussed in this paper point to the difficulties of generalisation, of assumptions of 'good' and 'bad', as they each have a story to tell in terms of choices made in particular contexts and at particular moments in time. Yet patterns can be detected—the search for economic security (in the context of extreme poverty), age and positionality of the woman concerned, the number of children, their age and sex, the responsibility demonstrated by the husband/ father as 'provider', to name a few. Facing resistance from her marital kin, an older woman like Hopni, for instance, remarried, hoping through this move, to help her daughter in the longer term. Each decision—should they separate or claim their share of property in case their husband brings a second wife, should they remarry or not if widowed—however, involves certain trade-offs, when analysed from the perspective of well-being—between material, personal and relational concerns.

The choices women have, how far they can push the boundaries and deviate from the norm, need to be located within an understanding of the social systems and structures, and how these are changing in the context of larger political and economic changes. In the forest cluster, the erstwhile *Damin-i-koh*, the voice of the *majhi* (headman) and community leaders was much more respected than in the plains, where even minor complaints are now lodged with the police and courts (Rao, 2008). Women then potentially have greater voice in the hilly tracts, with some of their customary entitlements likely to be respected, to maintain local peace and a sense of fairness within the community. This, however, cannot be generalised, as over the last decade, with the construction of a road through the forest, and enhanced interaction with the 'outside' world, perspectives are changing. While seen as a society with relative gender equality, the examples presented in this paper reveal that this claim may be far from the truth. Women need to fight for their rights, these are not automatically given to them. Their ability to fight is shaped by their economic (in)security, social standing and kin support, within the diverse ecological contexts in which they live. Without understanding the microcosm of women's lives and contexts, it is difficult to understand their everyday struggles and resistances, to create a better life for themselves and eventually their daughters.

Why have I focused only on the mother-daughter relationship and not on the primordial mother-son one? First of all, the quality of the mother-son relationship is of an entirely different order. The son is expected to look after the parents in their old age, and in many ways, to ensure her position and security in future years, the mother does not fail to shower favours on her son. There is clearly a material dimension to this relationship, an expectation of future returns. Further, in a patrilineal and patrilocal society, the son normally lives close to the parents, in the same house or in a different house in the same compound, so maintaining a cordial relationship becomes a necessity from a practical standpoint as well.

Daughters, on the other hand, leave home upon marriage, but are also not expected to contribute in any significant way to the lives of the parents in their old age. In the absence of material obligations, the relationship between a mother and a daughter tends to be honest, reflecting feelings of love and hate, of conflict and support, and provides an insight into the emotions of women, as they feel and experience them. There could be errors of judgement in this process that lead to tensions between the mother and daughter, but neither has much to gain from sustained conflict; in a sense, both occupy subordinate positions within a patriarchal social system. When things go wrong in the daughter's life, she may blame her mother for not giving her proper advice, or indeed for misguiding her. This is particularly the case when it comes to conjugal relations and their different understandings and expectations of it, from their particular subject-positions—as a mother and as a wife (possibly also a mother herself).

Starting from this insight, the paper has further pointed to the contradictions and conflicts between women's interests as women, and women's interests as mothers. Mothering is a significant life experience for women and often they tend to choose this identity over others. Living up to the identity of a mother is however not easy, as the cases here demonstrate, and often involve lives of struggle and hardship, of compromise and acceptance, of abuse, and even rejection.

This takes us to the multiple understandings of the notions of emotional pain and well-being. Women in different positions have different perceptions of well-being at particular moments in time. The choices and decisions are hard, for the mother as well as for the latter. Some of their own dilemmas in 'bargaining with patriarchy' (Kandiyoti, 1988) are then projected on to their daughters. While the mother is concerned about the welfare of her daughter, the daughter is perhaps looking for a different kind of support. It could be affirmation of her marriage, inspiration to carry on fighting to improve the relationship, rather than backing out of it. Of course, when the daughter is young, if the mother prioritises her own emotional well-being, this could potentially lead to physical separation. While justified in terms of future material support, this can be emotionally painful nevertheless (Rao, 2012).

An unexpected finding is the difference in the way these women define their rights and identities in contrast to the urban, middle class feminist movement in India. The women discussed in this paper have struggled to expand both their sex-related and employment-related capabilities to use Nussbaum's phraseology. They have struggled to push the boundaries of patriarchal control, for themselves, and for their children, often having to choose one struggle over the other. Compromising on their personal interests does not make them less conscious or aware of their selves; clearly it is an informed, though constrained, choice. It is an attempt to forge new opportunities for care through developing new forms of affiliation. An exploration such as this one into mother-daughter relationships then provides us with deeper insights into the nature of women's choices, the factors influencing their exercise of agency, and the outcomes of these choices. Often it is harder lives.

References

Ahmed, F.E. (2014). "Peace in the Household: Gender, Agency, and Villagers' Measures of Marital Quality in Bangladesh", *Feminist Economics* 20(4): 187-211.

Barnett, R.C. (1988). "On the Relationship of Adult Daughters to Their Mothers", *Journal of Geriatric Psychiatry* 21: 37-50.

Barnett, R.C., N. Kibria, G.K. Baruch and J.H. Pleck (1991). "Adult Daughter-parent Relationships and Their Associations with Daughters' Subjective Well-being and Psychological Distress", *Journal of Marriage and the Family* 53: 29-42.

Edholm, F., O. Harris and K. Young (1977). "Conceptualising Women", *Critique of Anthropology* 3(9 & 10): 101-30.

Fischer, L.R. (1986). *Linked Lives: Adult Daughters and Their Mothers*. New York: Harper and Row.

Gough, I., J.A. McGgregor and L. Camfield (2007). 'Theorising Well-being in International Development", in I. Gough and J.A. McGregor (eds.), *Well-being in Developing Countries: From Theory to Research*. Cambridge, UK: Cambridge University Press. pp.3-43.

Gulati, L and J. Bagchi (eds.) (2005). *A Space of her Own: Personal Narratives of Twelve Women*. New Delhi: Sage.

Hirsch, M. (1981). "Mothers and Daughters", *Signs* 7(1): 200-22.

Kandiyoti, D. (1988). "Bargaining with Patriarchy", *Gender and Society* 2(3): 274-90.

Krause, C.A. (1978). *Grandmothers, Mothers and Daughters: An Oral History Study of Ethnicity, Mental Health, and Continuity of Three Generations of Jewish, Italian and Slavic-American Women*. The Institute on Pluralism and Group Identity of the American Jewish Committee.

McCrindle, J. and S. Rowbotham (eds.) (1977). *Dutiful Daughters: Women Talk about their Lives*. London: Allen Lane.

McGregor, J.A. (2008). "Well-being, Development and Social Change in Thailand", *Thammasat Economic Journal* 26(2): 1-27.

Narayan, D. (2009). *Moving Out of Poverty: The Promise of Empowerment and Democracy in India*. London and Washington, D.C.: Palgrave Macmillan and The World Bank.

Nussbaum, M. (2000). *Women and Human Development: The Capabilities Approach*. New Delhi: Kali for Women.

Ortner, S.B. (1974). "Is Female to Male as Nature is to Culture?", in M.Z. Rosaldo and L. Lamphere (eds.), *Woman, Culture, and Society*. Stanford, CA: Stanford University Press. pp.68-87.

Rao, N. (2005a). "Questioning Women's Solidarity: The Case of Land Rights, Santal Parganas, Jharkhand, India", *Journal of Development Studies* 41(3): 353-75.

———. (2005b). "Kinship Matters: Women's Land Claims in the Santal Parganas, Jharkhand", *Journal of the Royal Anthropological Institute* 11(4): 725-45.

———. (2008). *Good Women do not Inherit Land: Politics of Land and Gender in India*. New Delhi: Social Science Press and Orient Blackswan.

———. (2012). "Breadwinners and Homemakers: Migration and Changing Conjugal Expectations in Rural Bangladesh", *Journal of Development Studies* 48(1): 26-40.

———. (2014). "Caste, Kinship and Life-course: Rethinking Women's Work and Agency in Rural South India", *Feminist Economics* 20(4): 78-102.

Rao, N. and A. Mitra (2013). "Migration, Representations and Social Relations: Experiences of Jharkhand Labour to Western Uttar Pradesh", *Journal of Development Studies* 49(6): 846-60.

Rich, A. (1976). *Of Woman Born: Motherhood as Experience and Institution*. New York and London: W.W. Norton and Company.

Ruddick, S. (1980). "Maternal Thinking", *Feminist Studies* 6(2): 342-67.

Sen, I. (ed.) (1994). *A Space within the Struggle: Women's Participation in People's Struggles*. New Delhi: Kali for Women.

White, S.C. (2010). "Analysing Well-being: A Framework for Development Practice", *Development in Practice* 20(2): 158-72.

Index

G

L

M

N

P

Q

R

S

T

W